Taylor's Guides to Gardening

A Chanticleer Press Edition

Taylor's Guide to Shrubs

Houghton Mifflin Company Boston

Based on Taylor's Encyclopedia of Gardening. Fourth Edition, copyright © 1961 by Norman Taylor, revised and edited by Gordon P. DeWolf, Jr.

Library of Congress
Cataloging-in-Publication Data
Taylor's guide to shrubs.
(Taylor's guides to gardening)
Based on: Taylor's encyclopedia of gardening. 4th edition. 1961.
Includes index.
1. Ornamental shrubs 2. Ornamental shrubs—Dictionaries. I. Taylor's encyclopedia of gardening. II. Title: Guide to shrubs. III. Series.
SB435.T43 1987 635.9'76 86-20024
ISBN 0-395-43093-3 (pbk.)

Prepared and produced by Chanticleer Press, Inc., New York
Cover photograph: Dexter hybrid rhododendron 'Scintillation' by Charles Marden Fitch

Designed by Massimo Vignelli

Color reproductions made in Italy
Printed in Hong Kong

First Edition.

DNP 10 9

Contents

Hal Bruce, author of the gardening essays, is Curator of Plant Collections at the Henry Francis du Pont Winterthur Museum in Winterthur, Delaware, with which he has been associated since 1960. He has taught at the University of Delaware and written numerous books and articles on gardening and horticulture, including *Winterthur in Bloom.*

Philip Chandler, special consultant on southern West Coast shrub species, is a landscape designer, horticultural writer, and lecturer. He lives in Santa Monica, California.

Gordon P. DeWolf, Jr., Ph.D., coordinator of the Horticultural Program at Massachusetts Bay Community College in Wellesley Hills, Massachusetts, revised and edited the fifth edition of *Taylor's Encyclopedia of Gardening,* upon which this guide is based. Dr. DeWolf previously served as Horticulturist at the Arnold Arboretum at Harvard University.

Pamela Harper, a principle photographer for this and other Taylor's Guides, is the coauthor of *Perennials: How to Select, Grow, and Enjoy,* published by HPBooks. A well-known horticultural writer, photographer, and lecturer, she has published articles in such magazines as *Flower and Garden, American Horticulturist,* and *Pacific Horticulture.* Harper has taken more than 80,000 photographs of plants and gardens.

Gordon E. Jones, general consultant for this book, is Director of Planting Fields Arboretum in Oyster Bay, New York. He has written numerous articles on woody ornamental plants and served as guest editor for the Brooklyn Botanic Garden handbook, *Rhododendrons and their Relatives.*

Steven M. Still, the editor of the plant descriptions and a contributing photographer, holds a Ph.D. in horticulture from the University of Illinois. He is a Professor at The Ohio State University in Columbus. Still's work has appeared in *American Nurseryman, HortScience,* and other periodicals, and he is the author of the book *Herbaceous Ornamental Plants.*

Katharine Widin, author of the essay on pests and diseases, holds an M.S. and a Ph.D. in plant pathology. She operates a private consulting firm, Plant Health Associates, in Stillwater, Minnesota.

Preface

Some of the most colorful members of the plant kingdom are shrubs. Think of mounds of golden forsythia, fiery summer-sweet, snowy spireas, bright-berried hollies, sky-blue hydrangeas, rich rose azaleas—the list is long, if not endless. Whatever its color, a shrub always presents a distinctive silhouette against the landscape. The flowers, fruit, and foliage are so effective because they are lifted off the ground. One forsythia blazing in an acre of lawn will catch your eye long before a bed of marigolds because it literally stands out.

One shrub can be planted as a single ornament or several massed as accents. Shrubs work well with other groups of plants—annuals, perennials, bulbs, ground covers, and trees—to add balance and dimension to a garden. Their varied shapes enhance environments that are open or enclosed, large or small, sunny or shaded, formal or informal. Many shrubs perfume the air with delightful fragrances—lilac, honeysuckle, magnolia, gardenia, and mock-orange, to name a few. Some shrubs will even attract butterflies and birds to your yard. You can watch cedar waxwings feed on cherries or flocks of juncoes dash for the cover of a thorny pyracantha.

As a special bonus, gardening with shrubs serves practical purposes in pleasing ways. A hedge or informal border can offer privacy, screen areas from view, or serve to separate your yard from your neighbor's. Large, hardy plants make effective windbreaks and noise buffers.

Whether you are interested in creating an entirely new landscape or improving an existing one, this book will introduce you to a bounty of beautiful shrubs and tell you exactly how to grow them. Your efforts will be rewarded season after season and year after year.

How to Use

Shrubs are among the most varied and versatile of garden plants. They fill the landscape with shape, color, and texture, serving purely as ornament or to balance an overall garden design. Shrubs provide year-round interest—flowers in spring, attractive foliage in summer, berries and bright leaves in fall, colorful stems or evergreen leaves in winter. And there is the added dimension of utility: Shrubs can serve architectural as well as decorative purposes.

Whether you live in Maine or California, there are countless shrubs just right for your garden. And although their size and permanence tend to intimidate beginning gardeners, there is really no mystery to growing shrubs. All that you need to know can be found in this guide. You'll see how easy it is to create a landscape that suits your particular needs and tastes. If you have been growing shrubs for years, this book will show you new varieties and fresh ways to use old favorites. It can also help you to identify and learn to use plants that you admire in other gardens or nurseries.

How This Book Is Organized

The species presented in this guide were selected for their ornamental qualities. Junipers and other conifers, which usually provide background rather than ornament, are not included. The book contains three types of material: color plates, plant descriptions, and essays by experts to guide you through every aspect of gardening with shrubs.

Color Plates

More than 300 of the most popular and attractive shrubs in cultivation today are illustrated in the color plates. The plates are arranged by plant shape to help you select the right shrub for the visual effect you desire. A view of an entire shrub is shown first, together with a detail of its flowers, foliage, or fruit, or with details of other, similar shrubs. Some photographs also present variations in flower color or seasonal changes. Flowering shrubs begin the color section, followed by shrubs grown for their striking foliage and showy fruit. The plates end with lush green foliage plants.

If you are a novice, browse through the color plates looking for plants that appeal to you. Even if you are unfamiliar with their common or scientific names, you will no doubt recognize many plants that you have seen before. To find out more about a particular shrub, turn to the page noted in the caption.

Visual Key

The color section begins with a visual key, which adds another dimension to the plates. It allows you to select shrubs according to the color of their flowers, foliage, or fruit. It also identifies those that bloom before their leaves appear and those with unusual or colorful stems.

This Guide

Captions
The captions that accompany the color plates provide essential information at a glance: how tall a shrub grows, the kind of soil it needs, and for flowering shrubs, when it blooms. Also given here are the scientific and common names of the plant, the size of individual flowers or flower clusters, and a zone number which indicates in what climate the shrub can be grown. Finally, a page reference directs you to the description of your plant in the Encyclopedia of Shrubs.

Encyclopedia of Shrubs
Here you will find a full description of each plant shown in the color plates and specific information on how to grow it. The descriptions are based on the authoritative *Taylor's Encyclopedia of Gardening,* revised and updated for this guide. Entries are arranged alphabetically by genus and cross-referenced by page number to the color plates. (If you are unfamiliar with scientific names, you can easily find a plant by looking up its common name in the comprehensive index, which starts on page 470.)
Each description begins with a heading indicating the genus name, followed by the common and scientific family names. Pronunciation of the scientific name precedes a brief overview of the genus.

Genus
This section describes the overall characteristics of the garden plants in the genus. It also outlines broad growing requirements for the genus, including when and how to prune and how to propagate.

Species, Hybrids, and Cultivars
After the genus description, you will find detailed information about each of the shrubs shown in the color plates and additional information about other popular cultivars. Each species description includes the plant's country of origin and the zone to which it is hardy. (You can find what zone you live in by referring to the map on page 22.) It also offers any growing tips that differ from the genus requirements, like the need for acid soil or a tendency to spread rapidly without pruning. A black-and-white illustration next to a species description depicts the whole plant and is also representative of other shrubs in the genus.

Gardening Essays
Written by experts, these essays explain every aspect of gardening with shrubs—how and when to plant and transplant, how to prune, and other important cultivation information, as well as tips on designing your garden.
In the section on botany, beginners will learn how shrubs differ from other plants and the importance of scientific names. The illustrations of shrub forms show you their different growth habits

and how they work in a landscape. A gardening calendar provides a practical schedule for seasonal maintenance activities. The essay on keeping records offers practical advice on how to remember what you plant and when and where you plant it. Should a shrub begin to falter, you can turn to the pest and disease chart to identify your problem and cure it. Common-sense advice on buying shrubs includes a list of nurseries and other sources. Finally, all the technical terms you may encounter are defined in the glossary.

Using the Shrub Chart

The chart beginning on page 424 allows you to see at a glance which shrubs are best suited to your desires and the conditions in your garden. For example, suppose you live in Pennsylvania (in zone 6) and want to plant a row of tall flowering shrubs along your back fence. You'd like them to bloom in late winter or early spring. Look in the chart for plants over eight feet tall and winter-to-spring blooming. (If a shrub blooms over two seasons, both will be indicated.) Then make sure these plants are hardy in your zone. Three shrubs may suit your needs: *Corylopsis glabrescens, Hamamelis* × *intermedia,* and *Lonicera fragrantissima.* The first needs acid soil, and yours is of average pH, so you can eliminate that from consideration. Turn to the color plates listed for the other two plants and read their descriptions to decide which appeals to you more.

Using the Color Plates to Plan Your Garden

Shrubs come in a wide array of shapes and colors, and today it is almost impossible to learn about every new hybrid or cultivar that is introduced. In this guide, the most popular varieties are illustrated, many in a detail as well as an overall view.

First, decide where you would like to plant shrubs and what visual effect you desire. Perhaps you are designing an azalea garden in your back yard. Look for the azaleas among the showy flowering shrubs in the color plates; examine the range of colors and shapes available and determine how you might mix and match different hybrids. Check the captions to see how tall the plants grow, when they bloom, and what conditions they require. Finally, turn to the plant descriptions for cultivation details, color variations, and related forms that may not be pictured.

Planning your garden is enjoyable and easy, and this guide will help you through every stage of growing shrubs for a lifetime of pleasure.

Basic Botany

It is not necessary to learn all about botany to be a successful gardener, but it certainly helps to know a few basics. Being able to communicate clearly about what you grow or want to grow can be satisfying as well as useful.

What Is a Shrub?

Shrubs are defined as woody, perennial plants, smaller than trees and usually with several stems or trunks. Although this is a good working definition, nature does not always conform to such convenient categories. There is no specific height boundary between shrubs and trees, and many shrubs may be trained to grow—or may even grow naturally—with a single trunk. The only invariable characteristics are that shrubs are woody and live more than two years.

If the term "perennial" in the definition confuses you, it may be because we most commonly use the word to describe certain flowers, and in that context it is really short for herbaceous perennial. The roots of herbaceous perennials survive winter after winter, but their stems die back to ground level in autumn and grow anew in spring. Woody perennials like shrubs survive winters without dying back, although they become dormant—a condition most evident in deciduous plants, which lose their leaves.

Some shrubs behave like herbaceous perennials if you grow them in climates colder than those to which they are native. Many soft-wooded, moderately tender shrubs like beautyberries, butterfly bushes, and some St. Johnsworts die back in cold winters. Instructions for growing them often say "treat as an herbaceous perennial." This simply means you should cut off the dead stems in late fall. The plant will produce new stems and bloom abundantly the following spring.

Subshrubs

There are a few plants that fall between herbaceous perennials and shrubs, and they are referred to as subshrubs, or suffruticose plants. Their stems die back partially in autumn, the extent depending on the severity of the weather. Rosemary and lavender are examples of subshrubs.

Evergreen, Semi-evergreen, or Deciduous?

The terms evergreen, semi-evergreen, and deciduous describe the length of time a shrub holds its leaves. Evergreen shrubs retain their leaves for more than one year. There are two classes of these: conifers or needled evergreens like pine, spruce, and juniper; and broad-leaved evergreens like box, camellia, and most rhododendrons. Deciduous shrubs, by contrast, shed their leaves—often after a glorious burst of color—in autumn, at the end of the growing season. Among the many deciduous garden shrubs are clethra, aronia, cornus, corylopsis, deutzia, and lilac. In between are

Cyme
A branching cluster in which the flowers bloom from the center toward the edges, and in which the tip of the axis always bears a flower

Spike
A raceme in which the individual flowers are stalkless

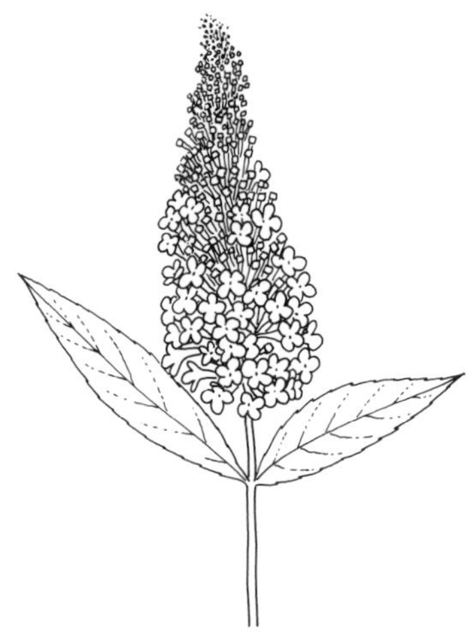

Umbel
A flower cluster in which the individual flower stalks grow from the same point

Shrubs bear flowers singly or in clusters of varying arrangement. This chart describes six of the most common cluster types.

Corymb
A flattened cluster in which stalks grow from the axis at different points and flowers bloom from the edges toward the center

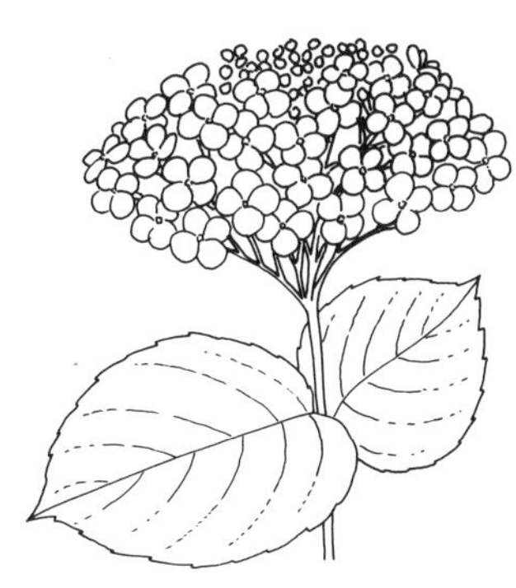

Panicle
An open flower cluster, blooming from bottom to top, and never ending in a flower

Raceme
A long cluster in which individual flowers are borne on short stalks from a central stalk

semi-evergreen shrubs, which retain at least part of their foliage well into winter. Many of the Asian species of azalea are semi-evergreen, as are *Lonicera fragrantissima* (which can remain green until after the New Year), *Abelia* × *grandiflora,* and *Viburnum* × *burkwoodii.* Semi-evergreen shrubs often remain fully evergreen in warm climates.

Scientific Names

Like all living things, shrubs enter into the system of classification perfected by the Swedish naturalist Linnaeus. In this system, each plant or animal is given a two-word name, or binomial. The first word—the generic name—indicates the genus of the plant. A genus is a group of closely related plants that stem from a common ancestor. Genera may include from one to several hundred species. The second name—the specific epithet—identifies the species, or particular member of the genus. A specific epithet is often an adjective describing some important characteristic of the species. Most binomials are Latin or Latinized Greek; they are printed in italics, usually with only the generic name capitalized. The importance of this system is that it is universal.

One or more genera descended from a common ancestor make up a family. All the members of a family are presumed to be more closely related to each other than to plants in other families. For example, the honeysuckle family contains several genera of shrubs with trumpet-shaped flowers. A family name usually ends in the suffix "-aceae," pronounced "ay'see-ee." Caprifoliaceae is the name for the honeysuckle family, which includes the genus *Weigela* and the species *Weigela florida.*

Common Names

Although common names are less intimidating than scientific names and often delightfully evocative, they are not universal. Rose-of-Sharon, for example, can mean either *Hibiscus syriacus* (also known as Shrub Althea) or *Hypericum calycinum,* a species of St. Johnswort. *Syringa* is the generic name of the lilacs, but some gardeners use syringa as the common name for *Philadelphus.* Mock-orange, the other common name for *Philadelphus,* is sometimes used in the South for *Pittosporum tobira.* As you can see, using common names can cause confusion. Moreover, for many plants, the generic and common names are the same: Abelia, magnolia, acacia, and forsythia are simply generic names used as common names. Others, like Korean Abelialeaf or White Forsythia for *Abeliophyllum distichum,* seem just as awkward and unwieldy as the scientific names. Time-honored common names like lilac and box are usually safe, but for clearest communication, know the scientific name as well.

Forms and Varieties

Below the level of species, plants are classified as forms and varieties. A form is a small but constant variation within a population, such as a white-flowered plant in a normally purple-flowered species. Variety is an often misused term for a plant of greater variation within a species. It may have a different leaf shape or growth habit. The term tends to be used more generally, however, to indicate any sort of variation in plant groups, including those produced artificially by horticulturists.

Hybrids

Many garden plants are hybrids—crosses between different species and sometimes between plants in different genera. Hybridization is relatively rare in nature, but horticulturists can breed plants to produce hybrids more ornamental or hardier than their parents. An example of a very successful hybrid group is the Dexter hybrid rhododendrons, which combine the exotic color and large flowers of Asian rhododendron species with the extreme hardiness of the American ones. Like many other hybrids, they are of complex parentage, with several species in their ancestry. The symbol × in a scientific name tells you that the plant is a hybrid.

Cultivars

An individual of a cultivated hybrid group is commonly called a cultivar. It is usually given a name in single quotation marks after the genus or species name—for example, *Camellia japonica* 'Rev. John G. Drayton'. This name is selected by the breeder of the plant as a sort of trademark. Indeed, cultivar names can be registered, and this assures you that the plant you buy will have the same characteristics as all others with that cultivar name.

Shrub Shapes

Prostrate

Rounded Spreading

The various growth habits of shrubs give them different silhouettes. This chart shows eight basic shapes that can be used singly or in combination to create certain landscape effects.

Low Spreading

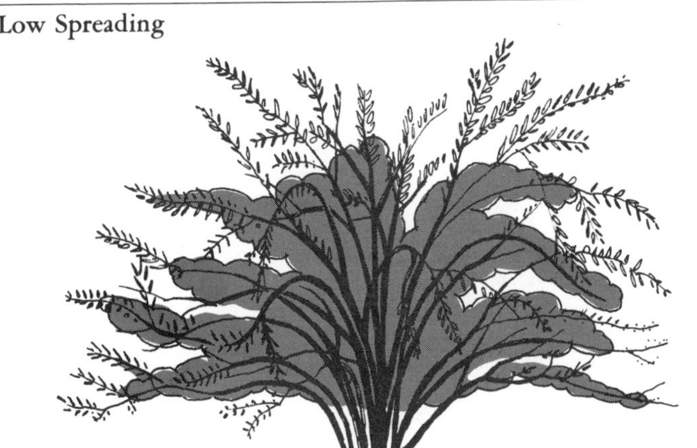

Open Spreading

Shrub Shapes

Globular

Columnar

Weeping

Pyramidal

Getting Started

The beauty and variety of shrubs is a wonderful asset, but choosing just a few for your garden can be somewhat overwhelming. There are certain practical considerations that will help narrow down the field. Not every shrub will thrive in every environment. Assessing conditions in your garden and learning about the needs of certain shrubs will help you not only to choose a plant, but also to keep it healthy and attractive.

Hardiness and Zones

A major factor affecting your choice of shrubs is the climate in your area. Some shrubs can tolerate cold winters; others require temperatures that stay within certain ranges. The ability of plants to survive harsh conditions is referred to as their hardiness. Although hardiness involves other elements like soil and water, temperature is the most important factor.

The United States Department of Agriculture has devised a map that divides the U.S. and Canada into ten zones based on average minimum temperatures. (See map on page 22.) These zones are numbered from north to south and are used in this book and other planting guides to suggest the best areas in which to grow certain plants. If your garden is located in zone 6, and the zone notation for the plant you are interested in growing is 6 or lower (zone 4 or 5, for example), you can expect it to thrive in your garden with proper care. Plants described as hardy to zone 7 or 8, on the other hand, will suffer in a zone 6 garden, and probably die in the first winter. The map is based on lowest temperatures, but extreme heat is as dangerous for some plants as cold. For example, certain northern shrubs will not live long on the warm coastal plain of the eastern United States. Some information on hardiness, therefore, involves a range of zones—for example, "zones 5–9." This tells you not only how far north a plant may be grown, but also how far south.

Microclimates

Within each hardiness zone, conditions can fluctuate because of variations in temperature, rainfall, or soil type. Even within your garden there are microclimates, some more favorable to certain plants than others. A woodland plant like rhododendron, for example, is much more likely to survive close to the north side of the house than in the middle of a windswept lawn facing south, or at the bottom of a slope, where frost will settle.

Choosing a Site

Once you determine that your winters aren't too cold or your summers too hot for a particular shrub, the next step is to choose the place in your garden where it will grow best. Take some time to learn about the shrub's needs. How much light does it require? How much exposure will it endure? Does it need much water? In what type of soil will it grow best? Landscape effects such as size, color, and bloom time should also be taken into account; these are discussed in the section on garden design. Think carefully about the conditions in your garden in general and the characteristics of certain areas within it to make the best match of shrub to site.

Sun and Shade

Most shrubs will tolerate mixed conditions of sun and shade, but some do much better with more of one than the other. Flowering shrubs, for example, need at least some sun in order to produce flowers. Some foliage plants, like pieris, grow well in almost constant shade.

Generally speaking, broad-leaved evergreens do best in shade and deciduous shrubs prefer more sun. Gray-leaved deciduous plants like elaeagnus, buddleia, tamarix, and certain willows are especially fond of sun. The most desirable situation for shade lovers is the high shade provided by tall trees with no low branches. You can tell that a shrub is growing in insufficient light if it becomes lanky, leans toward the strongest source of light, and blooms sparsely. These distress signals call for transplanting.

Assess the light available at the site you have in mind. How many hours of sun does it receive? Is it mainly morning or afternoon sun? Is it direct or filtered by trees? Watch the proposed site for a few days. Consider the movement of shadows and how you might provide more or less shade by adding plants or pruning existing ones.

Exposure

Few ornamental shrubs will stand up to constant strong winds, so it is important to know the wind patterns of your site. Is it shielded by your house, a fence, or other plants? Is it in the lee of a hill or at the exposed top? Some shrubs, like hollies and pittosporum, do tolerate high winds and can therefore serve as windbreaks for other, less sturdy shrubs. Newly planted or transplanted shrubs need special protection from winds.

Soil Types

Soils consist of particles of weathered rock mixed with organic material in the form of decaying plants and animals. The size of these rock particles determines soil type. If they are very small, the resulting soil is called clay. Very large particles create sand or gravel soils. In between there is loam, which contains medium-sized or mixed rock particles.

You can tell what type of soil you have by taking a moist—but not wet—handful and kneading it into a ball. Clay soils easily form a compact ball that will not crumble even if dropped from waist height. Sand will crumble at the slightest movement—if you succeed in kneading it into a ball at all. Loam soils form a ball easily but crumble when dropped.

Hardiness Zone Map

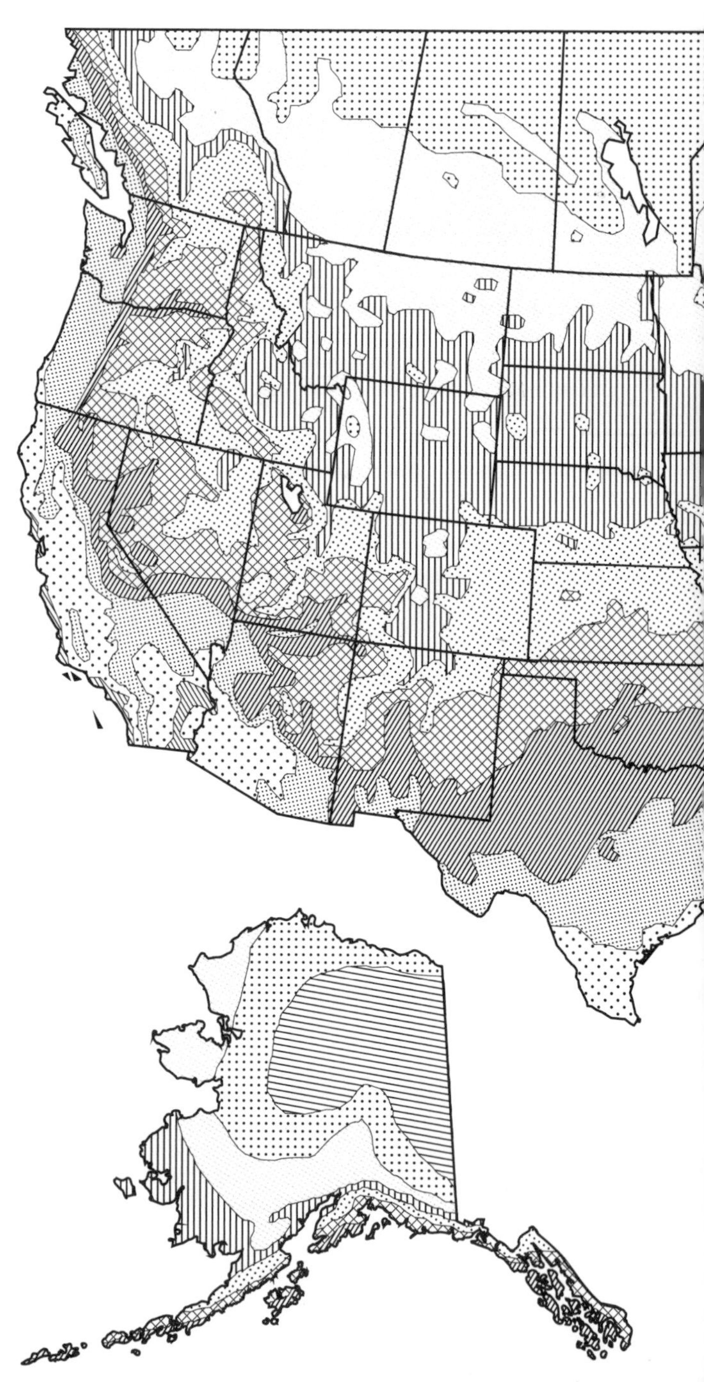

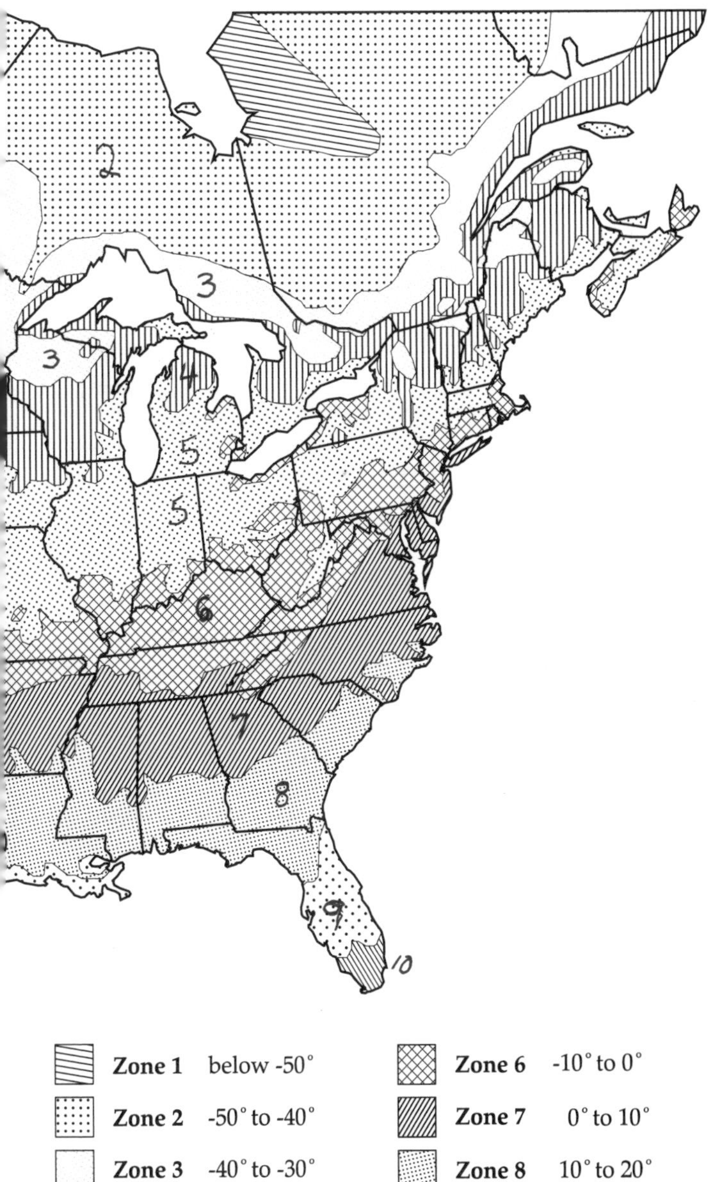

Zone 1	below -50°
Zone 2	-50° to -40°
Zone 3	-40° to -30°
Zone 4	-30° to -20°
Zone 5	-20° to -10°
Zone 6	-10° to 0°
Zone 7	0° to 10°
Zone 8	10° to 20°
Zone 9	20° to 30°
Zone 10	30° to 40°
Zone 11	above 40°

You may choose to have your soil tested by a local agricultural extension service, or you can buy an inexpensive soil test kit at any large nursery or garden center. These tests will tell you the characteristics of your soil and help you determine which shrubs are best suited to it.

If your soil contains mostly sand and gravel, it will dry out so rapidly that your plants will die of thirst. Clay, on the other hand, retains water so long that plant roots rot. When clay soil does dry out, it becomes as hard as concrete. Fortunately, you can improve all types of soil by adding organic matter, which makes sandy soils more water retentive and clay soils more open and aerated. Clay soils may also be treated with gypsum, or calcium sulphate, which helps separate the individual soil particles. Use gypsum in combination with large amounts of organic matter.

The importance of organic matter cannot be stressed too much. The most readily available—and expensive—form is peat, which comes in various forms. Since it is acidic, peat is applied in conjunction with materials like gypsum, bone meal, superphosphate, and chemical fertilizers, which are neutral or alkaline. Other forms of organic matter are leaf mold from deciduous trees, pine needles, animal manure, garden compost made up of lawn and garden clippings, and sawdust. Ideally, all these materials—especially manure and sawdust—should be aged at least one season before use.

pH Levels

The acidity or alkalinity of soil is measured on a pH scale from 1 to 14, with 7 representing a neutral level. Lower numbers indicate more acidity; higher ones more alkalinity. pH levels influence the degree to which vital minerals in the soil, such as calcium, magnesium, and iron, are available for plants to absorb. When soil has a neutral pH, most of these minerals can be absorbed. Calcium and magnesium are more abundant in neutral to alkaline soils than in acid ones. Plants have difficulty absorbing trace elements like iron, however, from alkaline soils. Leaves of plants such as azaleas, rhododendrons, and camellias turn yellow in neutral or alkaline soil because they cannot get the iron they need. If the pH is lowered, iron is freed in the soil and the plants can absorb it.

The test you buy or have done by an extension service will tell you the specific pH rating of your soil. Generally speaking, most areas in the East have soils that vary from neutral to very acid. This is because the underlying rock is granite, which produces acid. In much of the West and Midwest, on the other hand, the underlying rock is limestone, which is alkaline, so soils there are often—sometimes very strongly—alkaline.

Fertilizer

The major nutrients that plants require are nitrogen, phosphorus, and potassium. These ensure proper growth, flowering, and other life processes. As they grow, plants consume these elements, depleting the soil, so gardeners use fertilizers—either organic or chemical—to replace them.

Organic matter like humus, rotted leaves, or compost encourages the breakdown of soil particles to release plant nutrients. Some gardeners argue that organic fertilizers are safer to use than chemical ones. Although that is not strictly true—fresh manure, for example, will kill plants—it is true that most organic matter may be used safely in large amounts.

Chemical fertilizers provide specified amounts of each major element, indicating the percentages numerically. For example, a package marked 5-10-5 contains 5 percent nitrogen, 10 percent phosphorus, and 5 percent potassium. The remaining 80 percent is made up of inert, sterile particles or water. A typical mix for feeding shrubs in ordinary soils is 5-10-10. A soil test can tell you what type of fertilizer you need to grow a particular shrub.

Chemical fertilizers come in two forms. Granular types are spread on the ground; liquid forms are mixed with the water supply. Be sure not to exceed the recommended concentrations given on the container: Too much fertilizer can burn your plants. The best time to apply fertilizer is in the spring when plants grow most actively. If you fertilize too late, you run the risk of forcing new growth so late in the season that it will be damaged by frost. Since nitrogen forces growth, a chemical fertilizer high in nitrogen used in spring will help the plant form new leaves and branches. Concentrations of phosphorus, on the other hand, help to harden plants for winter. Fertilizer applied after midsummer should be low in nitrogen and high in phosphorus.

Watering

Garden plants die more often because of a lack of water than for any other single reason. Perhaps this is because some gardeners do not water correctly. Standing in the garden and sprinkling the tops of the plants each evening is not enough. You must get water to the root zone by soaking plants individually. Probably the best way to do this is with a perforated hose, which you can buy at a garden center for a reasonable price. It produces a fine spray that soaks the ground gradually but thoroughly.

Frequent, regular watering is especially important if summer droughts last longer than two weeks or if your soil is light, sandy, and drains quickly. Shallow-rooted plants like rhododendrons and azaleas need plenty of water, as do plants that have been recently planted or transplanted. In general, you should water plants whenever their leaves begin to wilt or droop.

Altering a Site

We all know you can't fool Mother Nature, but there are a few changes you can make in a site so that it will better suit the needs of a specific shrub. Transform a very shady site by thinning or cutting out plants that block the sun. Plant a living windbreak or build a fence to protect a shrub from high winds. Always place a windbreak so that the plants you wish to protect are between it and the prevailing winds. Improve soil fertility by adding whatever minerals are lacking, or dig in organic matter to make the soil hold more water.

You can alter the pH of a soil slightly by adding lime for alkalinity or sulfur for acidity. Sulfur comes in ground form or as ferrous (iron) sulfate, both of which are available at nurseries. Do not use aluminum sulfate for acidity because large amounts of aluminum are poisonous to plants. Be careful not to use more sulfur than recommended or you'll kill the shrub. You can also add peat moss to your soil to improve acidity slightly.

There are several forms of limestone available to make soil more alkaline; ask a nurseryman or your extension service about what type to use in your area. If you plan to apply any of these additives to your soil, do so as far in advance of planting as possible—a month or even a season is ideal—because the pH changes slowly.

If the pH of your soil is either very low or very high, do not expect to alter it permanently. Some gardeners in alkaline areas of the Midwest or Southwest have been known to succeed with acid-loving azaleas and rhododendrons by planting them in raised beds of pure peat moss, which is acidic. You can imagine what sort of work this entails, and even so these beds slowly return to their original alkalinity, as earthworms bring up calcium from the subsoil. The beds must be watched closely and renewed periodically. Your best bet is to choose a shrub suited to the natural conditions of your garden. Fortunately, there are many beautiful shrubs that tolerate a wide range of pH levels—from 5.5 to 8.0.

Buying Shrubs

Where can you find the beautiful shrubs you see in this guide, in other books and magazines, and in neighbors' gardens? Many are available at local garden centers and nurseries. Unusual and rare types can be acquired by mail through specialist nurseries.

Local Suppliers

There are several advantages to buying shrubs at local garden centers or nurseries. You can see a selection of plants, choose a specific one for its height, habit, flowers, or other characteristics, and be sure that it is healthy before spending your money. The plants have undergone less stress and are probably larger than those you would receive from a mail-order nursery. The varieties offered will be those hardy to and proven successful in your area.

The best nurseries have large and varied inventories and informed personnel who know the plants and your area and can give you detailed cultural information. If you admire a shrub but are unfamiliar with its needs, describe the site you have in mind. The clerk will tell you how the plant will fare in your environment and what special care you should provide. The plants themselves should look vigorous and healthy, with no dead stems. Make sure green leaves are free of brown patches, which indicate dead or dying tissue. Insufficient water is the greatest enemy of nursery stock; do not accept plants with severely wilted or dry foliage.

Ordering by Mail

Local nurseries and garden centers do not always stock rare or unusual shrubs. It is best to obtain those from mail-order nurseries specializing in rarities or specific groups of shrubs. Be sure to send your order in early in the season to get the best selection. Study catalogues in advance to become familiar with suppliers' policies on terms of sale, shipping dates, and plant guarantees. It is wise to request a shipping date that coordinates with the best planting time in your area, especially if the mail-order source is located in another part of the country. Specify delivery by United Parcel Service, which may cost more than the U.S. Postal Service, but your plants will arrive faster and in better condition. If you do receive a damaged shrub, write to the supplier, specifically describing the problem and indicating whether you want a refund or a replacement.

See page 454 for a list of reliable shrub sources around the country. Whether you buy from a local garden center or a mail-order nursery, beware of extravagant claims for plant performance. If it sounds too good to be true, chances are it is.

Planting

The old saying about the 25-cent hole for the 5-cent plant has much wisdom behind it. The most important part of the whole process of gardening with shrubs is preparing the medium in which they will grow.

The best way to do this is to dig a hole at least twice as large as the size of the shrub's root ball or the spread of its roots. Take out the topsoil—the first four or six inches of the soil—and pile it beside the hole. Then take out the subsoil—the paler, leaner soil below the topsoil—and cart it away to the compost pile or to a pile of soil to be used for grading. To the topsoil beside the hole add organic matter—an amount equivalent to the amount of subsoil you carted away. You can also add a small amount of fertilizer. Mix well and begin filling the hole.

Position the shrub in the hole so that its crown—the junction of the roots and trunk with the stems—is just about at soil level. In other words, don't plant it more deeply or shallowly than it was planted before it entered your garden. Continue filling, saving enough soil to make a raised ring around the edge of the hole so that you can run water into the basin this creates. Once the plant is established, you can rake this ring level.

Timing is important in planting shrubs. In regions where winters are very cold, early spring planting is usually best. In the South, where summer heat may be more lethal than winter cold, fall planting is usually better.

You will need to vary the basic planting techniques just described according to the way your shrub has been grown by the supplier. Shrubs are sold in three forms: bare-rooted, balled and burlapped, and container-grown. The last form is probably the most common today, but all three types have advantages and disadvantages.

Bare-rooted Shrubs

Since bare-rooted shrubs have no heavy soil attached to them, they are relatively easy to transport and can be sold in very large sizes. They should be planted only when dormant, in late fall or very early spring. This method of planting is the most traumatic to shrubs, so they need special care for a longer period of time than plants sold in other forms.

Never let the bare roots dry out. Fill a wash tub with water and add several shovelfuls of soil to make a thin, watery slurry. After pruning any crushed or broken roots, dip the roots in the slurry so that even the finest ones are coated. It is wise, in fact, to leave the plant propped up in the tub of slurry from time of purchase until actual moment of planting, which should be as soon as possible.

After planting, pour the slurry into the hole around the roots and back-fill with prepared soil. This is a good time to prune out some top growth to keep it from sapping too much strength from the roots. Shear off about one-third of the growth on all the branches and remove any weak or broken ones.

To plant a shrub, dig a hole twice as wide as the spread of the roots. Place the shrub so its crown is at soil level.

Fill the hole with a mixture of topsoil and organic matter. Make a ring of soil around the planted shrub to hold water.

Planting

Handle bare-rooted shrubs with care, and keep the roots wet until planting.

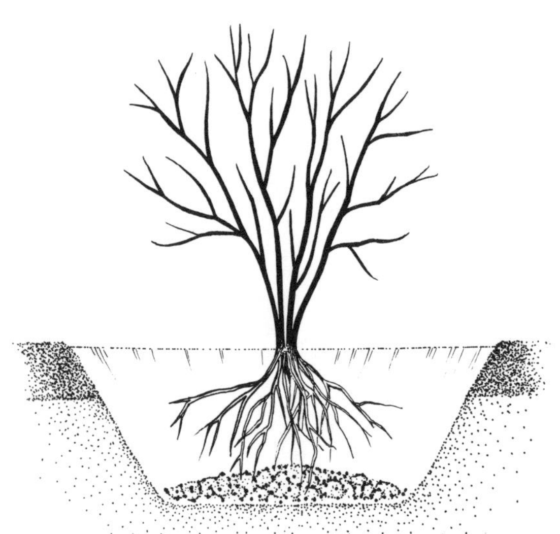

Prune branches to compensate for root damage. Stake to prevent toppling by winds.

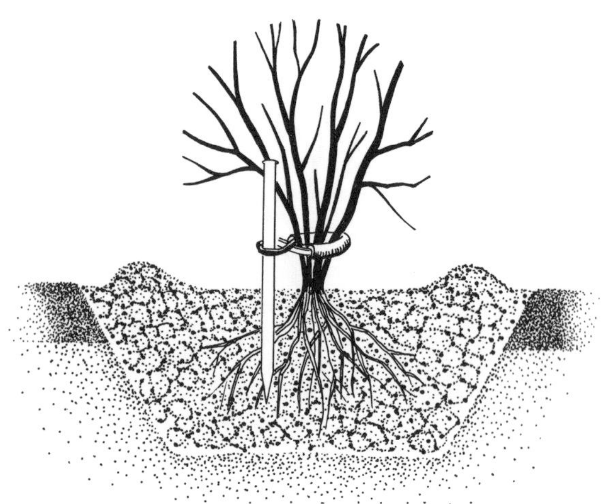

Bare-rooted shrubs, especially large ones, need staking after planting because they have no root ball to anchor them. In general, you can tell that a shrub needs staking if you see empty space around its stem at the soil line—the result of the plant whipping about in the wind. Drive a wooden stake into the ground close to the stem and on the side of the prevailing winds. Fasten the main stem securely to the stake with raffia or heavy twine. It is usually best to leave the stakes intact for the shrub's first winter in its new location.

Balled and Burlapped Shrubs
These plants are dug out of their growing medium so that a ball of soil surrounds the roots; the ball is wrapped in burlap or other material and tied up for transporting. Planting balled and burlapped shrubs involves less stress than planting bare-rooted shrubs, but you should still plant in spring or fall when the shrubs are at least partly dormant. A disadvantage of this method is that the soil ball is extremely heavy, so you may need help moving a large plant. Staking and subsequent watering is not quite so vital but still important.

Follow the general directions for planting, placing the shrub in the hole burlap and all. Partially back-fill the hole, cut the ropes tying the root ball, and pull the burlap away from the top of the ball, working it down along the sides. If the rope and covering materials are not real burlap and hemp but some form of plastic or polymer, leave as little of them around the root ball as possible. They will not break down in the soil and can eventually strangle the roots. Natural materials will rot, but do not leave burlap exposed above the soil, since it acts as a wick, drawing water away from the roots.

Container-grown Shrubs
At one time, plants grown in metal or plastic containers were heralded as the answer to all the dangers of moving plants. Indeed, such plants can be put into the ground at almost any time of the year with very little trauma. The problem is that many eventually die—not immediately, but after a year or more.

There are two reasons for this widespread mortality. First, container-grown shrubs are almost invariably pot-bound, with a mass of roots growing circularly around the edge of the root ball. Second, the medium in which they are grown is a soilless mix of peat, bark, perlite, and other very light materials. If such a plant is removed from its pot and put in ordinary garden soil as it is, its roots encounter the heavier soil and continue traveling in a circle as if they were still coming up against the barrier of the pot. Some eventually girdle and strangle the shrub's crown. If root strangulation doesn't get the plant, drought eventually does, because the roots never penetrate the subsoil in search of water.

When you plant container-grown shrubs, never stint on the soil preparation. Dig a hole much larger than the root ball, and prepare the soil so that it is at least 50 percent organic matter. Slide the shrub out of its container or cut the container off. Examine the roots and cut off any that you see encircling the crown, no matter how large they are. These girdling or potentially girdling roots should be cut as close to the crown as possible. Next, use a knife to make vertical cuts three to four inches deep into the root ball. The object of this is to stimulate new root growth at the cuts. You might also pry several long roots from the ball and direct them out into the new soil when you plant the shrub.

The point of all these actions is to induce the plant's roots to penetrate into the surrounding soil and grow. If the top growth of the shrub is extensive and its root ball has been cut, it is best to thin or prune back about a third of the branches to counteract that damage. Vary the amount you prune according to the structure of the plant and how much you are willing to sacrifice.

Growers are now experimenting with pots designed to prevent root strangulation. One successful design is a deep, square pot that induces roots to grow downward when they encounter its corners.

Growing Shrubs in Containers

For gardeners working with small spaces, or for anyone who wants to show off a small prized specimen or brighten a patio, planting a shrub in a container is a good idea. Choose compact or low-growing shrubs that are drought resistant, small-leaved, and fairly hardy. Some candidates are azaleas, false-cypresses, boxwood, heaths and heathers, and dwarf spireas.

Use a container with large drainage holes, which you can cover with pebbles to keep the soil from escaping. A light potting soil is usually adequate; if you use garden soil, add plenty of organic matter for good drainage. Plant the shrub so that its crown is at soil level and about three inches below the edge of the container. Make sure the stem is centered in the container and straight. If the plant becomes root-bound after several years, repot it or cut off some of its roots and prune its top growth to compensate. Water container plants thoroughly and often, and watch for dryness at the root zone in summer and freezing in the winter. It is a good idea to move container-grown shrubs to a greenhouse or cold frame over the winter.

Consider using shrubs that would be a shade too tender for your garden if grown in the ground—dwarf pomegranate, for example, or the West Coast ceanothus species, or carissa, jasmine, or cistus. A container holding a fragrant-leaved shrub like the Rockrose, *Cistus ladanifer,* situated near a doorway where you may brush against it and release its scent, is a wonderful addition to the garden.

Transplanting

Every gardener is eventually faced with rearranging his or her handiwork by transplanting. Although it is not difficult,

Place a balled and burlapped shrub in the hole with burlap still attached.

Partially fill the hole, cut ropes, and push burlap down into the hole. If wrapping is not biodegradable, remove it before planting.

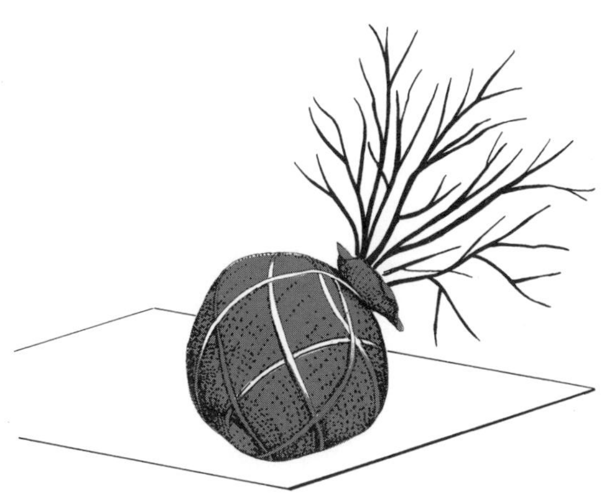

Planting

Container-grown shrubs may be pot-bound. Check for girdling roots and cut them off close to the crown. Pry long roots out of the root ball and direct them into the new soil.

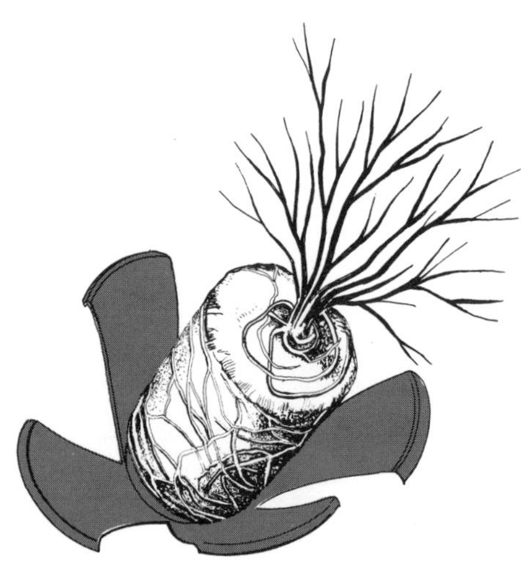

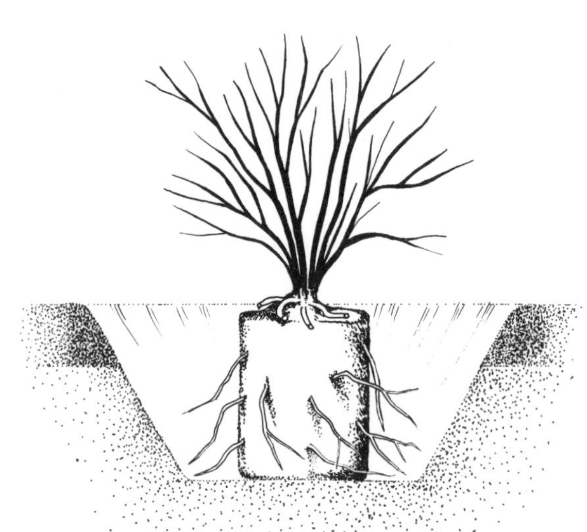

transplanting does require a certain amount of skill. If you are an amateur, don't try to move a very large shrub yourself. But if your plant is not over three feet tall, you can transplant it successfully by following a few rules. The most important consideration is water. Transplanted shrubs must never dry out, either while you are moving them or after they are planted.

It is best to transplant in early fall, after the summer heat has abated and autumn rains are beginning, or in early spring. Generally speaking, spring planting is better in areas of cold winters; fall planting is preferable farther south. In the warmest areas of the South and West, you may transplant all through the winter if there are no exceptional freezes. Move deciduous shrubs when they are totally dormant—that is, leafless. Broad-leaved evergreens and conifers are never truly dormant, but they should be moved after the new growth matures, or hardens, in late summer or early fall or before it sprouts in spring.

The aim in transplanting is to cut a symmetrical, root-filled ball of soil around the shrub and lift the whole thing out of the ground without losing the soil adhering to the roots. Use a regular garden spade to make a continuous cut as deep as the blade around the trunk or stems of the shrub. If you make the cut one blade length from the trunk—a distance of 10 to 12 inches—you'll create a root ball about 20 to 24 inches across, which is about the maximum size and weight you can handle safely.

Go around the cut at least twice, making sure that all roots are severed. If you encounter a root so large that you cannot cut it with the spade, dig back carefully from the cut to expose the root and cut it with a saw or heavy shears. On no account should you pull backward on the spade handle while you are cutting the ball. All this does is loosen the soil around the roots.

Once the ball is completely cut, put pressure on it gingerly by levering the spade handle backward. If there are no unsevered roots to hold it, the shrub should come out of the hole with relative ease. A helper with another spade is enormously valuable in this operation.

Have a tarpaulin or piece of sturdy canvas laid down next to the hole, and place the plant on it. You can now carry or drag the shrub to its new site. The new hole—prepared as described above—and a supply of water should be ready. Fill the hole with water and let it drain out partially. Then slip the transplant into it. Add soil, making sure that in the end the shrub is planted no more or less deeply than it was positioned originally. With the excess soil, make a ring around the transplant to hold water. Fill this ring with water repeatedly until it drains slowly. Later in the day, make sure that the surface of the soil beneath the plant is level and smooth and that no roots are exposed.

One task remains: Since a large percentage of the roots are invariably lost in transplanting, you should sacrifice some top growth in

Transplanting

1. *Use a spade to make a continuous cut 10–12 inches from the stem and 10–12 inches deep. Make sure all roots are severed.*

2. *Using the spade as a lever, lift the shrub carefully out of the soil. Carry or drag it on a tarpaulin to the new hole.*

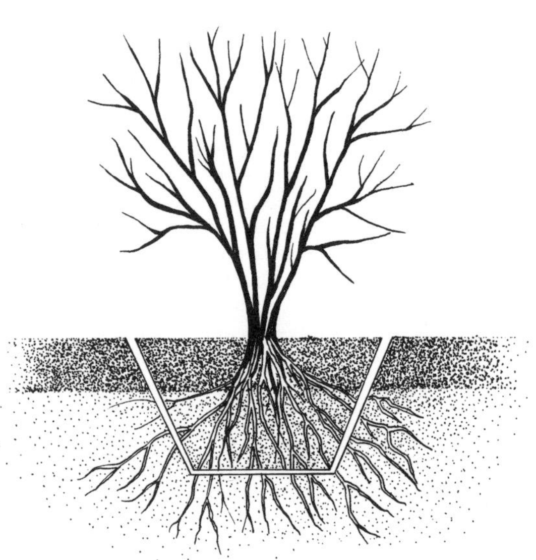

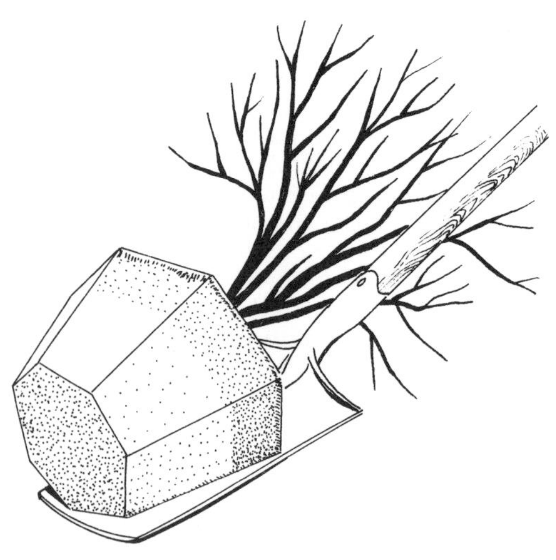

3. *Plant to the same depth as the shrub grew in the original hole.*

4. *Prune off about one-third of the top growth to compensate for severed roots and to encourage new growth.*

compensation. Prune out about a third of the top growth. It doesn't do any good to attempt to circumvent this requirement, because unpruned plants simply do not grow until their roots have re-established themselves. Plants that are pruned, however, will soon put out vigorous new growth.

Caring for Newly Planted Shrubs
Because they lack a set of deeply penetrating roots, newly planted or transplanted shrubs are more vulnerable to heat, drought, and winds than established plants. They are also more susceptible to water loss from desiccating winter winds and deeply frozen soils. Water these plants often during the summer heat and drought, and stake larger ones to prevent their being wind-thrown during storms. In winter, apply mulch around the crown to keep the soil from freezing. Evergreens may benefit from a screen of burlap wrapped around them to cut down the wind and block the winter sun.

Winter Care
All but the hardiest of shrubs benefit from special care in winter. Begin winter preparations early by discontinuing nitrogen fertilizer after about the Fourth of July. Instead, give your plants a shot of high-phosphorus fertilizer, which slows growth and promotes changes that enable them to resist extreme cold. Do not prune heavily late in the season, since pruning also stimulates growth. Broad-leaved evergreens benefit from a coating of the liquid material called Wilt Pruf, which slows water loss through leaves.

A mulch of leaves, pine needles, pine bark, cottonseed meal, or similar material is good for your plants, though not for the reason many people think. A mulch may keep the soil beneath it warmer than it would be otherwise, but its greatest benefit is that it stabilizes soil temperatures.

Put down your mulch after the first hard frost; mulching early will lock in too much heat. Do not make the pile more than four inches deep. So that the mulch area does not become a haven for mice and voles, put traps out.

Somewhat tender shrubs like vitex and *Buddleia davidii* can be protected with a mixture of soil, peat, and mulch mounded at the roots to a depth of about eight inches. This way the crown of the plant will survive even if its stems die back to ground level.

In some regions, box suffers from sunscald in the winter. You can prevent this by erecting a screen of burlap to the east of the plants. Another, related technique can be useful for deciduous, bushy shrubs like *Hydrangea macrophylla*. Place a circular cage of chicken wire around the plant and fill it with a light mixture of leaves and pine needles. Do not try this technique with evergreens, because it will kill their leaves by spring. Again, be careful that the leaf mass doesn't become a haven for mice and similar pests.

Pruning

There are many reasons to prune shrubs: for better shape, to induce new growth, to counteract the shock of transplanting, to keep a plant in scale, or to remove ailing branches. And there are several techniques to use, depending on your purpose and the growth habit of the shrub.

Thinning and Shearing

Done to shape or revitalize a shrub, thinning involves taking out selected branches and twigs with pruning shears or a saw. The branches may be cut back slightly or all the way to the main stems. At the opposite extreme is the technique called shearing, or heading, which is done with special long-bladed hedge clippers or an electrically powered hedge trimmer. Here all the branches are cut to alter the overall shape and size of the plant. Formal hedges and topiary are created by shearing plants into a specific form. Sometimes shearing involves "taking back"—cutting all of a shrub's stems down to the crown so it will renew itself in spring.

Because of differing habits, some plants look better when thinned, while others are perfect for shearing. Common lilac, for instance, with its heavy, upright branches, would look stubby if sheared but can be improved and kept vigorous by annual thinning out of the oldest stems. Forsythia is another shrub that should not be sheared; those that you sometimes see cut into globes always have fewer flowers than others allowed to assume their natural, arching shape. On the other hand, compact, twiggy shrubs with dense habits of growth, like privets, box, or Kurume hybrid azaleas, seem made for the hedge shears. They look bushier and neater after such grooming.

How and When to Prune

It pays to learn exactly how and when to prune, since improper pruning can expose a shrub to disease, prevent blooming, and result in unsightly dead or dying stubs. The cardinal rule is to cut back to a branch or node, so as not to leave a stub. In addition to being unsightly, stubs are a potential entryway for disease.

Timing is another vital element of good pruning, especially for flowering shrubs. There are two classes of flowering shrubs to be considered. Some bloom, usually in spring, on old wood—that is, wood formed during the previous growing season. Others bloom on new wood—wood produced during the current season. If you prune the first class in autumn or early spring, you will cut off most of the bud wood and the shrub will bloom sparsely, if at all. The proper time to prune shrubs that bloom on old wood is immediately after bloom fades. On the other hand, shrubs that flower on new wood should be pruned in fall, winter, or very early spring so that bud wood will develop during that growing season.

Some plants that should be pruned right after they bloom are azaleas, boxwood, flowering quince, forsythia, winter hazel, *Hydrangea macrophylla,* pieris, lilac, and some viburnums and spireas.

Thinning

Shearing

Always prune at an angle and cut back to a bud or branch.

Plants that bloom on new wood and can therefore be pruned hard in fall, winter, or early spring include beautyberries, *Hibiscus syriacus, Hydrangea arborescens,* and *H. paniculata,* the shrubby St. Johnsworts, and some spireas like *S. japonica.*

Unfortunately, there is no foolproof way to tell if a shrub blooms on old or new wood. In general, plants that bloom before the first of June do so on old wood, and those that flower later bloom on new wood. There are notable exceptions, so it is best to ask about the correct pruning time when you buy a shrub.

Pruning for Fruit or Colorful Growth

You may have a shrub with showy fruit as well as flowers—some examples are pyracantha, cotoneaster, crab apple, and many viburnums. Any time you prune these you will lose at least part of the fruit display. It is best just to thin these types lightly immediately after they flower; never shear them.

Shrubs with especially colorful young stems or new foliage are pruned for esthetic reasons alone. For example, *Cornus sericea* can have red or yellow stems, and some forms of smoke bush, *Cotinus coggyria,* have new foliage that is bright purple. Cutting *Cornus sericea* to the ground each winter encourages new, much more brightly colored branches to replace the old. Pruning a purple smoke bush each spring makes it a brighter addition to the landscape.

Hedges and Shrub Borders

One of the most popular landscape uses of shrubs is as a fence or screen. When a row of shrubs is pruned into a more or less formal shape, it is called a hedge; when it is allowed to grow naturally, it is called a shrub border. The individual plants in a hedge are placed much closer together than in a border—one to two feet apart, depending on the ultimate height desired. Shrubs in a border are usually three to five feet apart.

Almost any group of plants can make a hedge, if they are planted close together in a line and sheared occasionally. But some plants are not really suited for this and will never look like anything but a row of mutilated plants placed too close together. Hedge plants should be hardy and able to tolerate competition and poor, dry soil. They should have dense, twiggy natural growth and small leaves. Choose shrubs with inconspicuous flowers because shearing deprives hedges of bud wood and they don't flower well. Boxwood, euonymus, hollies, and privets are popular hedge shrubs. Large-flowered shrubs like azaleas, hibiscus, weigelas, and philadelphus, however, serve well in borders, where their showy blooms are not sheared.

Hedges and borders do not have to consist of only one species of shrub. The mixed, or tapestry, hedge of the Japanese is an interesting variation. In such a hedge different species are chosen so they contrast interestingly with each other. A mixed hedge of foliage plants might consist of enkianthus, cutleaf maple, euonymus, cherry, holly, and elaeagnus, all sheared in the rigid framework of a hedge but providing subtle contrasts in color, mass, and texture.

To plant a hedge, prepare the soil by digging in organic matter and fertilizer so that the plants get off to a good start. Space plants one to two feet apart, either in a trough or in separate holes, and begin shearing them as soon as new growth matures.

When it comes to frequency of pruning, a hedge is similar to a lawn. You can clip it infrequently if you don't mind a rough, informal appearance. If you want a tidier hedge, you must clip more often—every three or four weeks during the summer, or whenever you notice new growth to more than a couple of inches. In any case, the first clipping of the season should be in late spring, after the new growth has matured. Cut back to the line of the hedge, which is the point where old growth becomes new. This forces the plant to send out side branches, filling in the hedge. Shear again in late summer.

The mature hedge should be several inches wider at the bottom than at the top so that the leaves on lower branches can receive sunlight. If the lower branches of a hedge die, it is very difficult to induce them to resprout.

Topiary

The art of making plant sculpture, topiary, goes back to the Romans and was very popular in 18th-century formal gardens. The most popular subjects are animals and geometrical shapes, but nature and the imagination are the only limits to other possibilities. The average American gardener seldom tries much topiary because it demands large amounts of space, time, and work; but simple shapes like the popular "poodle" are sometimes grown in containers to decorate a doorway.

Topiary is created by shearing plants that are best for use in hedges—especially box, holly, and yew. The simplest method is to make, or have made for you, a wire frame in the shape you desire. Fit it over a suitable plant, and when its branches grow beyond the wire, shear them back. The wire is hidden by the leaves and branches of the plant but remains as a guide to proper shape.

There are good collections of topiary at several public gardens, which you may want to visit if you are interested in pursuing this art. The two best known are probably Ladew Gardens just outside of Baltimore and Green Animals near Newport, Rhode Island. Longwood Gardens in Pennsylvania has a topiary garden. And any fancier who visits Great Dixter, the home of the famous English garden writer Christopher Lloyd, will see strange, surrealistic figures that were cut out of yew by Lloyd's father many years ago. There are also whole books on the subject of topiary to give you instructions and ideas.

Espaliers

The word espalier—pronounced either *ess-pall-yay'* or *ess-pal'yer,* depending on your preference—refers to a plant that has been trained to grow flat against a wall or framework. The technique probably developed in areas too cold to grow tender fruit trees like nectarines, apricots, or plums in conventional orchards. Growing them flat against a southern or eastern wall protected them from winds and the coldest temperatures—a good example of the use of a microclimate.

Espaliers may be of any pattern, formal or informal, and can be made from almost any shrub with flexible growth. Pyracanthas, dogwoods, Japanese hollies, and other fruiting shrubs or trees are often used. One of the great advantages of any espalier is that it takes almost no ground space whatsoever, and thus is excellent for a small garden.

The first step in creating an espalier is to make a framework of stainless or vinyl-covered wire in the shape you desire. Attach it to the wall with special bolts designed to attach wire to masonry, which may be purchased at a hardware store. Once the framework is in place, plant your shrub six to twelve inches away from the wall and prune out all branches that will not be attached to the frame. As new branches sprout, either remove them or attach them to the frame, depending on how they fit its design. Planning which branches to prune and which to train onto the frame is not easy and is part of what makes espalier an art.

For details on growing espaliers, consult a large garden encyclopedia or a book like Harold Perkins' *Espaliers and Vines for the Home Gardener*.

Propagation

If you are a beginning shrub gardener, you will want to purchase full-grown shrubs to fill your garden. As your collection increases, you may enjoy experimenting with propagation—producing new plants from those you have.

Cold Frames

If you are going to grow plants from seed or do any form of plant propagation yourself, a cold frame is a useful and versatile device. It is a bottomless box with a top made of a transparent material like glass, polyethylene plastic, or fiberglass that can be opened or removed. Cold frames are unheated and vary in size; most are three feet by six feet. They can be portable or permanent.

Place a frame in a protected area on ground that is high enough to prevent surface water from seeping in. If you plan to grow seeds directly in the cold frame, the soil must be well drained and should have a quantity of leaf-mold or similar organic matter incorporated into it. If the plants are to be grown in pots, then line the bottom of the frame with builder's sand, fine gravel, or coal ash.

Starting Plants from Cuttings

The simplest way to propagate shrubs is by softwood cuttings—four- to six-inch branch tips cut off at an angle. The best time to take softwood cuttings is in spring or summer. Dip the cut ends into a rooting hormone and push them two to three inches deep and one inch apart into a pot of light rooting medium such as sand, a mixture of sand and peat, or perlite. Cover the cuttings with a moisture-retaining hood: A large jar or plastic bag will work fine. Provide bright light but no direct sun.

If you water your cuttings regularly, they should take root in one to two months. Transfer rooted cuttings outdoors to the cold frame and keep them there one year before planting them permanently. This method of propagation works especially well for evergreen azaleas, flowering quince, mock-oranges, box, and Japanese holly, among other shrubs.

Fast-growing deciduous shrubs like hydrangeas, forsythias, spireas, shrub dogwoods, and viburnums root easily from hardwood cuttings. The genus descriptions in this book will tell you if a particular shrub should be propagated by hardwood cuttings. These are twig tips or sections six to eight inches long, with the bottom end cut at an angle. They are taken in fall, as the shrub's leaves drop.

Wound the base of each cutting by slicing an inch of bark away to encourage the growth of root tissue. Dust the wounded base with a rooting hormone/fungicide powder mixture. Tie the finished cuttings in a bundle using string or rubber bands, and bury the bundle below the frost line in the garden or cold frame. Over the winter callused tissue, which later becomes roots, will form on the cuttings.

To propagate from hardwood cuttings, use branch tips or sections 6–8 inches long, cut at an angle.

Slice an inch of bark off the base of each cutting, tie them in a bundle, and bury in a cold frame until spring.

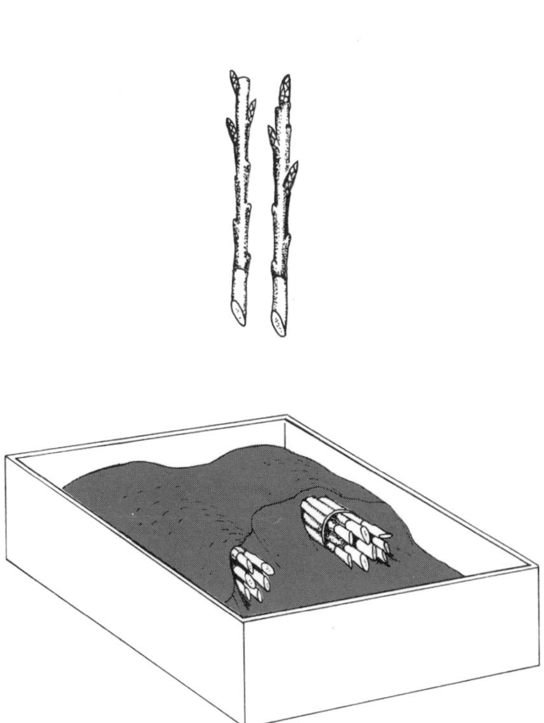

Propagation

To propagate by layering, bend a branch to the ground, anchor it with a stake, and cover with soil. After one year, cut branch and transplant the new shrub.

To start plants from softwood cuttings, cut off 4–6 inches of branch tips at an angle, just below a leaf joint. Remove the leaves at the base.

As soon as the ground can be worked in spring, dig up the bundle, separate the individual cuttings—do not let them dry out—and lay them out in a trench in the garden, burying all but an inch of the tips. As the weather warms, leaf growth will begin above the ground and root growth beneath. Leave the cuttings in place until the following spring, when you can transplant them.

Layering

Rhododendrons, fothergillas, and maples are among the harder-to-root shrubs that can be increased by ground layering. This technique involves bending supple branches to the ground and anchoring them until they take root. Layering is a slow process: It takes at least a year for new plants to form. But the process is reliable and easy to accomplish.

Mix peat, humus, or both, with the soil where the branch will be anchored. With a sharp knife, scrape the bark from the underside of the branch. Be careful not to make the wound so deep that the branch will snap off when you bend it. Cover the wounded area with a strong rooting powder and secure the branch to the ground at the wounded point with a wire or a forked stake. A rock or brick placed directly on top of the branch will anchor it more securely, although it may be unsightly. Cover the branch with some of the prepared soil and keep the area constantly moist. After the branch sends out roots, you can cut it from the parent plant and transplant the newly formed shrub.

Spring or early summer is the best time to try layering. Do not detach the branch until the next spring, and leave the new plant in place for at least three weeks before transplanting it.

A related method of propagation called air layering is often used by commercial greenhouses. It is less practical for home gardeners, not only because it involves considerable skill, but also because it is rather unattractive. Briefly, a section of stem is cut into, wedged open, and treated with rooting hormone. Moist sphagnum moss is placed around the wound and covered with clear plastic. It may take a full year for roots to fill the plastic, after which you sever the stem below the root mass and plant the newly formed shrub.

Dividing Shrubs

Some shrubs—for example, deciduous azaleas, lilacs, deutzias, and many spireas—spread underground by shoots that develop into independent stems, although they remain attached to the parent. Each of these stems and accompanying roots will develop into a new plant if separated from the others. This method of propagation, called division, is the easiest and quickest way for the home gardener to increase a plant.

If your plant is relatively small, dig up the whole root ball. Pull the roots apart gently or cut them with a knife into several pieces. Plant each piece to start a new shrub. For larger plants, use a sharp spade

To divide a large shrub, use a sharp spade to sever an outer stem from the main plant. Dig up the outer stem and its root ball and transplant.

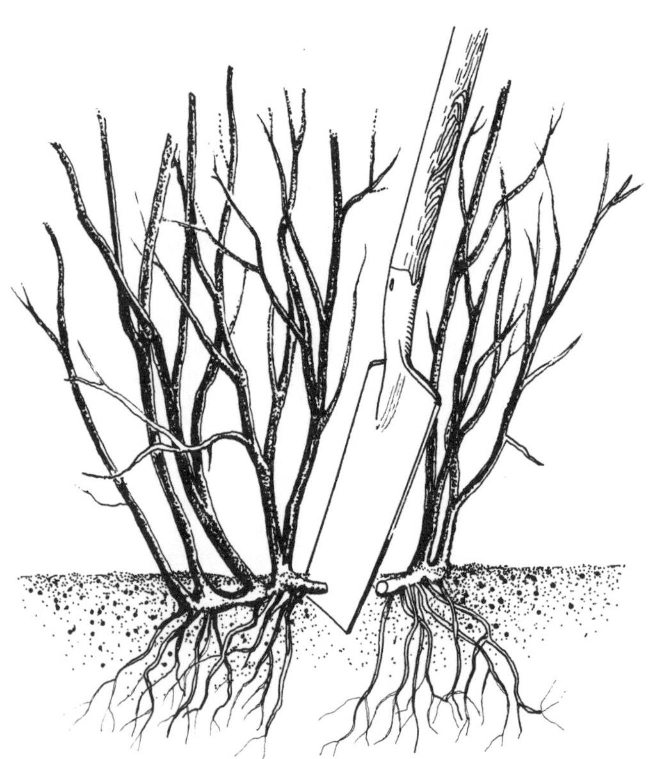

to sever an outer stem from the main plant. Then, move about a foot away from the stem and dig deeply under and toward it to loosen the accompanying roots. Preserve as much of the root ball as possible; you may have to go back behind the stem and dig more deeply. Plant the stem and its root ball as you would any new shrub, pruning it back to about one foot to encourage new growth.

Growing Shrubs from Seed

Not all ornamental shrubs can be grown from seed. The seeds of hybrids and cultivars are often sterile; even if not, they may produce plants that differ from the parent. Seeds from a species, however, will most likely "breed true."

The germination patterns of shrubs differ greatly from species to species. Azalea seeds, for example, will germinate immediately after you gather them if you provide warm, moist conditions. But it is better to store the seeds dry and plant them in spring. Many shrub seeds require a cold period—about 90 days between 30 and 40° F—before they will germinate. You can plant them out of doors immediately after gathering them in fall or after storing them for three months in a refrigerator. Roses and many of their relatives require after-ripening—a period of several weeks in a warm, moist medium, followed by about three months of cold—to induce germination.

Certain shrubs, viburnums among them, need what is called double dormancy—a cold period followed by a warm period, followed by another cold one. In nature, such seeds take two years—actually, two winters and one summer—to germinate. You can hurry them along by stratifying the seeds. Place them in a covered glass or plastic container with a moist medium, such as a mixture of sand and peat. A mayonnaise jar will do fine. Put them immediately into the refrigerator for three months. Keep the jar at room temperature for three more months, then put it back in the refrigerator for another three. The seeds should begin germinating in the stratification medium at the end of the cycle.

Seedling shrubs need special care for the first season of their lives. Leave them in the original pot for a couple of months after germination, if they are not too crowded. After they have developed two or more leaves, you can transplant them to separate flats, pots, or seed beds, where they will have abundant room to spread. Place slow growers two to three inches apart; fast growers twice that. If you start plants indoors in spring, treat them like annuals or perennials: Provide abundant light and take them out of doors when danger of frost is past.

Designing with

Whether you are starting a garden from scratch or making just a few changes in your landscape, it pays to think about elements of design. You do not have to be a specialist to recognize a few basic principles that will help you choose shrubs to complement each other and their surroundings.

There is an architecture to shrubs that is both beautiful and functional. Their shape, height, color, and texture are not only attractive in themselves, but also serve to link elements in a landscape—a lawn with a grove of trees or a flower bed with the hills beyond, for example. The size and longevity of shrubs make them useful in other, more concrete ways—such as to block out unpleasant views, noise, or wind.

Some homeowners, faced with large empty lots or the unacceptable choices of previous owners, elect to hire a landscape designer. That is certainly wise in some cases, but there can be great satisfaction in making your own choices and watching them work from season to season and year to year.

Mapping Your Space

Begin by taking account of what is in your garden now. Even if you have just moved into a newly built house, there are certain "givens" to work with—property boundaries, driveways and sidewalks, utility lines and pipes, and so forth. Draw a simple map or plan of your yard. Use graph paper to make sketching easier and to enable you to work in scale: 1 inch=10 feet, for example. Pencil in the scale at the lower corner of your plan so you don't forget it.

Identify and draw in the boundaries of your lot, the house and all other buildings, driveways and parking areas, and any other existing features. Locate your utilities—electricity or telephone cables, water or gas lines, well heads, sewers, septic tanks, and drainage fields. These will be marked on the property plan that goes with your deed. Sketch in existing plants, including trees, shrubs, hedges, and flower beds. Indicate microclimates, areas of sun and shade, low or moist places, and any other conditions that would affect the success of your shrubs. Indicate north with an arrow and show the direction of the prevailing winds, if you know it.

Once the existing features are keyed in, you are ready to think about how to use your space. Do you want a spacious lawn surrounded by shrubs? Or a large garden of flowering shrubs and other plants with walks winding through it? Do you want your garden open to the street or more private? Are there prospects such as parking lots, garbage cans, or nearby houses that you want to screen from view? Do you want to block wind or noise, line walkways, accent a doorway? Does a certain corner need brightening or a bare area filling in? What sort of feeling—formal or informal—do you want to create? To get ideas, you may want to look at other landscape designs in your area or visit botanical gardens, arboreta, or public gardens to see what designers there have attempted.

Shrubs

Make copies of your map, keeping the original for your records. Use the copies as worksheets on which to draw possible designs. This is a simple, systematic way both to keep track of the variables involved in choosing plants and to visualize the results of your plans.

Formal and Informal Designs

Garden designs can be as varied as the tastes of their creators, but they are often described as being either formal or informal in style. Formal designs are symmetrical and controlled, with geometrically shaped beds, clipped shrubs, and terracing; they usually have paths, stairs, pools, and other architectural—rather than horticultural—features. This type of design goes back to ancient Egyptian gardens; the 17th-century gardens of Williamsburg and Versailles are more modern, large scale examples.

Symmetry and balance, straight lines and right angles, with circular paths or beds for contrast, are the prized elements of formal design. Because clipped hedges and topiary are used, dense evergreen shrubs like hollies and boxwood are often found in formal gardens. Color usually comes from flower beds or specimen shrubs—perhaps four cherries anchoring the corners of the garden.

It takes time and effort to care for a formal garden. Frequent pruning, weeding, and general grooming are imperative to maintain the controlled look. But a simple formal design can be easier for an amateur to create than an informal one, precisely because there are strict rules and clearly evident patterns involved.

In informal designs, plants are allowed to assume their natural shapes. Curved lines, asymmetrical balance, and natural slopes are valued. The style descends from the Picturesque landscape school of 18th-century England and the naturalistic, or "wild garden" movement led by William Robinson and Gertrude Jekyll in the late 19th century. Informal gardens have a more varied selection of plants, and the emphasis is on subtle combinations of color, texture, and shape. The plants used tend to have loose or spreading habits, like forsythia and spirea. Shrubs may be massed—azaleas with winter-hazels and needled evergreens, for example—or used singly. Single specimens usually echo the shape of plants in other areas of the garden.

To design an informal garden, you need to know about the growth habits of plants and to be aware of the many varieties from which to choose. Some simple guidelines can help. When you plan for color and texture, consider foliage as much as flowers. Think also about bloom time and plant size. Choose and place plants to balance other areas of the landscape—for example, a large mass of perennials on one side of the yard can balance a mass of shrubs on the other. Plant in masses shaped roughly to echo the curve of a path or the shape of your yard. An informal garden will not require a great deal of grooming; it is the planning stage that is most important. Use your garden maps to sketch ideas before literally digging in.

Design for a Garden

Circle size indicates height: small for under 4 ft., medium for 4–8 ft., and large for over 8 ft.

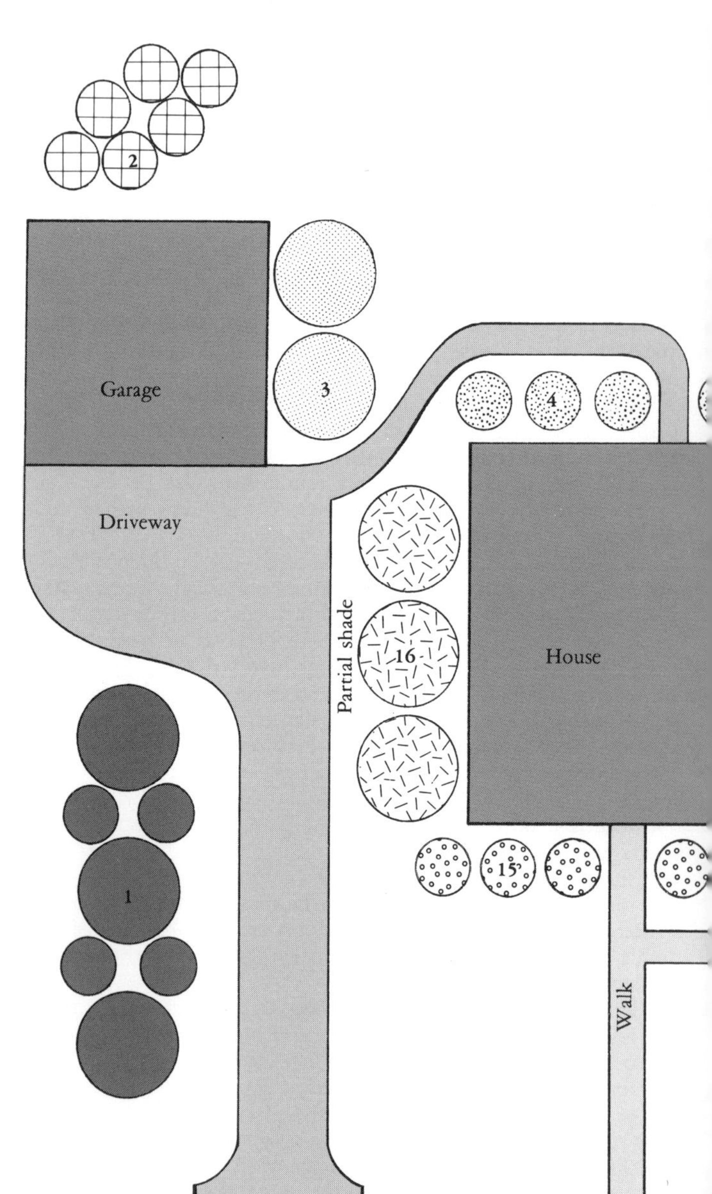

1. *Evergreen rhododendron hybrids*
2. *Gable hybrid rhododendrons*
3. *Rhamnus frangula*
4. *Leucothoe axillaris*
5. *Syringa vulgaris*
6. *Rhododendron mucronulatum*
7. *Prunus 'Hally Jolivette'*
8. *Corylopsis glabrescens*
9. *Berberis verruculosa*
10. *Callicarpa japonica*
11. *Ilex species*
12. *Corylus maxima*
13. *Viburnum species*
14. *Hamamelis mollis*
15. *Cotoneaster horizontalis*
16. *Camellia species*

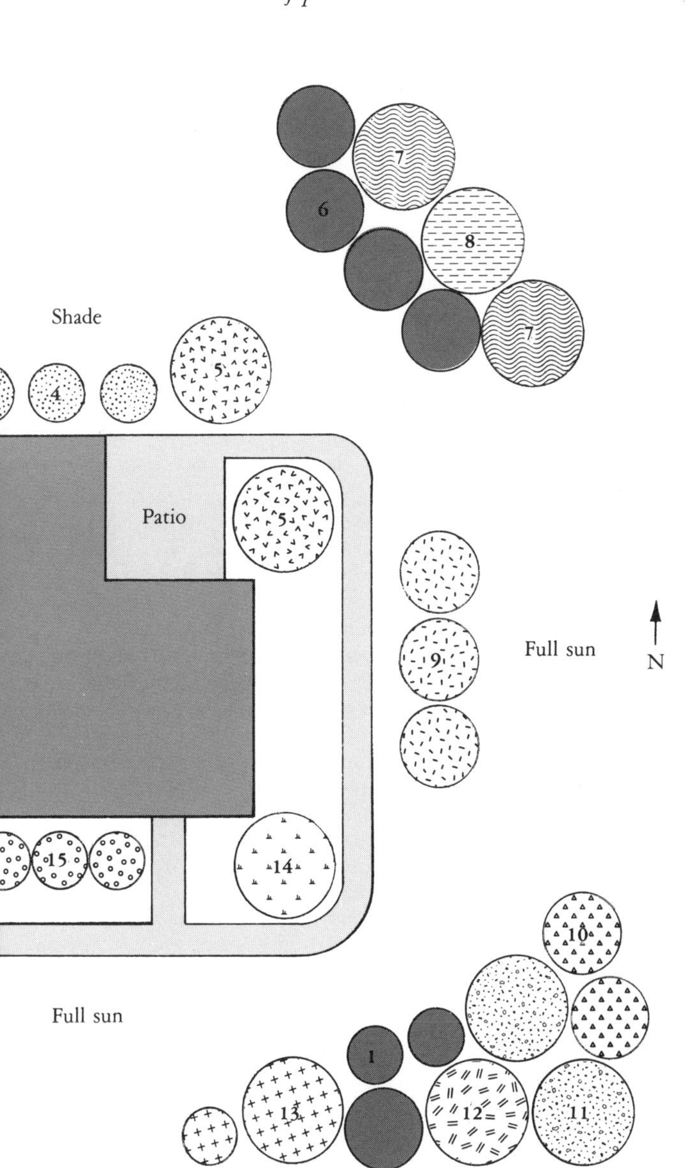

Specimens, Massings, and Groupings

A specimen shrub is one that is planted conspicuously alone, usually in a prominent place, so as to show off its ornamental qualities. Specimen plants are often large or treelike, with showy flowers, attractive fruits, conspicuous leaves, or a combination of these features. Some examples are hibiscus and buddleia for flowers, hollies and beautyberries for fruits, and *Acer palmatum* 'Dissectum' or *Baccharis halmifolia* for foliage.

In contrast, massed or grouped shrubs are planted in quantity, often so close together that their branches touch. They should be lower and bushier, with smaller leaves and flowers than specimen shrubs. A mass usually consists of plants of the same species, while a group more often contains shrubs of different species or cultivars. Some shrubs that are especially suitable for massing or grouping are barberries, forsythias, privets, spireas, and viburnums.

Foundation Plantings

Shrubs and other plants grown near the house for the purposes of decoration, hiding exposed concrete, or covering architectural flaws are called foundation plants. If you choose them carefully, they can also serve to balance the design of a house and tie it visually to its environment. Foundation plants should be durable, handsome throughout the year—evergreens are often chosen—and of slow growth or low stature. You do not want twenty-foot shrubs on either side of your front step in twenty years, and it is time-consuming to have to clip back robust shrubs all summer long. Use upright plants, but place them at corners or against large areas of blank wall rather than in front of windows.

A certain overused, ranch-house foundation planting syndrome has developed over the years, consisting of azaleas or spreading junipers under the picture window, globular box flanking the front entrance, and columnar conifers at each corner. Like most clichés, this design is basically sound—and overused for that reason; but with a little imagination you can turn a good working design into your own creation. Try using some unusual plants, trellised vines or espaliers, ground covers, and perennials or annuals in place of some of the old standbys. Remember to pay attention to the transition between the foundation planting and the design of the rest of your property.

Ground Covers

Another way to use shrubs in the landscape is for ground cover. Ground covers are usually low, spreading plants arranged in a mass. They clothe areas of the garden where grass will not thrive—in deep shade, for example—or where mowing would be difficult, such as on a steep slope. In addition to their usefulness, ground covers are esthetically appealing, with their colorful foliage, handsome flowers, or showy fruits. A few of the best ground covers featured in this book are the prostrate cotoneasters; *Calluna vulgaris,* which is colorful year-round; lavender, which survives heat, drought, and alkaline soil; and *Berberis thunbergii* 'Crimson Pygmy', with its rich burgundy foliage.

Working with Height and Shape

Knowing the ultimate height of a shrub will help you decide whether it is appropriate for a certain site, but you should also consider its overall shape and how it looks in relation to other plants. For example, a border of azaleas around a bed of perennials would obscure the flowers to all but air travelers. Obviously, tall plants should be placed behind shorter ones.

Each of the eight shrub forms illustrated in the front of this book can be used to achieve a different landscape effect. Compact shrubs like boxwood give a neat, essentially formal look, while those with spreading habits like forsythia and spirea lend a less formal airiness. Be careful, especially in informal designs, about combining shrubs with several kinds of habit. A good rule of thumb is that you can combine two shapes in a single planting but almost never three. For example, azaleas and winter-hazels of low, rounded spreading habits work well with upright pyramidal evergreens. But to introduce a totally different shape, like a weeping cherry, would reduce the group to a confused hodgepodge. This rule is less applicable in formal landscapes, where you can combine a clipped, rounded plant with both a prostrate spreader and a columnar or pyramidal shrub, because the plants are shaped artificially by shearing.

Using Color

Flowering shrubs offer a dazzling array of colors, but variations of hue occur in foliage as well. "Green" foliage can be almost black, light gray, or any shade in between, and some shrubs have red, purple, yellow, or variegated leaves. The changing seasons reveal other sources of color in shrubs—bright berries, fiery leaf hues, and colorful stems or bark. All of these features can be combined and used to advantage in your garden design if you recognize a few simple but time-honored rules.

The first has already been touched on: Green is the most common and constant color in any garden, but it is extremely variable in depth and value, and it influences any color planting you attempt. Another rule is that contrasting colors—such as blue and orange, yellow and violet, and red and green—go well together. Surprisingly, they do not clash, although combinations of pure, deep tones may exhaust the eye. This is due to the fact that pure colors may be described as "hot"—red, orange, yellow—or "cool"—blue, green, violet. Hot colors stand out in the landscape, while cool colors tend to recede. White is an exception, especially in shaded areas, where it carries a long way. Each of the three combinations of contrasting colors listed above consists of one hot and one cool color.

You can also make successful combinations without the benefit of contrast by staying within a family of colors—various shades of blue and purple, for example, or scarlet, orange, and bright yellow. Consider toning down the latter, "hot" arrangement with maroon- or purple-leaved plants. Dilute colors are usually safer in the garden than full-strength hues. Scarlet or crimson with royal blue tends to tire the eye, but pink and pale blue is a wonderful combination. Mixing light yellows and creamy white with pale green foliage is also pleasing.

The amount of gray in a shrub's color will also affect how it looks in combination with other plants. Gray may look impure or muddy next to more vivid colors, so it is best to group gray-toned plants together. For example, the dusky rose shades of heather (*Calluna vulgaris*), *Spiraea* × *bumalda,* and *S. japonica* work well with the mauve and lilac flowers of lavender. Taller shrubs could work in this group as well—tamarisks, with their rose flowers and grayish leaves, and vitex, with its silvery blue flowers and gray foliage.

Planting for Year-round Color

Beginning gardeners often choose flowering shrubs that bloom only in spring. Spring bloomers are indeed some of the most striking shrubs, but if you want color in your garden for more than a few months a year, learn to think of shrubs in terms of seasonal interest. This involves not only time of bloom but also the appearance and persistence of colorful features other than flowers.

For summer color, choose late-blooming plants such as *Hibiscus syriacus, Buddleia,* and some tamarisks. Shrubs with showy displays of fruit are most effective in fall and offer almost as much color diversity as those grown primarily for flowers. There are viburnums with glorious, glistening scarlet berries, the luscious delft blue of *Symplocos paniculata,* and beautyberries in lilac or white, for example. Fall color is enhanced by shrubs with stunning autumn foliage, like summersweet and certain Japanese maples. Evergreens give year-round interest but are especially valuable in winter. Chinese Witch Hazel (*Hamamelis mollis*) will open its yellow blossoms and perfume the air during every mild spell from January until spring, when the forsythia and azaleas appear to begin the color cycle all over again.

To ensure year-round color, you may stagger one-season plants: forsythia for spring, hibiscus for summer, viburnum for fall, and holly for winter. Or you may want to choose plants that are especially attractive for two or more seasons. Camellias, for example, are of interest throughout the year because their polished leaves are evergreen. They are truly showy when their exquisite red, pink, or white blossoms appear. Camellias are certainly four-season plants, while forsythia is a single-season one. All the evergreen hollies are four-season plants, especially those with red berries. Dogwoods, with their beautiful flowers in spring and wine-red foliage and scarlet berries in fall, are wonderful two-season plants.

A combination of plants of different seasonal interest allows some to star while others play supporting roles. Try broad-leaved evergreens with conifers—hollies and evergreen magnolias among pines, for example. The magnolias will bloom white against the dark greenery, and in winter the holly berries will shine scarlet. Add some rhododendrons or deciduous azaleas for contrast of color in spring and some camellias—*C. japonica* forms for winter and spring bloom and *C. sasanqua* forms for late autumn flowers. Now you have a landscape of truly year-round appeal.

Texture
For long-term display, a shrub's leaf texture can be more important than its flowers. Large leaves—simple, as in fringe trees and *Syringa villosa,* or compound, as in *Aralia spinosa, Rhus typhina,* sorbaria, and mahonia—produce a lush, tropical effect. Plants with smaller leaves like box, cotoneaster, and *Syringa microphylla* have a faintly formal, ordered air. They offer an interesting contrast when used with bold-leaved plants. Shrubs with glossy evergreen leaves—kalmia, pieris, leucothoe, *Prunus laurocerasus,* hollies, camellias, and some viburnums, for example—lend themselves to group planting. Their leaves range in size from seven inches on *Viburnum rhytidophyllum* and *Aucuba japonica* to less than one inch on box, Japanese holly, and *Lonicera nitida*. Mix the varous sizes for interesting textural contrasts within this otherwise homogeneous group. Try planting several red-twig dogwoods and one or two *Euonymus alata* or *Poncirus trifoliata* nearby for extreme textural contrast in winter.

Practical Considerations
Shrubs, unlike flowers, are architecturally useful as well as ornamental. They can offer privacy, screen unpleasant views, delineate boundaries, steer visitors to preferred paths, protect against intruders, and block wind and noise. On the map of your space, identify areas where such improvements are needed and follow the tips below to find the best shrubs for a specific purpose.

Screening and Fencing
A hedge or more informal shrub border can screen your yard from your neighbors', from the street, or from parking lots or trash pickup areas. Different growth habits and leaf textures can offer degrees of openness varying from opaque to lacy. Hedges or borders can also serve to mark the boundaries of your yard, keeping children and pets in and others out. A well-groomed formal hedge or a mixed border of shrubs that is in flower in spring, soothingly green in summer, and in fruit in fall is a much less threatening dividing line than most fences. For best relations, site a hedge or border so that your neighbor gets as good a view of the plants as you do, but check local ordinances about how far your hedge can extend over a property line and how high you may let it grow.

Controlling Access

Shrubs planted along driveways and walkways are not always there for purely esthetic reasons. A low border of sturdy shrubs like potentillas, barberries, or cotoneasters can deter strollers or bicyclists from leaving a path. If stronger deterrence is called for, you can resort to using shrubs that "bite." All the *Berberis* species, flowering quince, *Elaeagnus pungens,* and *Rosa hugonis* are prickly enough to discourage intimacy but insufficiently armed for real damage. (A plant with long and lethal thorns, like *Poncirus trifoliata,* would be too punishing.) Spiny plants can also make it painful for would-be intruders to get to a ground-floor window, so consider using them in foundation plantings as well. Unfortunately, these shrubs also make garden clean-up and pruning painful. Disarm them first by throwing a tarp or blanket over them.

Controlling Wind and Noise

Shrubs and trees have been used to offer protection against wind as long as gardens have existed. Their use as noise barriers is perhaps a bit newer. Today, both uses are of some importance. For either purpose, use tall, hardy, and dense plants. Evergreens of any sort are excellent, and—rather surprisingly—dense, twiggy, deciduous plants can be just as effective, even in winter. Even though sound waves and wind currents are different, the same principle applies in blocking them.

Sound waves do not bend easily but bounce off objects in their path and eventually dissipate. Therefore, every leaf, twig, and branch in a dense planting functions to dissipate the sound passing through it. When wind currents strike a solid surface, like the wall of a house, they simply travel over and around it with little diminishment in force. An object that is not solid, however, baffles or breaks up the force of the wind by channeling it into minor eddies and back-flows. This is the principle that the slatted snow fence works on, and it is the reason that some deciduous shrubs are as effective against wind as evergreens. They baffle the wind rather than block it.

Wind and sound barriers should be as tall and deep as practical. Plant sound barriers close to the source of noise, but position wind barriers closer to the garden areas you want to screen—within about 50 feet—to avoid having the wind regain its strength after flowing over or around the barrier.

Record Keeping

Because there are so many plants in a garden and so many plant names to remember, it pays to record what you have planted and where. This does not involve a load of paperwork or an elaborate filing system. You can choose from among five methods, used singly or in combination and to the extent you desire. These are photographs, labels, maps, acquisition lists, and diaries.

Photographs
Clearly, a photograph allows you to see exactly how your garden looked at a particular point in time. Maybe you're thinking of planting a low border of perennials this spring in front of your hydrangeas, which won't bloom until summer. A photograph will be much more reliable than your memory of the exact shade of the shrubs' flowers, helping you choose perennials that won't clash. However, in addition to being cumbersome, collections of garden photos cannot tell you the names of plants, how to care for them, or whether you were pleased with certain choices. They must be accompanied by written records—at least labeled as to name, date, and site—to be useful.

Labels
Plant labeling offers the advantage of placing documentation close to the plant itself. Since most shrubs do not die back in winter, you can attach labels to them permanently rather than relying on labeled stakes. These can be small and unobtrusive but helpful. Common sense will tell you where this method of documentation is useful and where other types might be more advisable.

Make permanent labels by embossing a plastic or metal strip and attaching it to your plant with wire. Do not use brass or copper wire because they are toxic to plants. Also, be careful not to tie the labels on so tightly that they strangle branches. The longest-lasting labels for home garden use are made of a soft aluminum alloy backed with cardboard. You simply write the plant name, and the date of planting and source, if you wish, on them using hard pencil or ball-point pen to engrave the information into the label.

Maps
Garden maps and charts may be of any size and complexity—from large overall to small sectional views, from rough sketches to precisely measured scale representations of an area. (See page 50 for instructions on making a map of your site.) Be sure to label everything carefully, including all plants, landmarks, and the sheet itself. Make all sorts of notations, such as an arrow pointing to a border of lilacs and the comment "underplanted with dwarf daffodils and *Scilla sibirica.*" Use specific names for certain areas in your garden—wild garden, cutting garden, azalea collection—or coin terms so that you can indicate clearly on the map which part of the garden it represents.

Acquisition Lists

An acquisition list records the source and date of purchase of new plants, as well as rough but helpful notations as to location. What is the name of that new white viburnum near the gate? Thumb through last year's acquisition list and find "1 *Viburnum* × *carlcephalum,* Blank Nurseries, next to front gate," and the date you planted it. Now you know not only what to tell admiring neighbors, but also how to order an identical shrub for the other side of the path.

Keep your list on three-by-five cards, arranged alphabetically in a file box. This way, you can add cards as you acquire new plants and pull them when plants are lost or discarded. Keep the pulled cards in a dead file, noting what the problem seemed to be. If you want to try one of these plants again later, you can consult the dead file for clues as to why it failed. Failures are as significant as successes in gardening. Perhaps you put the plant in an unsuitable place. It may have arrived in an already moribund condition from the nursery, or perhaps it was unadaptable to your soil. Knowing why it failed will strongly influence your decision about whether to try the plant again.

Every card in the acquisition file should give the following information: genus, species, and cultivar name (*Kerria japonica* 'Pleniflora', for example); source, number of plants, and date (Zee Nursery, 4 plants, 4/20/87); and location in the garden (in shade beside back shed). Record other interesting or important comments, such as subsequent purchases of the same cultivar, date of order or purchase, condition of the shrub on arrival, success or failure in the garden, unusual characteristics such as poor flowering or legginess, the plant's color, or any special growing information.

Stick to scientific names, at least in card headings. Most good nurseries send their plants out under those names, and common names are apt to be arbitrary or lacking. "Sunshine Shrub," for example, is *Hypericum kalmianum*. This name was coined by a nursery for selling purposes; the generally accepted common name for the plant is Kalm St. Johnswort. Alphabetizing under the Latin name avoids this confusion and also keeps the card next to those for other *Hypericum* species you may grow.

Garden Diaries

The primary intent of a gardening diary is to record daily, weekly, or seasonal changes—made by you or by nature—in your garden. At its simplest, a diary can be a "blooming list." This is an account of which plants are beginning, reaching their peaks, or ending their seasons and what tasks you performed at various intervals throughout the year. For example, "April 6: Transplanted wiegela from front to side yard." At its most complex, a diary can include many horticultural details and personal impressions.

Rereading your entries gives real insight into the effects of location,

soil, exposure, fluctuating temperatures, and climate on your garden. t shows you how variable blooming seasons can be and how much he variability depends on external factors. A diary also gives an ccurate performance record. Comments of three or four years unning like "bloom sparse on Kurume azalea 'Snow' " might tell ou that the plant is either poorly situated or unsuitable for your limate. Conversely, just one year of sparse flowering on a plant that he record says has previously bloomed well might be due to harsh veather, not to any fault in the plant or its site.
Iere is a sample diary entry:

Kurume azaleas beginning in back garden
Dexter rhododendrons in back beginning
Daffodils along walkway in full bloom
Bloodroot along walkway blooming—need more in south edge
Rhododendron mucronulatum along driveway fading; sparse bloom this year
Crocuses throughout garden fading
Vegetable garden and annual beds fertilized and spaded this weekend
Planted 1 Camellia japonica 'Showa No Sake' (Blank Nurseries) in front foundation bed.

Always include the date at the top of the page, along with a weather ntry—for example, "April 30, 1987, 70° at noon, sunny, mild reeze." Then list the plants currently in bloom, just coming into loom, or fading. If your garden is small, list the plants at random s you see them. If it is large, arrange your list by area, recording all elevant details on one section before moving on to the next. nclude comments on performance, such as "*Magnolia quinquepeta* eautiful this year" or "*Clethra alnifolia* 'Pinkspire' sparse in bloom." Note esthetic judgments like "*Syringa microphylla* in side yard clashes vith *Rhododendron kaempferi*—move next spring." Record any bservation or intention, because the chances are you will forget hese in time—"*Corylopsis pauciflora* blooms same time as *Rhododendron mucronulatum* and they look nice together." There is no limit to such commentary. It may be somewhat peripheral— "many more birds since pond was dug," or eminently practical— "wet spring spawned a plague of slugs," "watch for spider mites in ate summer."

As it grows, your diary becomes a record of your experience that can e almost as rewarding as the garden itself. It may even take the lace of labeling, mapping, and acquisition lists, if you faithfully ecord purchasing and planting data. In any case, by recording the hanges that time, labor, neglect, and fate bring to your garden, a liary serves as an ongoing cross-index to the other, static systems nd helps you keep them up to date.

Calendar

Once they are established, shrubs require little special attention. You can keep them in peak condition by performing just a few seasonal tasks. The guidelines below will serve as reminders but are not hard-and-fast rules. Your own enthusiasm for gardening, an understanding of local environmental conditions, and the particular requirements of shrubs you grow will help you decide how conscientious to be.

The calendar is organized by season rather than month, so it is adaptable to various areas of the country. Remember that the dates of the first and last frosts in your region are the best indicators of the beginning of winter and end of spring.

Late Winter to Early Spring

This is the season of promise for gardeners, when the bleak landscape quietly gathers its strength for the coming burst of color. Help your plants with the following preparatory steps:

1. Plant and transplant shrubs, especially in cold regions.
2. Cut out winter-damaged twigs and branches as soon as new growth begins.
3. Cut back summer-flowering shrubs like hydrangeas and *Spirea japonica* if desired.
4. Fertilize with a balanced fertilizer such as 5-10-10 or 10-10-10.
5. Apply lime in acid-soil areas around plants requiring alkaline or neutral soil.
6. Apply dormant oil sprays to branches of deciduous shrubs to kill insect pests.

Late Spring to Early Summer

After the first glorious wave of color has ebbed, some garden clean-up and rejuvenation are helpful, both esthetically and horticulturally, to the continuing cycle of growth. Follow these guidelines:

1. Deadhead—remove spent flowers to prevent seed from setting—all spring-flowering shrubs such as lilacs and rhododendrons after bloom season.
2. Prune spring-flowering shrubs as soon as possible after flowers fade.
3. Spray for pests like scale and leafminers at appropriate times.
4. Near the end of this period, apply high-phosphorus fertilizer to rhododendrons and other broad-leaved evergreens.

Midsummer

The lazy, hazy days need not be interrupted by many garden chores. Relax and enjoy the fruits of your labors. Cut some fragrant branches from an abelia or a *Vitex agnus-castus,* for example, and enjoy them indoors. Sit on the porch and watch butterflies feed on the *Buddleia davidii*. Break the reverie only to do the following:

1. Water regularly, frequently, and deeply, with special attention to newly planted shrubs.
2. Prune to correct appearance by cutting out stressed, damaged, or spindly twigs and branches.

Early Fall

Flowers may have faded, but glimmers of richer autumn hues are beginning to appear. As your plants move toward the dormant stage, there are just a few tasks to perform:

1. Plant and transplant shrubs, especially in warm regions.
2. Continue watering until temperatures fall and rains begin.

Late Fall to Winter

If you have been careful to choose shrubs hardy to your climate, they should weather the cold with little human help. Do as many of the following chores as common sense tells you is prudent in your area and for the particular shrubs you are growing:

1. Mound soil or mulch around bases of tender plants after first frost.
2. Install burlap screens around evergreens.
3. Spray Wilt Pruf on leaves of broad-leaved evergreens.
4. At the slightest evidence of damage from mice or voles—bark nibbled at base of plant, for example—place a solid chemical pesticide containing warfarin, such as Mouse-knots, in waterproof jars or cans with openings and bury them under mulch or compost so that beneficial wild animals and pets cannot get to them.

The Color Plates

Shrubs are the backbone of the garden, providing dimension, texture, and balance to the landscape. Because the overall shape of a shrub—not just its color—often determines its effectiveness in the garden, the color plates are arranged by plant shape. A view of an entire shrub is shown first, together with a detail of its flowers, foliage, or fruit, or with details of other, similar shrubs. Some photographs also present variations in flower color or seasonal changes.

Flowering shrubs begin the color section—from large, spreading lilacs to more compact, showy rhododendrons to lacy forsythia. Next are shrubs grown for their striking foliage and showy fruit, such as bushy barberries, rounded viburnums, spreading pyracanthas, and tall hollies. Finally, there are the foliage plants—glossy osmanthus; tall, bushy privets; tight, rounded boxwoods.

Visual Key

The Visual Key adds another dimension to the color plates, allowing you to select shrubs according to the color of their flowers, foliage, or fruit. Shrubs whose flowers appear before the leaves and those with especially colorful or unusual stems are also featured here. The chart is divided into fourteen groups: white flowers; pink flowers; blue to purple flowers; red to orange flowers; yellow flowers; flowers appearing before leaves; green foliage; colorful or variegated foliage; fall foliage; yellow or orange fruit; red fruit; purple or blue fruit; white, gray, or black fruit; and colorful or unusual stems.

Visual Key

White Flowers

Pink Flowers

Blue to Purple Flowers

Red to Orange Flowers

This chart allows you to select shrubs by the color of their flowers, foliage, and fruit. In addition, shrubs whose flowers appear before the leaves or whose stems are especially colorful or unusual in winter are identified here. These first four groups are flower colors.

Pages 72, 73, 78, 79, 84, 86–91, 96, 98–103, 105, 106, 113–115, 117, 118, 122, 123, 124–127, 130, 136, 138–140, 142–146, 148–151, 154, 155, 196, 198–200, 202–204, 206, 215–222, 224–229, 231, 232, 240, 245–247, 256, 258, 260, 261, 270–273, 275–277, 279, 284, 285

Pages 73, 81–85, 90, 91, 96, 98, 99, 103, 107, 108, 110, 111, 113, 114, 119–122, 130–132, 134, 135, 137, 141, 143, 145, 152, 153, 201, 236, 244

Pages 74–78, 106, 107, 116, 128, 129, 141, 148–152, 154, 155

Pages 80, 83, 92–95, 97, 104, 105, 109–112, 142, 156, 157, 170

Yellow Flowers

Flowers Appearing Before Leaves

Green Foliage

Colorful or Variegated Foliage

Fall Foliage

The fifth flower color group, yellow, is given here. Flowering shrubs that bloom before their leaves appear are also cross-listed by color.

The fall foliage group includes only plants with especially vivid autumn hues.

Pages 80, 97, 104, 137, 158–191, 230, 242, 275

Pages 82–84, 86–89, 134, 163, 165–173, 176, 177

Pages 172, 173, 184, 185, 194, 202, 206, 208, 210, 212, 224, 244, 248, 250, 264, 266, 268, 270–287

Pages 85, 97, 150, 182, 183, 190, 192, 193, 195, 200–207, 214, 247, 248, 259, 274, 275,. 277, 283

Pages 109, 138, 139, 192–194, 197, 199, 205, 207, 209, 211, 213, 228

Yellow or Orange Fruit

Red Fruit

Purple or Blue Fruit

White, Gray, or Black Fruit

Colorful or Unusual Stems

Fruiting shrubs are divided into four groups by berry color. Some of the pages listed for these shrubs also show them in flower.

The last group on this chart features shrubs whose stem color or shape is interesting in winter.

Pages 87, 184, 185, 234, 235, 243, 254–256, 260

Pages 81, 93, 190–193, 195, 197, 210, 214–217, 219–224, 233, 237, 239, 243, 245–247, 249–255, 257, 260, 261

Pages 188, 189, 229, 257, 259, 262, 263

Pages 147, 191, 197, 231, 233, 238, 240, 241, 265–267, 269

Pages 166, 168, 208, 209, 241

Syringa reticulata

Japanese Tree Lilac
Plant height: to 30 ft.
Clusters: to 12 in. long
Blooms in spring
Zone 4

Average soil
p. 411

Syringa vulgaris

Common Lilac
Plant height: to 15 ft.
Clusters: 6–8 in. long
Blooms in spring
Zone 4

Average soil
p. 412

Syringa patula
'Miss Kim'

Miss Kim Lilac
Plant height: 4–8 ft.
Clusters: 3 in. long
Blooms in spring
Zone 4

Average soil
p. 411

Syringa villosa

Late Lilac
Plant height: to 10 ft.
Clusters:
to 3–7 in. long
Blooms in spring
Zone 3

Average soil
p. 412

Syringa meyeri
'Palibin'

Meyer Lilac
Plant height: 4–8 ft.
Clusters: to 4 in. long
Blooms in spring
Zones 4–8

Average soil
p. 411

Syringa × persica

Persian Lilac
Plant height: 5–6 ft.
Clusters: to 3 in. long
Blooms in spring
Zone 4

Average soil
p. 411

***Syringa microphylla* 'Superba'**	*Littleleaf Lilac* *Plant height: to 7 ft.* *Clusters: 1–3 in. long* *Blooms in spring* *Zone 5*	*Average soil* *p. 411*

Syringa × chinensis	*Chinese Lilac* *Plant height: to 10 ft.* *Clusters: 4–6 in. long* *Blooms in spring* *Zone 4*	*Average soil* *p. 411*

Syringa vulgaris	*Common Lilac* *Plant height: to 15 ft.* *Clusters: 6–8 in. long* *Blooms in spring* *Zone 4*	*Average soil* *p. 412*

Ceanothus cyaneus **'Sierra Blue'**	*San Diego Ceanothus* *Plant height:* *10–12 ft.* *Clusters: 2–5 in. long* *Blooms in spring* *Zone 8*	*Dry soil* *p. 313*

Syringa × chinensis

Chinese Lilac
Plant height: to 10 ft.
Clusters: 4–6 in. long
Blooms in spring
Zone 4

Average soil
p. 411

Ceanothus griseus
var. horizontalis

Carmel Creeper
Plant height: 2–3 ft.
Clusters: to 2 in. long
Blooms in spring
Zone 8

Dry soil
p. 313

Vitex agnus-castus

Lilac Chaste Tree
Plant height: 7–20 ft.
Clusters: to 1 ft. long
Blooms in summer
Zone 7

Average soil
p. 420

Vitex negundo

Chaste Tree
Plant height:
10–15 ft.
Flowers: see detail
Zone 7

Average soil
p. 421

Vitex agnus-castus **'Alba'**	*Lilac Chaste Tree* *Plant height: 7–20 ft.* *Clusters: to 1 ft. long* *Blooms in summer* *Zone 7*	*Average soil* *p. 420*

Vitex negundo	*Chaste Tree* *Clusters: to 8 in. long* *Blooms in summer*	*p. 421*

Ribes sanguineum

Flowering Currant
Plant height: 5–12 ft.
Flowers: see detail
Zones 6–8

Average soil
p. 396

Ribes odoratum

Clove Currant
Plant height: 4–6 ft.
Clusters: 1½–2 in. long
Blooms in spring
Zone 5

Average soil
Tolerates shade
p. 396

Ribes sanguineum

Flowering Currant
Clusters: 2–4 in. long
Blooms in spring

p. 396

Ribes alpinum

Alpine Currant
Plant height: 5–8 ft.
Clusters: to 1 in. long
Blooms in spring
Zone 3

Average soil
Tolerates shade
p. 395

Weigela florida	*Old-fashioned Weigela* *Plant height: 7–10 ft.* *Flowers:* *to 1½ in. long* *Blooms in spring* *Zone 4*	*Average soil* *p. 421*

Cercis chinensis	*Chinese Redbud* *Plant height: to 10 ft.* *Flowers: see detail* *Zone 7*	*Average soil* *p. 314*

***Weigela florida* 'Bristoe Ruby'**	*Old-fashioned Weigela* *Plant height: 7–10 ft.* *Flowers:* *to 1½ in. long* *Blooms in spring* *Zone 4*	*Average soil* *p. 421*

Cercis chinensis	*Chinese Redbud* *Flowers: to ¾ in. long* *Blooms in spring*	*p. 314*

Prunus
'Hally Jolivette'

Hally Jolivette Cherry
Plant height: 8–15 ft.
Flowers: 1–1½ in. wide
Blooms in spring
Zone 5

Average soil
p. 386

Prunus glandulosa

Dwarf Flowering Almond
Plant height: to 5 ft.
Flowers: to ½ in. wide
Blooms in spring
Zone 5

Average soil
p. 386

Prunus × cistena

Purple-leaf Sand Cherry
Plant height: 8–10 ft.
Flowers: to ½ in. wide
Blooms in spring
Zone 3

Average soil
p. 386

Prunus tenella 'Fire Hill'

Dwarf Russian Almond
Plant height: 2–5 ft.
Flowers: to ½ in. wide
Blooms in spring
Zone 3

Average soil
p. 387

Amelanchier stolonifera

Running Serviceberry
Plant height: 3–6 ft.
Clusters: ⅝–1⅝ in. long
Blooms in spring
Zone 4

Average soil
p. 295

Poncirus trifoliata

Trifoliate Orange
Plant height: to 20 ft.
Flowers: to 2 in. wide
Blooms in spring
Zone 6

Acid soil
p. 384

Abeliophyllum distichum

Korean Abelialeaf
Plant height: stems 3–5 ft. long
Flowers: to ⅝ in. wide
Blooms in spring
Zone 5

Average soil
p. 291

Poncirus trifoliata

Trifoliate Orange
Fruit

p. 384

Chionanthus virginicus	*Fringe Tree* *Plant height: to 25 ft.* *Flowers: see detail* *Zone 4*	*Average soil* *p. 317*

Magnolia stellata	*Star Magnolia* *Plant height: to 15 ft.* *Flowers: see detail* *Zone 4*	*Average soil* *p. 368*

Chionanthus virginicus	*Fringe Tree* *Clusters: to 7 in. long* *Blooms in spring*	*p. 317*

Magnolia stellata	*Star Magnolia* *Flowers: to 3 in. wide* *Blooms in spring*	*p. 368*

Magnolia × loebneri	*Loebner Magnolia* *Plant height: to 30 ft.* *Flowers: see detail* *Zone 4*	*Average soil* *p. 368*

Magnolia quinquepeta	*Lily Magnolia* *Plant height: to 12 ft.* *Flowers: see detail* *Zone 5*	*Average soil* *p. 368*

Magnolia* × *loebneri	*Loebner Magnolia* *Flowers:* *to 3½ in. wide* *Blooms in spring*	*p. 368*

Magnolia quinquepeta	*Lily Magnolia* *Flowers: to 4 in. long* *Blooms in spring*	*p. 368*

Calycanthus floridus

Carolina Allspice
Plant height: 4–8 ft.
Flowers: to 2 in. wide
Blooms in spring
Zone 4

Average soil
Tolerates shade
p. 309

Illicium floridanum

Florida Anise Tree
Plant height: to 10 ft.
Flowers: to 1½ in. wide
Blooms in spring
Zone 8

Wet soil
Tolerates shade
p. 356

Feijoa sellowiana | *Pineapple Guava* | *Dry soil*
Plant height: to 20 ft.
Flowers: ¾–1½ in. long
Blooms in spring
Zone 8
p. 339

Ochna serrulata | *Bird's-Eye Bush* | *Tolerates dry soil*
Plant height: to 10 ft.
Flowers: to ⅜ in. wide
Blooms in summer
Zone 9
p. 374

Punica granatum	*Pomegranate* *Plant height:* *10–20 ft.* *Flowers: see detail* *Zone 8*	*Average soil* *p. 387*

Calliandra haematocephala	*Red Powderpuff* *Plant height: to 15 ft.* *Flowers: to 2 in. wide* *Blooms fall to winter* *Zone 10*	*Average soil* *p. 306*

Punica granatum

Pomegranate
Flowers:
to 1½ in. wide
Blooms in spring

p. 387

Callistemon citrinus

Crimson Bottle-brush
Plant height:
10–20 ft.
Clusters: 2–4 in. long
Blooms spring to summer
Zone 9

Acid soil
p. 308

Cotinus coggygria

Common Smoke Tree
Plant height:
10–15 ft.
Clusters: 7–10 in. long
Blooms in summer
Zone 5

Dry soil
p. 325

Tamarix ramosissima

Five-stamen Tamarisk
Plant height:
10–15 ft.
Clusters: 1–3 in. long
Blooms in summer
Zone 3

Average soil
p. 413

***Cotinus coggygria* 'Purpureus'**	*Common Smoke Tree* *Plant height: 10–15 ft.* *Clusters: 7–10 in. long* *Blooms in summer* *Zone 5*	*Dry soil* *p. 325*

Kolkwitzia amabilis	*Beauty Bush* *Plant height: 6–12 ft.* *Flowers: to ½ in. long* *Blooms in spring* *Zone 5*	*Average soil* *p. 359*

Enkianthus campanulatus	*Redvein Enkianthus* *Plant height: 8–12 ft.* *Flowers: see detail* *Zone 5*	*Acid soil* *p. 334*

Baccharis halimifolia	*Groundsel Bush* *Plant height: 6–12 ft.* *Flowers: see detail* *Zones 6–10*	*Average soil* *p. 299*

Enkianthus campanulatus

Redvein Enkianthus
Flowers: to ½ in. long
Blooms in spring

p. 334

Baccharis halimifolia

Groundsel Bush
Clusters: to 3 in. long
Blooms in summer

p. 299

Staphylea colchica | *Colchis Bladdernut* | *Average soil*
Plant height: 8–12 ft.
Flowers: see detail
Zone 5
p. 407

Exochorda racemosa | *Common Pearlbush* | *Average soil*
Plant height: to 15 ft.
Clusters: to 2 in. wide
Blooms in spring
Zone 5
p. 337

Staphylea colchica

Colchis Bladdernut
Clusters: 2–4 in. long
Blooms in spring

p. 407

Exochorda × _macrantha_ 'The Bride'

Pearlbush
Plant height: to 4 ft.
Clusters: 3–4 in. long
Blooms in spring
Zone 5

Average soil
p. 337

Deutzia × lemoinei	*Lemoine Deutzia* *Plant height: to 7 ft.* *Clusters: 2–4 in. wide* *Blooms in spring* *Zone 4*	*Average soil* *p. 330*

Deutzia scabra 'Candidissima'	*Fuzzy Deutzia* *Plant height: to 8 ft.* *Clusters: 3–5 in. long* *Blooms spring to summer* *Zone 5*	*Average soil* *p. 331*

Deutzia gracilis

Slender Deutzia
Plant height: to 5 ft.
Flowers: to ¾ in. wide
Blooms in spring
Zone 5

Average soil
p. 330

Deutzia scabra
'Flore-Pleno'

Fuzzy Deutzia
Plant height: to 8 ft.
Clusters: 3–5 in. long
Blooms spring to summer
Zone 5

Average soil
p. 331

***Rhododendron* 'J. Jennings'**	*Exbury Hybrid Azalea* *Plant height: to 4 ft.* *Flowers: to 3 in. wide* *Blooms in spring* *Zone 5*	*Acid soil* *p. 391*

Rhododendron* × *kosteranum	*Mollis Hybrid Azalea* *Plant height: 6–8 ft.* *Flowers:* *2½–3½ in. wide* *Blooms in spring* *Zone 6*	*Acid soil* *p. 392*

Rhododendron
'Aurora'

Exbury Hybrid Azalea
Plant height: to 4 ft.
Flowers: to 3 in. wide
Blooms in spring
Zone 5

Acid soil
p. 391

Rhododendron
'Toucan'

Exbury Hybrid Azalea
Plant height: to 4 ft.
Flowers: to 3 in. wide
Blooms in spring
Zone 5

Acid soil
p. 391

Rhododendron yakusimanum	*Yako Rhododendron* *Plant height: to 3 ft.* *Flowers: see detail* *Zone 5*	*Acid soil* *p. 393*

Rhododendron **PJM hybrid**	*PJM Rhododendron* *Plant height: 3–6 ft.* *Clusters: 3–5 in. wide* *Blooms in spring* *Zone 4*	*Acid soil* *p. 392*

Rhododendron yakusimanum

Yako Rhododendron
Pink-flowered form
Clusters: 6–10 in. wide
Blooms in spring

p. 393

Rhododendron catawbiense

Catawba Rhododendron
Plant height: 6–10 ft.
Clusters: 6–10 in. wide
Blooms in spring
Zone 5

Acid soil
p. 391
Evergreen
Reliable, Cold Tolerant

***Rhododendron mucronulatum* 'Cornell Pink'**

Korean Rhododendron
Plant height: to 8 ft.
Clusters: 6–10 in. wide
Blooms in spring
Zone 5

Acid soil
p. 392

Rhododendron schlippenbachii

Royal Azalea
Plant height: 6–10 ft.
Flowers: to 2½ in. wide
Blooms in spring
Zone 5

Acid soil
p. 393

Rhododendron kaempferi

Torch Azalea
Plant height: to 8 ft.
Flowers: to 2 in. wide
Blooms in spring
Zone 5

Acid soil
p. 392

Rhododendron schlippenbachii

Royal Azalea
In fall

p. 393

Chaenomeles japonica

Japanese Quince
Plant height: to 3 ft.
Flowers: to 1 in. wide
Blooms in spring
Zone 5

Average soil
p. 315

Chaenomeles speciosa 'Toyo Nishiki'

Common Flowering Quince
Plant height: 6–10 ft.
Flowers: 1–2 in. wide
Blooms in spring
Zone 5

Average soil
p. 315

Chaenomeles* × *superba **'Mandarin'**	*Flowering Quince* *Plant height:* *stems to 5 ft.* *Flowers: 1–2 in. wide* *Blooms in spring* *Zone 5*	*Average soil* *p. 316*

Chaenomeles speciosa **'Phylis Moore'**	*Common Flowering* *Quince* *Plant height: 6–10 ft.* *Flowers: 1–2 in. wide* *Blooms in spring* *Zone 5*	*Average soil* *p. 315*

Rhododendron 'Stewartstonian'	*Gable Hybrid Azalea* *Plant height: 3–4 ft.* *Flowers: to 2 in. wide* *Blooms in spring* *Zone 6*	*Acid soil* *p. 392*

Rhododendron 'Hino-Crimson'	*Kurume Hybrid Azalea* *Plant height: 4–6 ft.* *Flowers:to 1½ in. wide* *Blooms in spring* *Zone 7*	*Acid soil* *p. 392*

Rhododendron **'Coral Bells'**	*Kurume Hybrid Azalea* *Plant height: 4–6 ft.* *Flowers: to 1½ in. wide* *Blooms in spring* *Zone 7*	*Acid soil* *p. 392*

Rhododendron **'Snow'**	*Kurume Hybrid Azalea* *Plant height: 4–6 ft.* *Flowers: to 1½ in. wide* *Blooms in spring* *Zone 7*	*Acid soil* *p. 392*

Kalmia latifolia

Mountain Laurel
Plant height: 7–15 ft.
Flowers: see detail
Zone 5

Acid soil
p. 358

Kalmia angustifolia 'Rubra'

Sheep Laurel
Plant height: 2–3 ft.
Clusters: 2–3 in. wide
Blooms in spring
Zone 3

Acid soil
p. 358

Kalmia latifolia 'Fuscata'

Mountain Laurel
Plant height: 7–15 ft.
Clusters: 4–6 in. wide
Blooms in spring
Zone 5

Acid soil
p. 358

Kalmia latifolia

Mountain Laurel
Clusters: 4–6 in. wide
Blooms in spring

p. 358

Cistus × purpureus	*Orchid Rockrose* *Plant height: 3–4 ft.* *Flowers: 2–3 in. wide* *Blooms in summer* *Zone 8*	*Dry, alkaline soil* *p. 318*

Alyogyne huegelii	*Blue Hibiscus* *Plant height: to 8 ft.* *Flowers: 4–5 in. wide* *Blooms year-round* *Zone 9*	*Dry soil* *p. 294*

Cistus ladanifer

Crimson-spot Rockrose
Plant height: to 4 ft.
Flowers: to 3½ in. wide
Blooms in summer
Zone 7

Dry, alkaline soil
p. 318

Romneya coulteri

Matilija Poppy
Plant height: to 8 ft.
Flowers: to 6 in. wide
Blooms in summer
Zone 7

Tolerates dry soil
p. 396

Cistus × hybridus	*White Rockrose* *Plant height: 2–4 ft.* *Flowers: to 1½ in. wide* *Blooms spring to summer* *Zone 8*	*Dry, alkaline soil* *p. 318*

Rosa wichuraiana	*Memorial Rose* *Plant height: to 1½ ft.* *Flowers: to 2 in. wide* *Blooms in summer* *Zone 6*	*Dry soil* *p. 398*

Cistus × pulverulentus	*Hybrid Rockrose* *Plant height: to 2 ft.* *Flowers: to 1 in. wide* *Blooms in summer* *Zone 8*	*Dry, alkaline soil* *p. 318*

Rosa rugosa	*Rugosa Rose* *Plant height: 4–6 ft.* *Flowers: to 3½ in. wide* *Blooms in summer* *Zone 3*	*Average soil* *p. 398*

Hibiscus syriacus
'Althea'

Rose-of-Sharon
Plant height: 5–15 ft.
Flowers: 3–5 in. wide
Blooms summer to fall
Zone 5

Average soil
p. 348

Camellia japonica
'Rev. John G. Drayton'

Common Camellia
Plant height: 20–25 ft.
Flowers: 3–5 in. wide
Blooms fall to spring
Zone 8

Acid soil
p. 310

Hibiscus rosa-sinensis **'Agnes Gault'**	*Rose-of-China* *Plant height: 8–15 ft.* *Flowers: 4–6 in. wide* *Blooms in summer* *Zone 10*	*Average soil* *p. 347*

Camellia sasanqua **'Showa No Sakae'**	*Sasanqua Camellia* *Plant height: 6–10 ft.* *Flowers: 2–3 in. wide* *Blooms fall to winter* *Zone 8*	*Acid soil* *p. 310*

Nerium oleander

Common Oleander
Plant height: 8–20 ft.
Flowers: see detail
Zones 8–10

Dry soil
p. 373

Rhodotypos scandens

Jetbead
Plant height: 4–6 ft.
Flowers: to 2 in. wide
Blooms in spring
Zone 5

Average soil
Tolerates shade
p. 393

Nerium oleander

Common Oleander
White-flowered form
Flowers: to 2½ in. wide
Blooms in summer

p. 373

Gardenia jasminoides

Gardenia
Plant height: 2–5 ft.
Flowers: 2–3½ in. wide
Blooms spring to fall
Zone 8

Acid soil
p. 342

Ligustrum japonicum	*Japanese Privet* *Plant height: 7–10 ft.* *Clusters: 4–6 in. long* *Blooms in spring* *Zone 7*	*Dry soil* *Tolerates shade* *p. 364*

Ligustrum obtusifolium* var. *regelianum	*Regel's Privet* *Plant height: 8–12 ft.* *Flowers: see detail* *Zone 4*	*Dry soil* *p. 364*

Ligustrum vulgare	*European Privet* *Plant height: 5–15 ft.* *Clusters: to 3 in. long* *Blooms in spring* *Zone 4*	*Dry soil* *p. 364*

Ligustrum obtusifolium* var. *regelianum	*Regel's Privet* *Clusters: to 1½ in. long* *Blooms in spring*	*p. 364*

Philadelphus coronarius

Common Mock-Orange
Plant height: to 10 ft.
Flowers: see detail
Zone 5

Average soil
p. 377

Philadelphus × lemoinei

Lemoine Mock-Orange
Plant height: 4–6 ft.
Flowers: to 1½ in. wide
Blooms in spring
Zone 5

Average soil
p. 377

Philadelphus coronarius

Common Mock-Orange
Flowers: to 1½ in. wide
Blooms in spring

p. 377

Philadelphus* × *virginalis

Virginal Mock-Orange
Plant height: 5–10 ft.
Clusters: 3–5 in. wide
Blooms in spring
Zone 5

Average soil

p. 378

***Brunfelsia pauciflora* 'Floribunda'**

Yesterday, Today, and Tomorrow
Plant height: 8–10 ft.
Flowers: to 2 in. wide
Blooms spring to summer
Zone 9

Acid soil
p. 302

Tibouchina urvilleana

Princess Flower
Plant height: 4–15 ft.
Flowers: 3–4 in. wide
Blooms year-round
Zones 9–10

Acid soil
p. 415

Brunfelsia pauciflora	*Brazil Raintree* *Plant height: to 2 ft.* *Flowers: to 2 in. wide* *Blooms spring to summer* *Zone 9*	*Acid soil* *p. 302*

Polygala × dalmaisiana	*Sweet-Pea Shrub* *Plant height: 3–6 ft.* *Clusters: 2–4 in. wide* *Blooms in spring* *Zone 9*	*Average soil* *p. 383*

Abelia* × *grandiflora	*Glossy Abelia* *Plant height: 3–6 ft.* *Flowers: to ¾ in. long* *Blooms summer to fall* *Zones 5–9*	*Acid soil* *p. 290*

Grewia occidentalis	*Lavender Starflower* *Plant height: to 10 ft.* *Flowers: to 1 in. wide* *Blooms in spring* *Zone 9*	*Average soil* *p. 345*

***Abelia* 'Edward Goucher'**	*Edward Goucher Glossy Abelia* *Plant height: 4–5 ft.* *Flowers: to ¾ in. long* *Blooms summer to fall* *Zone 7*	*Average soil* *p. 290*

Escallonia rubra	*Red Escallonia* *Plant height: 10–15 ft.* *Clusters: to 3 in. long* *Blooms spring to summer* *Zone 8*	*Average soil* *p. 335*

Raphiolepis umbellata 'Springtime'

Yeddo Raphiolepis
Plant height: 4–6 ft.
Flowers: to ¾ in. wide
Blooms in spring
Zone 8

Tolerates dry soil
p. 389

Raphiolepis indica 'Rosea'

Indian Hawthorn
Plant height: to 5 ft.
Flowers: to ½ in. wide
Blooms in spring
Zone 8

Tolerates dry soil
p. 389

Raphiolepis umbellata	*Yeddo Raphiolepis* *Plant height: 4–6 ft.* *Flowers: to ¾ in. wide* *Blooms in spring* *Zone 8*	*Tolerates dry soil* *p. 389*

Raphiolepis indica	*Indian Hawthorn* *Plant height: to 5 ft.* *Flowers: to ½ in. wide* *Blooms in spring* *Zone 8*	*Tolerates dry soil* *p. 389*

Daphne mezereum

February Daphne
Plant height: to 5 ft.
Clusters: to 1½ in. wide
Blooms in spring
Zone 6

Average soil
Tolerates shade
p. 329

Daphne cneorum
'Eximea'

Rose Daphne
Plant height: to 12 in.
Clusters: to 1½ in. wide
Blooms in spring
Zone 5

Average soil
p. 329

Daphne* × *burkwoodii
'Somerset'

Burkwood Daphne
Plant height: to 4 ft.
Clusters: to 2 in. wide
Blooms in spring
Zone 4

Average soil
p. 329

Daphne odora

Fragrant Daphne
Plant height: to 4 ft.
Clusters: to 1 in. wide
Blooms in spring
Zone 7

Average soil
Tolerates shade
p. 330

Choisya ternata

Mexican Orange
Plant height: 6–8 ft.
Flowers: 1–1½ in. wide
Blooms in spring
Zone 8

Acid soil
p. 317

× Fatshedera × lizei

Fatshedera
Plant height: to 6 ft.
Clusters: 8–10 in. long
Blooms in fall
Zone 8

Average soil
Requires shade
p. 338

Ceanothus ovatus

Inland Ceanothus
Plant height: 2–3 ft.
Clusters: 1–2 in.
Blooms in spring
Zone 5

Dry soil
p. 313

Fatsia japonica

Japanese Aralia
Plant height:
10–12 ft.
Clusters:
to 18 in. long
Blooms in fall
Zone 8

Average soil
Requires shade
p. 338

Hydrangea quercifolia

Oakleaf Hydrangea
Plant height: to 6 ft.
Flowers: see detail
Zone 5

Average soil
p. 351

Hydrangea quercifolia

Oakleaf Hydrangea
In fall

p. 351

Hydrangea quercifolia

Oakleaf Hydrangea
Clusters: to 10 in. long
Blooms in summer

p. 351

Hydrangea quercifolia

Oakleaf Hydrangea
In fall

p. 351

Hydrangea arborescens 'Annabelle'

Smooth Hydrangea
Plant height: 3–5 ft.
Clusters: 2–5 in. wide
Blooms in summer
Zone 4

Average soil
p. 350

Hydrangea paniculata 'Grandiflora'

Panicle Hydrangea
Plant height: 8–30 ft.
Flowers: see detail
Zone 4

Average soil
p. 350

Hydrangea macrophylla

Bigleaf Hydrangea
Plant height: to 6 ft.
Clusters: 6–10 in. long.
Blooms in summer
Zone 7

Average soil
p. 350

***Hydrangea paniculata* 'Grandiflora'**

Panicle Hydrangea
Pink-flowered form
Clusters: 8–12 in. long
Blooms in summer

p. 350

***Spiraea × bumalda* 'Froebelii'**	*Bumald Spirea* *Plant height: to 3 ft.* *Clusters: 4–6 in. wide* *Blooms in summer* *Zone 4*	*Average soil* *p. 406*

Physocarpus opulifolius	*Common Ninebark* *Plant height: 5–10 ft.* *Clusters: to 2 in. wide* *Blooms in spring* *Zone 3*	*Tolerates dry soil* *p. 380*

Spiraea japonica
'Little Princess'

Japanese Spirea
Plant height: 4–6 ft.
Clusters: to 3 in. wide
Blooms in spring
Zone 4

Average soil
p. 406

Cephalanthus occidentalis

Button Bush
Plant height: 5–12 ft.
Flowers: to 1 in. wide
Blooms in summer
Zone 5

Wet soil
p. 314

Aesculus parviflora

Bottlebrush Buckeye
Plant height: 8–12 ft.
Clusters:
to 12 in. long
Blooms in summer
Zone 4

Average soil
Tolerates shade
p. 294

Sorbaria sorbifolia

Ural False Spirea
Plant height: to 10 ft.
Clusters: 4–10 in. long
Blooms in summer
Zone 3

Average soil
p. 404

Clethra alnifolia 'Pink Spires'

Summersweet Clethra
Plant height: 3–8 ft.
Clusters: to 5 in. long
Blooms in summer
Zone 4

Wet, acid soil
p. 319

Prunus laurocerasus 'Otto Luyken'

Cherry Laurel
Plant height: to 4 ft.
Clusters: 2–5 in. long
Blooms in spring
Zone 7

Average soil
Tolerates shade
p. 386

Prunus laurocerasus

Cherry Laurel
Plant height: to 20 ft.
Clusters: 2–5 in. long
Blooms in spring
Zone 7

Average soil
Tolerates shade
p. 386

Prunus laurocerasus
'Schipkaensis'

Plant height: 4–5 ft.
Clusters: 2–5 in. long
Blooms in spring
Zone 5

Average soil
Tolerates shade
p. 386

Prunus laurocerasus *Cherry Laurel* *p. 386*
Fruit

Prunus besseyi *Sand Cherry* *Dry soil*
Plant height: 4–6 ft. *p. 386*
Zone 4

Buddleia davidii **hybrid**

Orange-eye Butterfly Bush
Plant height: 6–10 ft.
Flowers: see detail
Zones 5–9

Average soil
p. 303

Buddleia davidii

Orange-eye Butterfly Bush
Plant height: 6–10 ft.
Clusters: 5–12 in. long
Blooms summer to fall
Zones 5–9

Average soil
p. 303

Buddleia davidii **hybrid**

Orange-eye Butterfly Bush
Clusters: 5–12 in. long
Blooms summer to fall

p. 303

Buddleia davidii **'Black Knight'**

Orange-eye Butterfly Bush
Plant height: 6–10 ft.
Clusters: 5–12 in. long
Blooms summer to fall
Zones 5–9

Average soil
p. 303

Spiraea nipponica 'Snowmound'

Snowmound Spirea
Plant height: 4–6 ft.
Clusters: 1½–2 in. wide
Blooms in spring
Zone 4

Average soil
p. 406

Buddleia alternifolia 'Argentea'

Alternate Leaf Butterfly Bush
Plant height: to 20 ft.
Clusters: to ¾ in. long
Blooms in summer
Zones 6–8

Average soil
p. 303

Spiraea × vanhouttei	*Vanhoutte Spirea* *Plant height: 6–8 ft.* *Clusters: 1–2 in. wide* *Blooms in spring* *Zone 4*	*Average soil* *p. 407*

Lavandula dentata	*French Lavender* *Plant height: 1–3 ft.* *Clusters: to 2½ in. long* *Blooms in summer* *Zone 9*	*Dry soil* *p. 361*

***Calluna vulgaris* 'Million'**

Scotch Heather
Plant height: to 18 in.
Clusters: to 10 in. long
Blooms summer to fall
Zone 5

Acid soil
p. 308

Andromeda polifolia

Bog Rosemary
Plant height: to 12 in.
Clusters: to 1¼ in. long
Blooms in spring
Zone 2

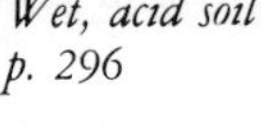

Wet, acid soil
p. 296

Erica × darleyensis	*Darley Heath* *Plant height: to 2 ft.* *Clusters: 3–6 in. long* *Blooms fall to spring* *Zone 6*	*Acid soil* *p. 335*

Gaylussacia brachycera	*Box Huckleberry* *Plant height: 8–16 in.* *Flowers: to ¼ in. long* *Blooms in spring* *Zone 6*	*Acid soil* *p. 343*

Caryopteris* × *clandonensis **'Kew Blue'**	*Bluebeard* *Plant height: to 2 ft.* *Flowers: to 3/8 in. long* *Blooms in summer* *Zone 5*	*Average soil* *p. 312*

Rosmarinus officinalis **'Collingwood Ingram'**	*Rosemary* *Plant height: to 6 ft.* *Flowers: to 1/2 in. long* *Blooms fall to winter* *Zone 7*	*Tolerates dry soil* *p. 399*

Caryopteris* × *clandonensis
'Blue Mist'

Bluebeard
Plant height: to 2 ft.
Flowers: to ⅜ in. long
Blooms in summer
Zone 5

Average soil
p. 312

Rosmarinus officinalis
'Albus'

Rosemary
Plant height: to 6 ft.
Flowers: to ½ in. long
Blooms fall to winter
Zone 7

Tolerates dry soil
p. 399

Grevillea rosmarinifolia	*Rosemary Grevillea* *Plant height: to 6 ft.* *Clusters: to 2 in. long* *Blooms in summer* *Zone 8*	*Dry soil* *p. 345*

***Grevillea* 'Constance'**	*Constance Grevillea* *Plant height: to 8 ft.* *Clusters: to 2 in. long* *Blooms in spring* *Zone 8*	*Dry soil* *p. 345*

***Grevillea* 'Canberra'**	*Canberra Grevillea* *Plant height: to 8 ft.* *Clusters: to 2 in. long* *Blooms in spring* *Zone 8*	*Dry soil* *p. 345*

Leptospermum scoparium	*New Zealand Tea Tree* *Plant height: 10–25 ft.* *Flowers: to ½ in. wide* *Blooms spring to summer* *Zone 9*	*Tolerates dry soil* *p. 361*

Lantana camara

Red Sage
Plant height: to 4 ft.
Clusters: 1–2 in. wide
Blooms year-round
Zone 9

Average soil
p. 360

Potentilla fruticosa

Shrubby Cinquefoil
Plant height: 1–4 ft.
Flowers: 1–1½ in. long
Blooms in summer
Zone 3

Dry soil
p. 385

Rosa hugonis	*Hugo Rose* *Plant height: 6–8 ft.* *Flowers: to 2 in. wide* *Blooms in spring* *Zone 5*	*Average soil* *p. 397*

Hypericum calycinum	*Aaronsbeard St. Johnswort* *Plant height: to 18 in.* *Flowers: to 2 in. wide* *Blooms in summer* *Zone 6*	*Dry soil* *p. 351*

***Hypericum patulum* 'Hidcote'**	*Hidcote Goldencup St. Johnswort* *Plant height: to 18 in.* *Flowers: to 2 in. wide* *Blooms in summer* *Zone 7*	*Dry soil* *p. 352*

Hypericum frondosum	*Golden St. Johnswort* *Plant height: to 4 ft.* *Flowers: to 2 in. wide* *Blooms in summer* *Zone 6*	*Dry soil* *p. 351*

Hypericum prolificum	*Shrubby St. Johnswort* *Plant height: 2–3 ft.* *Flowers: to ¾ in. wide* *Blooms in summer* *Zone 4*	*Dry soil* *p. 352*

Hypericum kalmianum	*Kalm St. Johnswort* *Plant height: to 3 ft.* *Flowers: to 1 in. wide* *Blooms in summer* *Zone 5*	*Dry soil* *p. 352*

Fremontodendron californicum	*Common Flannel Bush* *Plant height:* *10–25 ft.* *Flowers:* *to 1½ in. wide* *Blooms in spring* *Zone 8*	*Dry soil* *p. 342*

Kerria japonica	*Japanese Kerria* *Plant height: 4–6 ft.* *Flowers:* *¾–1½ in. wide* *Blooms in spring* *Zone 5*	*Average soil* *Tolerates shade* *p. 358*

Jasminum nudiflorum

Winter Jasmine
Plant height: 4–5 ft.
Flowers: ¾–1 in. wide
Blooms winter to spring
Zone 7

Average soil
Tolerates shade
p. 357

***Kerria japonica* 'Pleniflora'**

Japanese Kerria
Plant height: 4–6 ft.
Flowers: ¾–1½ in. wide
Blooms in spring
Zone 5

Average soil
Tolerates shade
p. 358

Michelia figo

Banana Shrub
Plant height:
10–15 ft.
Flowers:
1–1½ in. wide
Blooms in spring
Zone 9

Average soil
p. 370

Dirca palustris

Leatherwood
Plant height: 3–5 ft.
Flowers: see detail
Zone 5

Wet soil
Tolerates shade
p. 332

Chimonanthus praecox	*Fragrant Wintersweet* *Plant height: to 10 ft.* *Flowers: to 1 in. wide* *Blooms in winter* *Zone 7*	*Average soil* *p. 316*

Dirca palustris	*Leatherwood* *Clusters: to 1 in. wide* *Blooms in spring*	*p. 332*

Corylopsis pauciflora	*Buttercup Winter Hazel* *Plant height: to 6 ft.* *Flowers: see detail* *Zone 6*	*Acid soil* *p. 323*

***Corylus avellana* 'Contorta'**	*Harry Lauder's Walking Stick* *Plant height: 10–15 ft.* *Zone 4*	*Average soil* *p. 324*

Corylopsis pauciflora	*Buttercup Winter Hazel* *Flowers: to ¾ in. long* *Blooms winter to spring*	*p. 323*

Corylopsis glabrescens	*Fragrant Winter Hazel* *Plant height: 8–15 ft.* *Flowers: to ½ in. long* *Blooms winter to spring* *Zone 5*	*Acid soil* *p. 323*

Salix **'Melanostachys'**	*Black Pussy Willow* *Plant height: 6–10 ft.* *Clusters:* *1–1½ in. wide* *Blooms in spring* *Zone 5*	*Tolerates wet soil* *p. 400*

Salix sachalinensis **'Sekka'**	*Japanese Fantail Willow* *Plant height:* *10–15 ft.* *Zone 5*	*Tolerates wet soil* *p. 401*

Salix discolor 'Nana'

Common Pussy Willow
Plant height: 10–20 ft.
Clusters: to 1 in. wide
Blooms in spring
Zone 3

Tolerates wet soil
p. 400

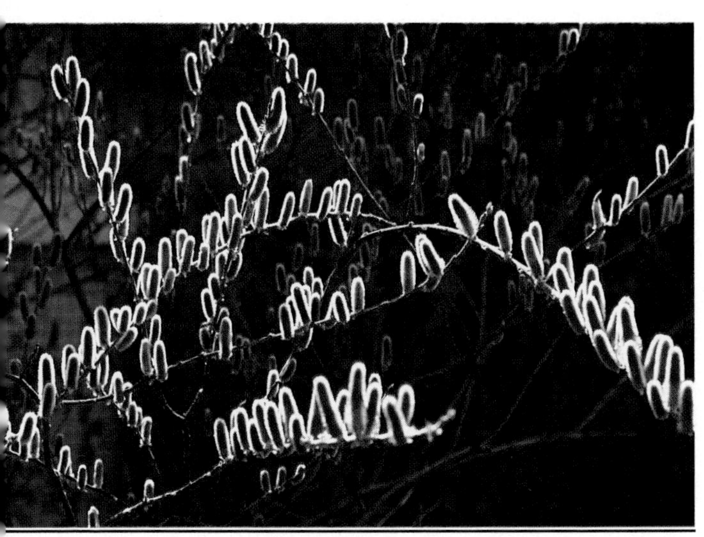

Salix gracilistyla

Rosegold Pussy Willow
Plant height: 4–10 ft.
Clusters: to 1¼ in. wide
Blooms in spring
Zone 6

Tolerates wet soil
p. 400

Hamamelis × _intermedia_ 'Ruby Glow'

Hybrid Witch Hazel
Plant height: to 20 ft.
Flowers: to ¾ in. long
Blooms winter to spring
Zone 5

Average soil
p. 346

Hamamelis virginiana

Common Witch Hazel
Plant height: to 20 ft.
Flowers: to ¾ in. long
Blooms in fall
Zone 4

Average soil
Tolerates shade
p. 347

***Hamamelis mollis* 'Brevipetala'**	*Chinese Witch Hazel* *Plant height: to 15 ft.* *Flowers: to ¾ in. long* *Blooms in winter* *Zone 6*	*Average soil* *p. 346*

Hamamelis vernalis	*Vernal Witch Hazel* *Plant height: to 10 ft.* *Flowers: to ½ in. long* *Blooms in winter* *Zone 5*	*Average soil* *p. 346*

Forsythia* × *intermedia	*Border Forsythia* *Plant height: to 10 ft.* *Flowers: see detail* *Zone 5*	*Average soil* *p. 340*

Forsythia viridissima **'Bronxensis'**	*Bronx Greenstem Forsythia* *Plant height: 12–18 in.* *Zone 5*	*Average soil* *p. 340*

Forsythia* × *intermedia

Border Forsythia
Flowers: to 1½ in. long
Blooms in spring

p. 340

Forsythia suspensa* var. *sieboldii

Weeping Forsythia
Plant height: to 12 ft.
Zone 5

Average soil

p. 340

Loropetalum chinense

Loropetalum
Flowers: to 1 in. long
Blooms in spring

p. 367

Dierviilla sessilifolia

Southern Bush Honeysuckle
Plant height: to 5 ft.
Clusters: 2–3 in. wide
Blooms in summer
Zone 4

Average soil
p. 331

Loropetalum chinense	*Loropetalum* *Plant height: 6–12 ft.* *Flowers: see detail* *Zone 7*	*Acid soil* *Tolerates shade* *p. 367*

Holodiscus discolor	*Cream Bush* *Plant height: 3–20 ft.* *Clusters: to 9 in. long* *Blooms in summer* *Zone 4*	*Dry soil* *p. 349*

Cytisus × praecox

Warminster Broom
Plant height: to 10 ft.
Flowers: see detail
Zone 7

Dry soil
p. 328

Cytisus racemosus

Easter Broom
Plant height: 6–8 ft.
Flowers: see detail
Zone 8

Dry soil
p. 328

Cytisus × praecox *Warminster Broom* *p. 328*
Flowers: to 1 in. long
Blooms in spring

Cytisus racemosus *Easter Broom* *p. 328*
Clusters: to 6 in. long
Blooms in spring

Cytisus scoparius 'Goldfinch'

Scotch Broom
Plant height: 4–9 ft.
Flowers: to 1 in. long
Blooms in spring
Zone 6

Dry soil
p. 328

Caragana arborescens

Siberian Pea Shrub
Plant height: to 20 ft.
Flowers: to ¾ in. long
Blooms in spring
Zone 2

Tolerates dry soil
p. 310

Cytisus scoparius	*Scotch Broom* *Plant height: 4–9 ft.* *Flowers: to 1 in. long* *Blooms in spring* *Zone 6*	*Dry soil* *p. 328*

Colutea arborescens	*Common Bladder Senna* *Plant height: to 8 ft.* *Flowers: to 1 in. long* *Blooms spring to summer* *Zone 6*	*Average soil* *p. 320*

Spartium junceum	*Spanish Broom* *Plant height: 6–8 ft.* *Clusters:* *to 1½ ft. long* *Blooms summer to fall* *Zone 8*	*Dry soil* *p. 405*

Genista lydia	*Lydia Woodwaxen* *Plant height: to 2 ft.* *Flowers: to ¼ in. wide* *Blooms in summer* *Zone 7*	*Dry soil* *p. 344*

Phlomis fruticosa

Jerusalem Sage
Plant height: 2–4 ft.
Flowers: to 1 in. wide
Blooms in summer
Zone 7

Dry soil
p. 378

Genista tinctoria

Woadwaxen
Plant height: to 3 ft.
Clusters: 1–3 in. long
Blooms in spring
Zone 5

Dry soil
p. 344

Santolina chamaecyparissus	*Lavender Cotton* *Plant height: 1–2 ft.* *Flowers: see detail* *Zone 6*	*Dry soil* *p. 402*

Cassia artemisioides	*Feathery Cassia* *Plant height: to 4 ft.* *Clusters: 2–6 in. long* *Blooms spring to summer* *Zone 9*	*Tolerates dry soil* *p. 312*

Santolina chamaecyparissus	*Lavender Cotton* *Flowers: to ¾ in. wide* *Blooms in summer*	*p. 402*

Caesalpinia gilliesii	*Bird-of-Paradise Bush* *Plant height: to 10 ft.* *Flowers: 4–5 in. long* *Blooms in summer* *Zones 9–10*	*Average soil* *p. 305*

Comptonia peregrina

Sweet Fern
Plant height: to 5 ft.
Zone 3

Acid soil
p. 320

Cyrilla racemiflora

Swamp Cyrilla
Plant height:
10–15 ft.
Clusters: to 6 in. long
Blooms in summer
Zone 6

Acid soil
p. 327

Comptonia peregrina	*Sweet Fern* *Detail*	*p. 320*

Cyrilla racemiflora	*Swamp Cyrilla* *In fall*	*p. 327*

Acacia longifolia

Golden Wattle
Clusters:
to 2¼ in. long
Blooms in summer

p. 292

Acacia redolens
var. *prostrata*

Acacia
Plant height: 1–2 ft.
Clusters: to 2 in. wide
Blooms in spring
Zone 9

Dry soil

p. 292

Acacia longifolia

Golden Wattle
Plant height: to 20 ft.
Flowers: see detail
Zone 8

Dry soil
p. 292

Buddleia × weyeriana 'Sun Gold'

Weyer Butterfly Bush
Plant height: 10–15 ft.
Clusters: to ¾ in. wide
Blooms in summer
Zones 7–10

Average soil
p. 303

Mahonia lomariifolia	*Mahonia* *Plant height: to 12 ft.* *Clusters: 3–7 in. long* *Blooms winter to spring* *Zone 9*	*Average soil* *Tolerates shade* *p. 370*

Mahonia aquifolium	*Oregon Grape Holly* *Plant height: 3–6 ft.* *Clusters: to 3 in. long* *Blooms in spring* *Zone 5*	*Average soil* *Tolerates shade* *p. 369*

Mahonia lomariifolia
Mahonia
Fruit
p. 370

Mahonia bealei
Leatherleaf Mahonia
Plant height: to 12 ft.
Zone 7
Average soil
Tolerates shade
p. 369

***Berberis thunbergii* 'Aurea'**	*Japanese Barberry* *Plant height: 4–6 ft.* *Zones 4–8*	*Average soil* *p. 301*

Berberis koreana	*Korean Barberry* *Plant height: to 6 ft.* *Clusters: to 2⅜ in. long* *Blooms in spring* *Zones 3–7*	*Tolerates dry soil* *p. 301*

Berberis verruculosa	*Warty Barberry* *Plant height: to 6 ft.* *Flowers: to ¾ in. wide* *Blooms in spring* *Zones 6–8*	*Average soil* *p. 301*

Berberis koreana	*Korean Barberry* *Fruit*	*p. 301*

Berberis thunbergii
'Crimson Pygmy'

Crimson Pygmy Barberry
Plant height: to 2 ft.
Zones 4–8

Average soil
p. 301

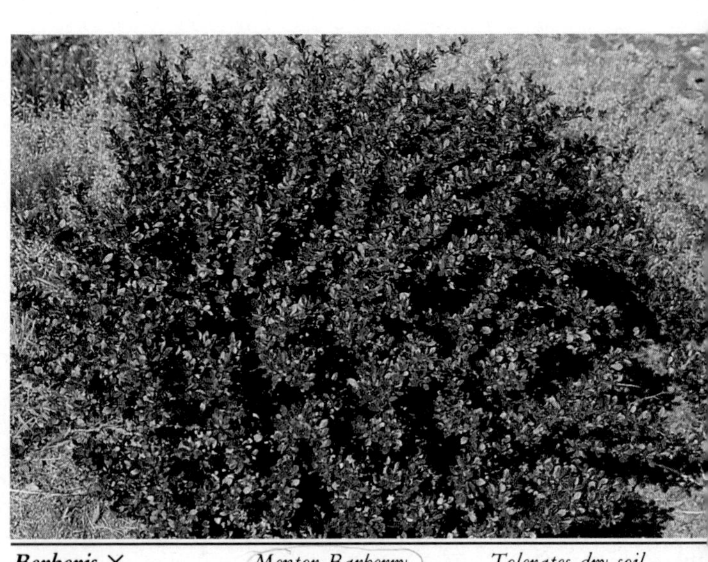

Berberis* × *mentorensis

Mentor Barberry
Plant height: 5–7 ft.
Zones 4–8

Tolerates dry soil
p. 301

Berberis *thunbergii*
'Atropurpurea'

Japanese Barberry
Plant height: 4–6 ft.
Zones 4–8

Average soil
p. 301

Berberis *thunbergii*

Japanese Barberry
Plant height: 4–6 ft.
Zones 4–8

Average soil
p. 301

Euonymus alata | *Winged Euonymus*
Plant height: 12–15 ft.
Zone 4
Average soil
p. 336

Euonymus kiautschovica 'Manhattan'
Spreading Euonymus
Plant height: 6–10 ft.
Zone 6
Average soil
p. 336

Euonymus japonica 'Matanzaki'	*Japanese Euonymus* *Plant height: to 15 ft.* *Zone 7*	*Average soil* *Tolerates shade* *p. 336*

Euonymus japonica 'Silver Knight'	*Japanese Euonymus* *Plant height: to 15 ft.* *Zone 7*	*Average soil* *Tolerates shade* *p. 336*

Aronia arbutifolia

Red Chokeberry
Plant height: to 8 ft.
Clusters: 1½ in. wide
Blooms in spring
Zone 4

Tolerates dry or wet soil
p. 298

Aronia melanocarpa

Black Chokeberry
Plant height: to 4 ft.
Clusters: 1½ in. wide
Blooms in spring
Zone 3

Tolerates dry or wet soil
p. 298

Aronia arbutifolia *Red Chokeberry* *p. 298*
Fruit

Aronia melanocarpa *Black Chokeberry* *p. 298*
Fruit

Fothergilla gardenii

Dwarf Fothergilla
Plant height: to 3 ft.
Flowers: see detail
Zone 5

Acid soil
p. 341

Fothergilla major

Large Fothergilla
Plant height: 4–10 ft.
Clusters: 1½–4 in. long
Blooms in spring
Zone 5

Acid soil
p. 341

Fothergilla gardenii *Dwarf Fothergilla* *p. 341*
Clusters: to 1 in. long
Blooms in spring

Fothergilla major *Large Fothergilla* *p. 341*
In fall

Pieris floribunda

Mountain Pieris
Plant height: 3–6 ft.
Clusters: 2–4 in. long
Blooms in spring
Zone 5

Acid soil
p. 381

Pieris forrestii

Chinese Pieris
Plant height: to 10 ft.
Zone 7

Acid soil
p. 381

***Pieris japonica* 'Wada'**	*Japanese Pieris* *Plant height: 3–10 ft.* *Clusters: 3–5 in. long* *Blooms in spring* *Zone 5*	*Acid soil* *p. 381*

Pieris japonica	*Japanese Pieris* *Plant height: 3–10 ft.* *Zone 5*	*Acid soil* *p. 381*

Leucophyllum frutescens

Texas Ranger
Plant height: 6–8 ft.
Zone 9

Dry soil
p. 362

Leucothoe fontanesiana

Drooping Leucothoe
Plant height: to 6 ft.
Clusters: to 3 in. long
Blooms in spring
Zone 5

Acid soil
Tolerates shade
p. 363

Leucothoe axillaris

Coast Leucothoe
Plant height: to 4 ft.
Clusters: 1–2 in. long
Blooms in spring
Zone 6

Acid soil
Tolerates shade
p. 363

Leucothoe fontanesiana 'Scarletta'

Drooping Leucothoe
Plant height: to 6 ft.
Zone 5

Acid soil
Tolerates shade
p. 363

Itea virginica

Virginia Sweet Spire
Plant height: 5–10 ft.
Clusters: to 6 in. long
Blooms in summer
Zone 5

Average soil
Tolerates shade
p. 356

Corylus maxima 'Purpurea'

Purple Giant Filbert
Plant height: 10–20 ft.
Zone 5

Average soil
p. 324

Itea virginica *Virginia Sweet Spire* *p. 356*
In fall

***Corylus maxima* 'Purpurea'** *Purple Giant Filbert* *p. 324*
Detail

Photinia × fraseri

Fraser Photinia
Plant height: to 15 ft.
Zone 8

Average soil
p. 379

Photinia serrulata

Chinese Photinia
Plant height: 10–30 ft.
Clusters: 4–6 in. wide
Blooms in spring
Zone 8

Average soil
p. 379

Photinia glabra *Japanese Photinia*
Plant height: to 12 ft.
Zone 8
Average soil
p. 379

Photinia villosa *Oriental Photinia*
Plant height: to 15 ft.
Zone 5
Average soil
p. 379

Acer ginnala	*Amur Maple* *Plant height: to 20 ft.* *Zone 2*	*Average soil* *p. 292*

Acer palmatum **'Dissectum'**	*Cutleaf Japanese Maple* *Plant height: to 12 ft.* *Zone 5*	*Average soil* *p. 293*

Acer japonicum 'Aconitifolium'

Fernleaf Maple
Plant height: 8–10 ft.
Zone 6

Average soil
p. 293

Acer palmatum 'Dissectum'

Cutleaf Japanese Maple
In fall

p. 293

Rhus typhina

Staghorn Sumac
Plant height: 10–30 ft.
Zone 4

Tolerates dry soil
p. 395

Rhus aromatica

Fragrant Sumac
Plant height: 2–6 ft.
Zone 3

Dry soil
p. 394

Rhus typhina *Staghorn Sumac* *In fall* *p. 395*

Rhus aromatica *Fragrant Sumac* *In fall* *p. 394*

Parrotia persica

Persian Parrotia
Plant height:
20–40 ft.
Zone 5

Acid soil
p. 376

Parrotia persica

Persian Parrotia
Detail

p. 376

Parrotia persica *Persian Parrotia* *In fall* *p. 376*

Parrotia persica *Persian Parrotia* *Detail* *p. 376*

Aucuba japonica var. variegata | *Gold-Dust Tree* | *Average soil*
Plant height: 4–15 ft. | *Requires shade*
Zone 7 | *p. 298*

Ruscus aculeatus | *Butcher's Broom* | *Average soil*
Plant height: 2–3 ft. | *Tolerates shade*
Zone 8 | *p. 399*

Aucuba japonica

Japanese Aucuba
Plant height: 4–15 ft.
Zone 7

Average soil
Requires shade
p. 298

Carissa grandiflora

Natal Plum
Plant height: to 15 ft.
Flowers: to 2 in. wide
Blooms year-round
Zone 10

Average soil
p. 311

Viburnum* × *pragense	*Prague Viburnum* *Plant height: 10–12 ft.* *Clusters: 2–3 in. wide* *Blooms in spring* *Zone 6*	*Average soil* *p. 418*

Viburnum prunifolium	*Black Haw* *Fruit*	*p. 418*

Viburnum prunifolium	*Black Haw* *Plant height:* *10–15 ft.* *Clusters: to 4 in. wide* *Blooms in spring* *Zone 4*	*Average soil* *p. 418*

Viburnum prunifolium	*Black Haw* *Fruit*	*p. 418*

Viburnum dilatatum

Linden Viburnum
Plant height: 6–10 ft.
Clusters: to 5 in. wide
Blooms in spring
Zones 5–8

Average soil
p. 417

Viburnum lentago

Nannyberry
Plant height: 20–30 ft.
Clusters: to 5 in. wide
Blooms in spring
Zone 3

Average soil
p. 417

Viburnum rhytidophyllum	*Leatherleaf Viburnum* *Plant height:* *10–15 ft.* *Clusters: to 8 in. wide* *Blooms in spring* *Zone 5*	*Average soil* *p. 418*

Viburnum lantana	*Wayfaring-tree Viburnum* *Plant height:* *10–15 ft.* *Zone 4*	*Average soil* *p. 417*

Viburnum* × *rhytidophylloides	*Lantanaphyllum Viburnum* *Plant height: 8–15 ft.* *Clusters: 3–4 in. wide* *Blooms in spring* *Zone 5*	*Average soil* *p. 418*

Viburnum sargentii	*Sargent Viburnum* *Plant height: 10–15 ft.* *Zone 4*	*Average soil* *p. 419*

Viburnum suspensum	*Sandankwa Viburnum* *Plant height: 6–12 ft.* *Clusters:* *to 1½ in. wide* *Blooms in spring* *Zone 9*	*Tolerates dry soil* *p. 419*

Viburnum setigerum	*Tea Viburnum* *Plant height: 7–12 ft.* *Zone 5*	*Average soil* *p. 419*

Viburnum trilobum

American Cranberry Bush
Plant height: 8–12 ft.
Clusters: to 4 in. wide
Blooms in spring
Zones 3–7

Average soil
p. 419

Viburnum plicatum var. tomentosum

Doublefile Viburnum
Plant height: 8–10 ft.
Clusters: to 3 in. wide
Blooms in spring
Zone 5

Average soil
p. 418

Viburnum dilatatum	*Linden Viburnum* *Plant height: 6–10 ft.* *Zones 5–8*	*Average soil* *p. 417*

Viburnum sieboldii	*Siebold Viburnum* *Plant height: to 20 ft.* *Zone 4*	*Average soil* *p. 419*

Viburnum opulus **'Roseum'**

Common Snowball Viburnum
Plant height: 6–10 ft.
Clusters: 3–4 in. wide
Blooms in spring
Zone 4

Average soil
p. 417

Viburum opulus **'Nanum'**

Dwarf European Cranberrybush Viburnum
Plant height: to 3 ft.
Zone 4

Average soil
Tolerates shade
p. 417

Viburnum plicatum

Japanese Snowball
Plant height: 8–10 ft.
Clusters: to 3 in. wide
Blooms in spring
Zone 4

Average soil
p. 418

Viburnum opulus 'Compactum'

Compact European Cranberrybush Viburnum
Plant height: 4–5 ft.
Zone 4

Average soil
p. 417

Viburnum × juddii	*Judd Viburnum* *Plant height: 6–8 ft.* *Clusters: to 3 in. wide* *Blooms in spring* *Zone 5*	*Average soil* *p. 417*

Viburnum carlesii	*Koreanspice Viburnum* *Plant height: to 5 ft.* *Clusters: to 3 in. wide* *Blooms in spring* *Zone 5*	*Average soil* *p. 416*

Viburnum* × *burkwoodii	*Burkwood Viburnum* *Plant height: to 6 ft.* *Clusters: to 3 in. wide* *Blooms in spring* *Zone 4*	*Average soil* *p. 416*

Viburnum* × *carlcephalum	*Carlcephalum Viburnum* *Plant height: 6–10 ft.* *Clusters: 5 in. wide* *Blooms in spring* *Zone 5*	*Average soil* *p. 416*

Viburnum wrightii

Wright Viburnum
Plant height: 7–10 ft.
Clusters: to 4 in. wide
Blooms in spring
Zone 5

Average soil
p. 420

Viburnum dentatum

Arrowwood
Plant height: 10–15 ft.
Zone 3

Average soil
p. 417

Viburnum tinus	*Laurustinus* *Plant height: 7–10 ft.* *Clusters: to 3 in. wide* *Blooms winter to spring* *Zone 7*	*Average soil* *p. 419*

Viburnum davidii	*David Viburnum* *Plant height: to 4 ft.* *Zone 8*	*Average soil* *p. 416*

Skimmia japonica

Japanese Skimmia
Plant height: 3–5 ft.
Flowers: see detail
Zone 8

Average soil
Requires shade
p. 404

Aralia spinosa

Hercules'-Club
Plant height:
15–20 ft.
Clusters:
12–18 in. long
Blooms in summer
Zone 5

Average soil
p. 296

Skimmia japonica *Japanese Skimmia* *p. 404*
Clusters: to 2 in. wide
Blooms in spring

Aralia spinosa *Hercules'-Club* *p. 296*
Fruit

Sambucus canadensis

American Elder
Plant height: 6–10 ft.
Clusters: to 4 in. wide
Blooms in summer
Zone 4

Average soil
p. 401

Sambucus nigra

European Elder
Plant height: to 30 ft.
Clusters: to 3 in. wide
Blooms in spring
Zone 6

Average soil
p. 402

Sambucus canadensis	*American Elder* *Fruit*	*p. 401*

Sambucus pubens	*American Red Elder* *Plant height: 8–12 ft.* *Zone 4*	*Average soil* *p. 402*

***Pyracantha fortuneana* 'Graberi'**	*Graberi Fire Thorn* *Plant height:* *10–15 ft.* *Zone 7*	*Average soil* *p. 388*

Pyracantha coccinea	*Scarlet Fire Thorn* *Plant height:* *10–15 ft.* *Zone 6*	*Average soil* *p. 388*

Pyracantha **'Navaho'**

Navaho Fire Thorn
Plant height: to 6 ft.
Zone 7

Average soil
p. 388

Pyracantha **'Teton'**

Teton Fire Thorn
Plant height: to 15 ft.
Zone 7

Average soil
p. 389

Lonicera tatarica	*Tatarian Honeysuckle* *Plant height: 8–10 ft.* *Flowers: ¾–1 in. long* *Blooms in spring* *Zone 4*	*Average soil* *p. 367*

Ternstroemia gymnanthera	*Ternstroemia* *Plant height: 4–10 ft.* *Flowers: to ½ in. wide* *Blooms in summer* *Zone 7*	*Acid soil* *Tolerates shade* *p. 414*

Lonicera maackii	*Amur Honeysuckle* *Plant height:* *10–15 ft.* *Zone 3*	*Tolerates dry soil* *p. 366*

Ternstroemia gymnanthera	*Ternstroemia* *Fruit*	*p. 414*

***Nandina domestica* 'Alba'**	*Nandina* *Plant height: 6–8 ft.* *Zone 7*	*Average soil* *Tolerates shade* *p. 373*

Symphoricarpos albus	*Snowberry* *Plant height: to 4 ft.* *Zone 3*	*Average soil* *Tolerates shade* *p. 409*

Nandina domestica

Nandina
Plant height: 6–8 ft.
Zone 7

Average soil
Tolerates shade
p. 373

Symphoricarpos × chenaultii

Chenault Coralberry
Plant height: 3–6 ft.
Zone 5

Average soil
Tolerates shade
p. 409

Cornus sericea	*Red Osier* *Plant height: to 6 ft.* *Zone 3*	*Average soil* *p. 322*

Cornus racemosa	*Gray Dogwood* *Clusters: to 2 in. wide* *Blooms in spring*	*p. 322*

Cornus alba

Tartarian Dogwood
Plant height: 6–10 ft.
Zone 3

Average soil
p. 321

Cornus racemosa

Gray Dogwood
Plant height: 8–15 ft.
Flowers: see detail
Zone 4

Average soil
Tolerates shade
p. 322

Lindera benzoin

Spicebush
Plant height: 6–12 ft.
Clusters: to ⅓ in. long
Blooms in spring
Zone 4

Tolerates dry soil
p. 365

Cornus mas

Cornelian Cherry
Plant height:
20–25 ft.
Flowers: to ¾ in. wide
Blooms in spring
Zone 5

Average soil
p. 322

Lindera benzoin *Spicebush* *Fruit* *p. 365*

Cornus mas *Cornelian Cherry* *Fruit* *p. 322*

Cotoneaster adpressus	*Creeping Cotoneaster* *Plant height: 12–18 in.* *Zone 5*	*Tolerates dry soil* *p. 325*

Cotoneaster apiculatus	*Cranberry Cotoneaster* *Plant height: to 3 ft.* *Flowers: ¼–⅜ in. wide* *Blooms in spring* *Zone 5*	*Tolerates dry soil* *p. 326*

Cotoneaster dammeri 'Skogsholm'

Bearberry Cotoneaster
Plant height: to 18 in.
Flowers:
⅜–½ in. wide
Blooms in spring
Zone 6

Tolerates dry soil
p. 326

Cotoneaster horizontalis

Rockspray Cotoneaster
Plant height: to 2 ft.
Zone 5

Tolerates dry soil
p. 326

Cotoneaster divaricatus	*Spreading Cotoneaster* *Plant height: 3–7 ft.* *Flowers: to ¼ in. wide* *Blooms in spring* *Zone 5*	*Tolerates dry soil* *p. 326*

Cotoneaster lacteus	*Parney Cotoneaster* *Plant height: to 12 ft.* *Zone 7*	*Tolerates dry soil* *p. 326*

Cotoneaster multiflorus

Many-flowered Cotoneaster
Plant height: 8–10 ft.
Flowers: to ½ in. wide
Blooms in spring
Zone 4

Tolerates dry soil
p. 327

Cotoneaster salicifolius

Willowleaf Cotoneaster
Plant height: 7–12 ft.
Zone 6

Tolerates dry soil
p. 327

Ilex cornuta
'Rotunda'

Dwarf Chinese Holly
Plant height: to 6 ft.
Zone 7

Tolerates dry soil
p. 353

Ilex aquifolium
'Silver Edge'

English Holly
Plant height:
10–15 ft.
Zone 7

Average soil
p. 353

Ilex cornuta | *Chinese Holly*
Plant height: 8–15 ft.
Zone 7
Tolerates dry soil
p. 353

Ilex aquifolium
English Holly
Plant height: 10–15 ft.
Zone 7
Average soil
p. 353

Ilex × attenuata 'Fosteri'

Foster Holly
Plant height:
10–15 ft.
Zone 6

Average soil
p. 353

Ilex opaca

American Holly
Plant height:
15–30 ft.
Zone 6

Acid soil
p. 355

Ilex pendunculosa

Longstalk Holly
Plant height: to 20 ft.
Zone 5

Average soil
p. 355

Ilex opaca
'East Palatka'

American Holly
Plant height:
15–30 ft.
Zone 6

Acid soil
p. 355

Ilex cornuta
'Burfordii'

Burford Chinese Holly
Detail

p. 353

Ilex × altaclarensis
'Wilsonii'

Wilson Altaclara
Holly
Plant height:
10–15 ft.
Zone 8

Average soil

p. 353

Ilex cornuta 'Burfordii'

Burford Chinese Holly
Plant height: to 10 ft.
Zone 7

Tolerates dry soil
p. 353

Ilex × meserveae

Meserve Holly
Plant height: 8–12 ft.
Zone 5

Average soil
p. 354

Ilex verticillata

Common Winterberry
Plant height: 5–15 ft.
Zone 4

Acid soil
Tolerates wet soil
p. 355

Ilex decidua

Possum Haw
Plant height:
10–30 ft.
Zone 5

Tolerates wet soil
p. 354

Ilex verticillata 'Chrysocarpa'

Common Winterberry
Plant height: 5–15 ft.
Zone 4

Acid soil
Tolerates wet soil
p. 355

Ilex decidua

Possum Haw
Plant height: 10–30 ft.
Zone 5

Tolerates wet soil
p. 354

Hippophae rhamnoides	*Sea Buckthorn* *Plant height:* *10–25 ft.* *Zone 4*	*Average soil* *p. 348*

Symplocos paniculata	*Sapphire Berry* *Plant height:* *10–20 ft.* *Clusters: 2–3 in. wide* *Blooms in spring* *Zone 4*	*Average soil* *p. 410*

Symphoricarpos orbiculatus	*Indian Currant* *Plant height: 3–5 ft.* *Zone 3*	*Average soil* *Tolerates shade* *p. 409*

Symplocos paniculata	*Sapphire Berry* *Fruit*	*p. 410*

Vaccinium corymbosum	*Highbush Blueberry* *Plant height: 8–12 ft.* *Flowers: to ⅓ in. long* *Blooms in spring* *Zone 4*	*Wet, acid soil* *p. 415*

Elaeagnus pungens	*Thorny Elaeagnus* *Plant height: to 15 ft.* *Flowers: to ½ in. wide* *Blooms in fall* *Zone 7*	*Dry soil* *Tolerates shade* *p. 333*

Vaccinium corymbosum	*Highbush Blueberry Fruit*	*p. 415*

Elaeagnus pungens 'Variegata'	*Variegated Thorny Elaeagnus Plant height: to 15 ft. Zone 7*	*Dry soil Tolerates shade p. 333*

Elaeagnus umbellata

Autumn Elaeagnus
Plant height: to 4 ft.
Flowers: to 1 in. wide
Zone 4

Dry soil
p. 333

Elaeagnus angustifolia

Russian Olive
Plant height: to 20 ft.
Zone 3

Dry soil
p. 332

Elaeagnus multiflora	*Cherry Elaeagnus* *Plant height: to 6 ft.* *Flowers: to ⅜ in. wide* *Blooms in spring* *Zone 5*	*Dry soil* *p. 333*

Elaeagnus umbellata	*Autumn Elaegnus* *Fruit*	*p. 332*

Callicarpa dichotoma	*Purple Beautyberry* *Plant height: 2–4 ft.* *Zone 5*	*Average soil* *p. 307*

Callicarpa japonica	*Japanese Beautyberry* *Plant height: to 6 ft.* *Zones 6–8*	*Average soil* *p. 307*

Callicarpa americana	*French Mulberry* *Plant height: 5–8 ft.* *Zone 7*	*Average soil* *p. 307*

Callicarpa japonica	*Japanese Beautyberry* *Detail*	*p. 307*

Ilex vomitoria

Yaupon
Plant height: 15–25 ft.
Zone 7

Tolerates wet or dry soil
p. 355

Ilex crenata 'Helleri'

Japanese Holly
Plant height: 5–10 ft.
Zone 6

Average soil
Tolerates shade
p. 354

Ilex glabra

Inkberry
Plant height: to 6 ft.
Zone 5

Acid soil
Tolerates wet soil
p. 354

Ilex crenata
'Convexa'

Japanese Holly
Plant height: 5–10 ft.
Zone 6

Average soil
Tolerates shade
p. 354

Berberis julianae
Wintergreen Barberry
Plant height: 6–8 ft.
Zones 6–8
Average soil
p. 300

Berberis candidula
Paleleaf Barberry
Plant height: 2–4 ft.
Zones 6–8
Average soil
p. 300

Berberis julianae *Wintergreen Barberry* *p. 300*
Fruit

Berberis × chenaultii *Chenault Barberry* *Average soil*
Plant height: 3–4 ft. *p. 300*
Zones 6–8

Myrica pensylvanica	*Northern Bayberry* *Plant height: 3–10 ft.* *Zone 3*	*Dry soil* *p. 371*

Myrica cerifera	*Wax Myrtle* *Plant height:* *10–20 ft.* *Zone 7*	*Dry soil* *p. 371*

Myrica pensylvanica *Northern Bayberry* *p. 371*
Fruit

Myrica cerifera *Wax Myrtle* *p. 371*
Fruit

Osmanthus heterophyllus	*Holly Osmanthus* *Plant height:* *15–20 ft.* *Clusters: 1–1½ in. wide* *Blooms in fall* *Zone 7*	*Acid soil* *Tolerates shade* *p. 375*

Osmanthus americanus	*Devilwood* *Plant height:* *20–30 ft.* *Clusters: to ½ in. long* *Blooms in spring* *Zone 7*	*Acid soil* *p. 375*

***Osmanthus heterophyllus* 'Myrtifolius'**

Holly Osmanthus
Plant height: 15–20 ft.
Clusters: 1–1½ in. wide
Blooms in fall
Zone 7

Acid soil
Tolerates shade
p. 375

Sarcococca hookerana* var. *humilis

Himalayan Sarcococca
Plant height: to 6 ft.
Zone 7

Average soil
Requires shade
p. 403

Osmanthus* × *fortunei	*Fortune's Osmanthus* *Plant height:* *10–20 ft.* *Zone 7*	*Acid soil* *p. 375*

Osmanthus heterophyllus	*Holly Osmanthus* *Plant height:* *15–20 ft.* *Clusters: 1–1½ in. wide* *Blooms in fall* *Zone 7*	*Acid soil* *Tolerates shade* *p. 375*

Osmanthus fragrans | *Fragrant Tea Olive*
Plant height: to 25 ft.
Flowers: to ¼ in. wide
Blooms fall to winter
Zone 8

Acid soil
p. 375

Osmanthus americanus | *Devilwood*
Plant height: 20–30 ft.
Clusters: to ½ in. long
Blooms in spring
Zone 7

Acid soil
p. 375

Pittosporum tobira **'Wheeler's Dwarf'**	*Wheeler's Dwarf Pittosporum* *Plant height: to 3 ft.* *Zone 9*	*Dry soil* *Tolerates shade* *p. 382*

Pittosporum tobira **'Variegatum'**	*Japanese Pittosporum* *Plant height: 6–18 ft.* *Flowers: see detail* *Zone 9*	*Dry soil* *Tolerates shade* *p. 382*

Pittosporum tobira

Japanese Pittosporum
Plant height: 6–18 ft.
Clusters: 2–3 in. wide
Blooms in spring
Zone 9

Dry soil
Tolerates shade
p. 382

Pittosporum tobira
'Variegatum'

Japanese Pittosporum
Clusters: 2–3 in. wide
Blooms in spring

p. 382

Ligustrum amurense

Amur Privet
Plant height: 10–15 ft.
Zone 4

Dry soil
p. 363

Ligustrum vulgare

European Privet
Plant height: 5–15 ft.
Clusters: to 3 in. long
Blooms in spring
Zone 4

Dry soil
p. 364

Ligustrum lucidum

Glossy Privet
Plant height: to 30 ft.
Clusters:
to 10 in. long
Blooms in spring
Zone 8

Dry soil
p. 364

Ligustrum × vicaryi

Golden Vicary Privet
Plant height:
10–12 ft.
Zone 5

Dry soil
p. 364

Buxus sempervirens **var. *suffruticosa***	*Edging Box* *Plant height: to 20 ft.* *Zones 5-8*	*Average soil* *p. 304*

Buxus microphylla **var. *koreana***	*Korean Littleleaf Box* *Plant height: to 6 ft.* *Zone 5*	*Average soil* *p. 304*

Buxus microphylla	*Littleleaf Box* *Plant height: to 6 ft.* *Zone 6*	*Average soil* *p. 304*

***Myrtus communis* 'Compacta'**	*Compact or Dwarf Myrtle* *Plant height: 2–3 ft.* *Flowers: to ¾ in. wide* *Blooms in summer* *Zone 9*	*Tolerates dry soil* *p. 372*

Paxistima canbyi

Canby Paxistima
Plant height: to 12 in.
Zone 4

Average soil
p. 377

Coprosma repens

Mirror plant
Plant height: to 10 ft.
Zone 9

Average soil
Tolerates dry soil
p. 321

Arctostaphylos uva-ursi	*Bearberry* *Plant height: 2 in.* *Zones 2–6*	*Acid soil* *p. 297*

Stephanandra incisa **'Crispa'**	*Cutleaf Stephanandra* *Plant height: 1½–3 ft.* *Zone 4*	*Average soil* *p. 408*

Lonicera fragantissima	*Winter Honeysuckle* *Plant height: 5–10 ft.* *Flowers: to ½ in. long* *Blooms winter to spring* *Zone 5*	*Average soil* *p. 366*

***Lonicera xylosteum* 'Claveyi'**	*European Fly Honeysuckle* *Plant height: 3–6 ft.* *Flowers: to ½ in. wide* *Blooms in spring* *Zone 5*	*Average soil* *Tolerates dry soil* *p. 367*

***Lonicera nitida* 'Aurea'**

Boxleaf Honeysuckle
Plant height: to 6 ft.
Flowers: to 1/4 in. long
Blooms in spring
Zone 7

Average soil
p. 366

Syzygium paniculatum

Brush Cherry
Plant height: to 40 ft.
Flowers: ½–1 in. wide
Blooms in spring
Zone 10

Average soil
p. 412

Rhus ovata

Sugar Bush
Plant height: 5–10 ft.
Clusters: 3–4 in. long
Blooms in spring
Zone 9

Dry soil
p. 394

Rhamnus frangula
'Columnaris'

Tallhedge Buckthorn
Plant height: 10–15 ft.
Zone 3

Average soil
p. 390

Rhus integrifolia	*Lemonade Sumac* *Plant height: 5–10 ft.* *Clusters: to 3 in. long* *Blooms in spring* *Zone 9*	*Dry soil* *p. 394*

Xylosma congestum	*Xylosma* *Plant height: to 10 ft.* *Zone 9*	*Tolerates dry soil* *p. 422*

Podocarpus macrophyllus* var. *maki	*Maki Podocarpus* *Plant height: 6–8 ft.* *Zone 9*	*Average soil* *p. 383*

***Rhamnus frangula* 'Asplenifolia'**	*Feathery Buckthorn* *Plant height:* *10–12 ft.* *Zone 3*	*Average soil* *p. 390*

Podocarpus macrophyllus* var. *maki	*Maki Podocarpus Detail*	*p. 383*

***Rhamnus frangula* 'Asplenifolia'**	*Feathery Buckthorn Detail*	*p. 390*

Encyclopedia of Shrubs

Abelia

Honeysuckle family
Caprifoliaceae

A-bee′li-a. A group of Asiatic and Mexican evergreen or deciduous shrubs grown for their clusters of small but showy flowers. Of about 25 species and hybrids, only a few are common in American gardens.

Description
Leaves opposite, nearly stalkless. Flowers mostly in leafy terminal clusters, the corolla bell- or funnel-shaped. Fruit small, leathery, dry, one-seeded.

How to Grow
The species below prefer well-drained acid soil, with leaf mold added, and full sunlight. Increase by softwood cuttings in summer or by hardwood cuttings in fall. Can also be propagated by layers or by seed sown as soon as ripe. Since flowers appear on new growth, prune in winter or early spring. To encourage new growth, remove old stems to ground level after several years.

'Edward Goucher' *p. 131*
Edward Goucher Glossy Abelia. Evergreen to deciduous shrub, 4–5 ft. (1.2–1.5 m) high, young twigs minutely hairy. Leaves oval, 1 in. (2.5 cm) long, hairy on the midrib below. Flowers rosy lavender, funnel-shaped, ¾ in. (19 mm) long. Hybrid derived from *A. grandiflora* and *A. schumannii*. Blooms summer to fall. Zone 7.

× ***grandiflora*** *p. 130*
Glossy Abelia. Semievergreen shrub, 3–6 ft. (0.9–1.8 m) high, young twigs minutely reddish-hairy. Leaves oval, 1 in. (2.5 cm) long. Flowers white flushed with pink, bell-shaped, ¾ in. (19 mm) long. Most commonly cultivated form. Hybrid derived from *A. chinensis* and *A. uniflora*. Blooms summer to fall. Zones 5–9. Cultivar 'Prostrata' is low-growing, 2 ft. (60 cm) high, and blooms in summer. Zone 6.

Abeliophyllum

Olive family
Oleaceae

A-bee-li-o-fill′um. A single deciduous, shrubby species, native to Korea, grown for its fragrant, white forsythia-like flowers in early spring.

Description
Leaves opposite, short-stalked, minutely hairy on both sides. Flowers bell-shaped, in short fingerlike racemes.

How to Grow
Easy to grow in most garden soil. Increase by softwood cuttings in summer, hardwood cuttings in fall, or by seed sown as soon as ripe. Flowers appear on wood of the previous year, so prune immediately after flowering. To encourage new growth, remove old stems to the ground after several years. Flowers can be forced during winter.

distichum *p. 87*
Korean Abelialeaf. Stems arching and spreading, 3–5 ft. (0.9–1.5 m) long. Leaves ovalish with smooth edges, 1–3 in. (2.5–7.5 cm) long. Flowers white, ⅝ in. (16 mm) wide. Fruit flattened, 1 in. (2.5 cm) across. Blooms in early spring. Zone 5.

Acacia
Pea family
Leguminosae

A-ka′si-a, also a-ka′sha. An enormous genus of quick-growing, free-flowering shrubs and trees found all over the tropical world. A few grow in subtropical regions. About 20 species are cultivated, most of them originating in Australia.

Description
Some species are thorny. Leaves normally twice-compound, the leaflets very numerous and small. Flowers very small but crowded into dense, finger-shaped or globular clusters, all yellow in the species below. The clusters may be solitary, but are more often arranged in variously branched sprays, and therefore very handsome. Fruit like a pea pod, but often somewhat woody in maturity, and sometimes twisted.

How to Grow
Acacias are easy to grow in sunny locations, but they are not long-lived. This should be taken into account in planning your garden. Propagate by seed, which should be scarified. Even after scarification, some species take 4

or 5 weeks to germinate. You can also propagate acacias by semi-hardwood cuttings. Water plants freely at first, but less as they become established, since most species are drought-resistant.

longifolia *pp. 186, 187*
Golden Wattle; Sydney Golden Wattle. Shrub or small tree, to 20 ft. (6 m) high, without prickles. Phyllodia 3–6 in. (7.5–15.0 cm) long, narrow and oblong. Flowers in oblong spikes to 2¼ in. (5.5 cm) long. E. Australia. Blooms in summer. Zone 8.

redolens* var. *prostrata *p. 186*
A dense-growing evergreen, 1–2 ft. (30–60 cm) high, with bright green foliage and yellow flowers in 2 in. (5 cm) clusters. A good choice to quickly cover dry banks that receive full sun. Australia. Blooms in spring. Zone 9.

Acer
Maple family
Aceraceae

A'sir. Maple. About 150 species of north-temperate zone, mostly deciduous trees and large shrubs. The species listed here are small- or slow-growing maples suitable for use as shrubs.

Description
Leaves opposite, simple and lobed, or compound. Flowers commonly unisexual, small, in terminal panicles or corymbs. Two-winged fruit.

How to Grow
All maples are strong and easy to transplant. They will grow in any good soil in areas with a sufficient amount of rainfall. *A. ginnala* tolerates drier areas, while *A. japonicum* and *A. palmatum* 'Dissectum' grow best in moist but well-drained soils. Hot and dry summers cause leaf scorch on the latter two species. All 3 species can be propagated from seed or softwood cuttings.

ginnala *p. 208*
Amur Maple. Shrub or small tree, to 20 ft. (6 m) high, branches smooth and slender. Leaves 3-lobed, 1½–4 in. (4–10 cm) long, the central lobe usually much longer than

those at the sides, with marginal teeth, dark green and shiny above, light green beneath, turning scarlet in fall. Flowers yellowish white, fragrant, in terminal panicles 1½ in. (4 cm) long. Fruit smooth, with wings nearly parallel. Cen. and n. China; Manchuria and Japan. Blooms in spring. Zone 2.

japonicum *p. 209*
Fullmoon Maple. Shrub or small tree, 12–25 ft. (3.5–7.5 m) high. Leaves commonly 7- to 11-lobed, 3–5½ in. (7.5–14.0 cm) across, with marginal teeth or lobes; generally hairy on veins below, light green, turning an exceptional crimson in fall. Flowers purple, about ½ in. (13 mm) across, in drooping, hairy corymbs ½ in. (13 mm) long. Fruit with wings spreading almost horizontally. Cultivar 'Aconitifolium' has deeply divided leaves, a round habit, and grows 8–10 ft. (2.4–3 m). Japan. Blooms in spring. Zone 6.

palmatum **'Dissectum'** *pp. 208, 209*
Cutleaf Japanese Maple. Slow-growing shrub, to 12 ft. (3.5 m) high with weeping branches; develops into a broad mound at maturity. Leaves 5- to 9-lobed, 2–5 in. (5.0–12.5 cm) wide, the lobes deeply cut, creating a fern-like texture, turning bright red in fall. Flowers in small erect corymbs. Fruit with wings spreading, the nutlet smooth. Korea and Japan. 'Dissectum' is an aristocrat of the landscape. Zone 5.

Aesculus
Horse-chestnut family
Hippocastanaceae

Es′kew-lus. Highly prized flowering shrubs and trees. Of the 15 known species, which are chiefly North American and Eurasian, those below are much cultivated as shrubs for streets and lawns.

Description
Very scaly, gummy-coated buds in the spring, and large, compound, long-stalked leaves, the 5–9 leaflets arranged finger-fashion and toothed. Flowers very showy in a large, many-flowered cluster, the calyx bell-shaped or tubular and 4- to 5-toothed. Petals 4–5, narrowed into long claws. Fruit a large, 3-valved, often spiny capsule containing one or two very large seeds, the horse-chestnuts.

How to Grow
The species described below tolerates shade and any ordinary garden soil. The shrubs can be propagated by stratifying seeds and by mound layering. They are extremely handsome specimen plants for the lawn or shrub border, but they need plenty of room.

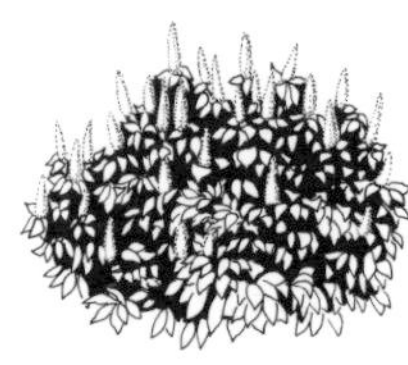

parviflora *p. 144*
Bottlebrush Buckeye. A widely spreading shrub, 8–12 ft. (2.4–3.5 m) high. Leaflets 5–7, practically stalkless, elliptic to oblongish, but a little broader at the tip, 3½–8 in. (9–20 cm) long. Flowers white, ½ in. (13 mm) long, the clusters cylindric, nearly 12 in. (30 cm) long. Stamens pink, protruding and showy. Fruit inverted egg-shaped, 1¾ in. (4.5 cm) long. S.C. to Ala. and Fla. Blooms in summer. Zone 4.

Alyogyne
Mallow family
Malvaceae

Al′yo-ghin. A genus of 6 species of small shrubs native to Australia. The species below is popular in the w. U.S., where its colorful flowers bloom intermittently throughout the year.

Description
Leaves may be unlobed, deeply dissected, or divided. Flowers hibiscus-like, pale lilac, often deeply spotted at the base. Calyx 5-lobed, longer than bracts, petals very large.

How to Grow
Grow Blue Hibiscus in full sun in a dry, well-drained soil. Pinch or prune occasionally to maintain a compact habit.

huegelii *p. 116*
Blue Hibiscus. An evergreen shrub, to 8 ft. (2.4 m) high. Leaves have 3 or 5 lobes which are again divided, dark green, with a coarse texture, about 3 in. (7.5 cm) long. Flowers 4–5 in. (10.0–12.5 cm) across, with glossy, lilac petals. Blooms year-round. Zone 9.

Amelanchier

Rose family
Rosaceae

Am-e-lank′i-er. These plants are variously called shadbush, serviceberry, and Juneberry, and the profusion of white bloom is commonly called shadblow. They are beautiful in early spring, with their white flowers, and later, with a profusion of small, often brightly-colored fruit.

Description
Leaves alternate, toothed, the buds prominently pointed. Flowers white, in terminal, rather profuse racemes, usually with 5 strap-shaped petals. Fruit like a miniature apple, but bony inside, sometimes used for jellies.

How to Grow
The species below is very easy to grow in any ordinary garden soil. Propagate by sowing ripe seeds, or by stolons. Keep in mind that these plants are alternate hosts for the fungus of some juniper rusts.

stolonifera *p. 86*
Running Serviceberry. A low, more or less sprawling shrub, 3–6 ft. (0.9–1.8 m) high, often forming patches because of its underground stolons. Leaves oblongish, or rounder, white-hairy on the underside when young, ultimately greenish throughout. Flower cluster upright, ⅝–1⅝ in. (1.6–4.1 cm) long. Fruit sweet, black-purple, with a slight bloom. Sometimes cultivated for its jelly-making fruit. Easy to propagate by its stolons. Ne. North America. Blooms in spring. Zone 4.

Andromeda

Heath family
Ericaceae

An-drom′i-da. A genus comprising only 2 species, grown throughout the cooler parts of North America.

Description
Both species are bog shrubs with evergreen leaves, the margins of which are rolled. Flowers very small, pink, urn- or bell-shaped, in small drooping clusters. Fruit a capsule.

How to Grow
Grow only in very acid soils, preferably in the bog garden or in specially prepared soil in the rock garden. Easy to propagate by division or by layering.

polifolia *p. 152*
Bog Rosemary. A low shrub, up to 12 in. (30 cm) high, with creeping roots. Leaves oblong, to 1½ in. (4 cm). Flowers urn-shaped, white, with a touch of pink, in 1¼ in. (3 cm) clusters. A difficult, slow-growing species that should be planted in peat soil or soil artificially amended with peat. The soil must be moist and cool; summer heat and dry soil are usually fatal. N. North America, n. Europe, n. Asia. Blooms in spring. Zone 2.

Aralia
Ginseng family
Araliaceae

A-ray'li-a. A genus of 30 species of mostly spiny shrubs and trees, or perennial herbs, grown for ornament. All but a few are native to North America or e. Asia.

Description
Leaves alternate, compound, or twice- or thrice-compound, often very large and showy. Flowers greenish or whitish, in umbels, the latter often grouped in a large terminal panicle. Fruit berrylike, with 2–5 flattened stones.

How to Grow
The shrubby Hercules'-Club needs a rich, moist soil and full sun to partial shade. Propagation of this species is by seeds sown in frames in the spring or by root cuttings over bottom-heat.

spinosa *pp. 230, 231*
Hercules'-Club; also called Devil's-Walking-Stick and Angelica Tree. A North American spiny-trunked shrub or small tree, usually 15–20 feet (4.5–6.0 m) high. Leaves twice-compound, long-stalked, the leaflets prickly, ovalish, 4 in. (10 cm) long, pale on the underside. Flowers whitish in large, hairy panicles 12–18 in. (30–45 cm) long. Fruit black. Large thorns along main stems. This is a striking plant that is quite tolerant of harsh situations.

Cen. Pa. to Fla. and Tex., naturalized in N.Y. and Conn. Blooms in summer. Zone 5.

Arctostaphylos

Heath family
Ericaceae

Ark-to-staff'i-los. A very large genus of woody plants, mostly North American, containing such handsome garden plants as the Bearberry and Manzanita.

Description
Shrubs or small trees, one a prostrate ground cover, with handsome, smooth-edged evergreen leaves. Flowers small, urn- or bell-shaped, often nodding. Fruit red or dull, fleshy.

How to Grow
Bearberry grows best in well-drained, sandy, acid soil and has good salt tolerance. It should be transplanted as a container plant in early spring or late summer.

uva-ursi *p. 281*
Bearberry; Kinnikinnick. Prostrate, in. (5 cm) high, the stems often to 7 ft. (2.1 m) long and rooting at the joints to form large patches of handsome evergreen foliage that turns bronzy in winter. Leaves slightly broader upwards, 1 in. (2.5 cm) long and ⅓ in. (8 mm) wide, the margins rolled and minutely fringed with hairs. Flowers white or pink, ⅙ in. (4 mm) long. Fruit red. Very good as a ground cover. Eur., n. Asia, North America. Blooms in spring. Zones 2–6.

Aronia

Rose family
Rosaceae

A-rone'i-a. A small genus of North American shrubs, often grown in informal shrubberies for their showy white flowers and persistent, colored fruits, whose bitter taste explains the common name, chokeberry.

Description
Leaves alternate, always toothed. Flowers in terminal clusters, blooming early in May, the white petals and black anthers making an

attractive contrast. Fruit fleshy, small, and berrylike.

How to Grow
These shrubs are very easy to grow in a variety of soils and can adapt to dry or wet conditions. They are easy to propagate by seeds, cuttings, or layering.

arbutifolia *pp. 196, 197*
Red Chokeberry. Not over 8 ft. (2.4 m) high, usually half that. Leaves gray beneath, oblongish, 2 in. (5 cm) long. Fine red foliage in fall. Flower clusters 1½ in. (4 cm) long. Fruit brilliant red, winter-persisting. Cultivar 'Brilliantissima' is said to have even more brilliantly red fruit. Mass. to Fla. Blooms in spring. Zone 4.

melanocarpa *pp. 196, 197*
Black Chokeberry. Also called *Aronia nigra*. A low shrub, rarely exceeding 4 ft. (120 cm). Leaves shiny and hairless. Flower clusters ½ in. (13 mm) wide. Fruit shiny black, but shriveling and soon dropping. Nova Scotia to Fla. Blooms in spring. Zone 3.

Aucuba
Dogwood family
Cornaceae

Aw-kew'ba. A small genus of Asiatic evergreen shrubs, very popular as foliage plants, especially for city window boxes in the North.

Description
Leaves opposite, without marginal teeth or distantly toothed. Male and female flowers on different plants, small and greenish or red. Fruit an orange or scarlet berry.

How to Grow
The species described below grows vigorously in the open, where it spreads, or in a tub, where its brightly-colored berries can be better seen. Propagate by cuttings of semi-hardwood, taken when convenient, rooted in a cutting bench under glass. Provide shade and plenty of moisture for best growth.

japonica *pp. 214, 215*
Japanese Aucuba. 4–15 ft. (1.2–4.5 m) high

in the wild, usually much smaller as cultivated. Leaves glossy, dark green, more or less oval, 4–8 in. (10–20 cm) long, rather distantly toothed. Berry ½ in. (13 mm), mostly scarlet, and not produced without male plants. Var. *variegata,* often called the Gold-Dust Tree, has yellow-spotted leaves. There are other varieties with narrower leaves, with coarse teeth, and otherwise marked. E. Asia. Blooms in spring. Zone 7.

Baccharis
Daisy family
Compositae

Bak'kar-is. A very large genus of American shrubs, usually found in salt marshes or alkali deserts.

Description
Leaves thick and more or less fleshy. Flowers very small, yellowish or dirty white, all tubular and crowded in small heads. Fruit a showy, white collection of pappus bristles.

How to Grow
The species here is a salt-marsh shrub in the northern part of its range, useful for seaside planting because of its resistance to salt spray. It will also grow in ordinary garden soil if given open sunshine. Easy to propagate by cuttings, and may be dug from the wild.

halimifolia *pp. 98, 99*
Groundsel Bush or Groundsel Tree. A much-branched shrub, 6–12 ft. (1.8–3.5 m) high. Leaves wedge-shaped at the base and coarsely toothed, more or less resinous, to 2½ in. (6 cm), gray-green. Flowerheads ¼ in. (6 mm) long, crowded in dense clusters, the fruiting head snowy white. New England to Tex. Blooms in summer. Zones 6–10.

Berberis
Barberry family
Berberidaceae

Ber'ber-iss. The barberries are very popular shrubs, often used as hedges. The genus includes almost 500 species of evergreen or deciduous shrubs, all more or less spiny, scattered throughout the north temperate zone, with a few in North Africa and South America.

Description
Yellow wood and inner bark, usually 3-branched spines at most of the axils. Leaves simple, appearing in small clusters at the ends of short spurs, turning to scarlet, orange, or yellow in the fall. Flowers yellow, in longish racemes or in closer clusters, all spring-blooming. Petals and stamens 6; the stamens explosively discharging pollen when touched. Fruit a berry, which may shrivel or lose its color toward winter.

How to Grow
Most of the species are easy to grow in ordinary garden soil. Raise from seed or from cuttings made in late spring and rooted in moist sand, preferably in a shaded hotbed.

candidula *p. 266*
Paleleaf Barberry. A low evergreen shrub, 2–4 ft. (60–120 cm) high, related to *B. verruculosa,* but more dwarfed. Leaves elliptic, ¾ in. (19 mm) long, the margin rolled and nearly hiding the few marginal spiny teeth; green above, hoary beneath. Flowers ½ in. (13 mm) wide, solitary, yellow, followed by a small blue fruit with a bloom. Prized for its bright green foliage, which withstands pruning well. Can also be used as a ground cover. Cen. China. Blooms in late spring. Zones 6–8.

× ***chenaultii*** *p. 267*
Chenault Barberry. An evergreen, 3–4 ft. (90–120 cm) high, with arching habit. Leaves bright green, about 1 in. (2.5 cm) long and toothed. Flower clusters ½ in. (13 mm) long. Hybrid derived from *B. verruculosa* and *B. gagnepainii*. Blooms in late spring. Zones 6–8.

julianae *pp. 266, 267*
Wintergreen Barberry. An upright evergreen shrub, 6–8 ft. (1.8–2.4 m) high. Leaves narrowly elliptic, 1½–3 in. (4.0–7.5 cm) long, the margins toothed and spiny, dark green above, pale beneath. Flowers in close clusters 2 in. (5 cm) wide. Fruit bluish-black, with a bloom. The hardiest of the evergreen species and one of the most popular of all the Chinese species. Cen. China. Blooms in spring. Zones 6–8.

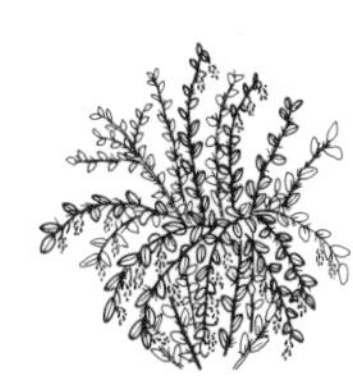

koreana *pp. 190, 191*
Korean Barberry. A deciduous shrub, to 6 ft. (1.8 m), the young branches grooved, reddish, and with a bloom, ultimately dark brown. Leaves rounded at the tip, wedge-shaped at the base, 1½–3 in. (4.0–7.5 cm) long, pale beneath. Flowers yellow, in dense, nearly stalkless racemes to 2⅜ in. (6 cm) long. Fruit bright red, holding its color well into the fall. Suitable for mass plantings. Tolerates dry soil. Korea. Blooms in spring. Zones 3–7.

× *mentorensis* *p. 192*
Mentor Barberry. A spiny hybrid, evergreen in mild regions, 5–7 ft. (1.5–2.1 m) high. Leaves elliptic, spiny-toothed, 1–2½ in. (2.5–6.0 cm) long, pale beneath. Flowers yellow, 1 or 2 in the ¾-in. (19 mm)-wide cluster. Fruit dark red, football-shaped. Makes an impenetrable thorny hedge and will tolerate drought. Hybrid derived from *B. julianae* and *B. thunbergii*. Blooms in spring. Zones 4–8.

thunbergii *pp. 190, 192, 193*
Japanese Barberry. Usually 4–6 ft. (1.2–1.8 m) high, mature branches purple-brown. Leaves variable, usually broader toward the tip, ½–1½ in. (1.3–4.0 cm) long, without teeth, brilliant scarlet in fall. Flowers yellow, red-tinged outside, ⅓ in. (8 mm) wide, solitary or in close clusters of 2–5. Fruit bright red, winter-persisting. More widely cultivated than almost any other shrub, and available in many varieties. 'Aurea' has yellow leaves and 'Atropurpurea' dark purple ones. Cultivar 'Kobold' has a compact habit similar to boxwood. Without pruning, it becomes mound-shaped, 2–3 ft. (60–90 cm) high. Flowers and fruit generally sparse. Useful in rock gardens or landscape areas where Japanese holly or boxwood would not grow well. 'Crimson Pygmy', a purple-leaved cultivar, also very popular for its compact habit, is about 2 ft. (60 cm) high. Japan. Blooms in spring. Zones 4–8.

verruculosa *p. 191*
Warty Barberry. Evergreen and not over 6 ft. (1.8 m) high, the branches warty. Leaves ovalish or elliptic, ¾–1½ in. (2–4 cm) long, glossy green, spiny-toothed, and pale beneath. Flowers larger than in most barberries, golden yellow, ¾ in. (19 mm) wide. Fruit bluish black, with a bloom. W. China. Blooms in spring. Zones 6–8.

Brunfelsia

Potato family
Solanaceae

Brun-felz′i-a. A genus of 40 species of tropical American shrubs or trees, the species given below grown in greenhouses for its extremely fragrant flowers.

Description
Leaves alternate and without marginal teeth. Flowers usually solitary, the calyx bell-shaped, the corolla funnel-shaped with a long tube. Stamens 4. Fruit fleshy.

How to Grow
Brunfelsia should be planted in fertile, moist, acid soil. Give them light shade for best foliage and flowers. Fertilize and water liberally during the summer and prune in the spring.

pauciflora *pp. 128, 129*
Brazil Raintree. An erect or somewhat sprawling evergreen shrub, generally not over 2 ft. (60 cm) high, but sometimes reaching 9 ft. (2.7 m). Leaves oblongish, 2½–4 in. (6–10 cm) long, bright green above, paler beneath. Flowers nearly 2 in. (5 cm) wide, in a terminal cyme, dark purple with white eye. The cultivar 'Floribunda,' 8–10 ft. (2.4–3.0 m) high, has an interesting trait that endears it to most gardeners. Over a 3-day period, the flowers change color from purple to lavender to white. Brazil. Blooms spring to summer. Zone 9.

Buddleia

Buddleia family
Loganiaceae

Bud′lee-a. Sometimes spelled *Buddleja*. The butterfly bushes, so called because they attract butterflies in profusion when in flower, comprise about 100 species of mostly tropical shrubs. They are among the most outstanding of late-flowering garden plants.

Description
All but one species have opposite leaves. Flowers usually in panicles or spikes, calyx bell-shaped and 4-lobed. Corolla tubular or bell-shaped, 4-lobed, the 4 stamens hidden inside. Fruit a 2-valved capsule, usually surrounded by the withered flower.

How to Grow
Plants need sunny locations and a rich, but not heavy, soil that is well-drained. They are easy to propagate by cuttings of semi-hardwood rooted in the fall in the greenhouse. Not all species are hardy in the North, but most will survive if given winter protection. If they should be winter-killed, cut them back to the ground, since the roots usually survive. Some growers prefer to cut back most of the cultivated species and mulch the crowns with light, strawy manure.

alternifolia *p. 150*
Alternate Leaf Butterfly Bush or Fountain Buddleia. The only cultivated species with alternate leaves. Shrub 10–20 ft. (3–6 m). Leaves lance-shaped, 1–4 in. (2.5–10.0 cm) long, green above, grayish and scurfy beneath. Flowers fragrant, lilac-purple, ½ in. (13 mm) long, in short, dense, leafy clusters to ¾ in. (19 mm) long. These appear on last year's branches, so prune after flowering. A beautiful plant, with arching or pendulous branches. Cultivar 'Argentea' has silky-haired leaves that give it a silvery sheen. Blooms in summer. Zones 6–8.

davidii *pp. 148, 149*
Orange-eye Butterfly Bush. Shrub 6–10 ft. (1.8–3.0 m) high, but often much lower in those cut back for the winter. Leaves oval-lance-shaped, 6–9 in. (15.0–22.5 cm) long, finely toothed, green above, white-felty beneath. Flowers fragrant, lilac, orange at the throat, in usually-nodding spikes, 5–12 in. (12.5–30.0 cm) long. The best known of the cultivated species and the hardiest. Var. 'Charming' has deep pink flowers. 'Black Knight', with dark purple flowers, 'Dubonnet', with reddish-purple flowers, and 'White Bouquet' are also popular; there are many other cultivars. China. Blooms summer to fall. Zones 5–9.

× ***weyeriana*** **'Sun Gold'** *p. 187*
Weyer Butterfly Bush. Shrub, to 15 ft. (4.5 m) high. Leaves lance-shaped. Flowers orange-yellow, with ball-shaped heads ¾ in. (19 mm) wide. Hybrid derived from *B. davidii* and *B. globosa*. Blooms in summer. Zones 7–10.

Buxus
Box family
Buxaceae

Bucks'us. Of the 30 known species of boxwood, only 2 are commonly grown. But these, and their numerous horticultural varieties, have added an atmosphere of grace, charm, and solidity to many historic gardens. Since the days of the Romans, this has been the best of all plants for hedges and topiary work.

Description
Leaves opposite, evergreen, without marginal teeth. Flowers small and inconspicuous, without petals, flowering in spring, male and female on the same plant, but not together, the female flowers usually above the male. Female flowers with 6 sepals, male with 4. Fruit a 3-horned capsule, usually shedding seed in June.

How to Grow
Boxwood is easy to grow and does best in well-drained soil in sun or light shade. Because its roots are close to the surface, use a compost or bark mulch around the base to help keep them cool and reduce the need for cultivation. Transplant as a balled and burlapped plant or as a container plant. The key to successful growth is in placing the plant where it will not be damaged by winter winds and temperatures.

microphylla *pp. 278, 279*
Littleleaf Box. A Japanese evergreen shrub, rarely over 6 ft. (1.8 m) high, and resembling *B. sempervirens,* but with its leaves smaller and broadest above the middle, and its branchlets prominently 4-angled or winged. Hardier than Common Box, especially in the variety *koreana,* which can be grown in zone 5. Var. *japonica* is a bit taller and has a more open habit. The var. *koreana* (from Korea), is shorter than the typical form, rarely exceeding 3 ft. (90 cm). It turns yellowish-brown in winter, but var. 'Wintergreen' retains its green foliage. Zone 6.

sempervirens *p. 278*
Common Box; English or American Box. Ranges from a dwarf, globular shrub to a tree 20 ft. (6 m) high, the latter only in the most favorable sites. Leaves broadest at or below the middle, ¾–1½ in. (2–4 cm) long,

lustrous green both sides, but darker above, rounded and slightly notched at the tip. Weeping, pyramidal, globe-shaped, and treelike varieties, some with variegated foliage. One of the best is var. *suffruticosa,* Edging Box, a permanent dwarf used for centuries to edge beds and in formal gardens. S. Europe, n. Africa, and w. Asia. Zones 5–8.

Caesalpinia

Bean family
Leguminosae

See-zal-pin′i-a. A genus of about 70 showy tropical trees or shrubs, widely grown for ornament in warm regions. In the U.S. they can be grown only in zones 9 and 10.

Description

The commonly cultivated species are shrubs with alternate, twice-compound leaves, the many leaflets arranged pinnately, without an odd one at the end. Flowers not pealike, the 5 broad, separate, showy petals slightly unequal. Stamens 10, distinct and protruding. Fruit a narrow, flattened pod (legume).

How to Grow

The species below is grown throughout most of Fla. and the Gulf states, and in Calif. It will thrive in full sun and almost any well-drained soil. Propagate by seeds soaked in warm water for several hours to encourage germination and sown in pots. Transfer outdoors when the plants have reached 1–2 ft. (30–60 cm) high.

gilliesii *p. 183*

Bird-of-Paradise Bush. A shrub or small tree, to 10 ft. (3 m) high, the branches straggling and sticky-hairy. Leaflets very numerous and small, making the foliage graceful and feathery. Flowers yellow, the clusters 4–5 in. (10.0–12.5 cm) long, the bright red, showy stamens protruding 4–5 in. (10.0–12.5 cm). Pods 3–4 in. (7.5–10.0 cm) long. The blossoms will attract hummingbirds. Previously known as *Poinciana gilliesii*. South America. Blooms in summer. Zones 9–10.

Calliandra

Pea family
Leguminosae

Kal′li-an-dra. A large genus of tropical evergreen shrubs and trees that differ only slightly from those in the genus *Acacia.* Unlike many acacias, however, these plants are not usually thorny.

Description
Leaves twice-compound, the leaflets numerous and small. Flowers small, crowded in dense, globular heads covered by the silky, protruding stamens. Fruit a flattened, and sometimes curled, legume.

How to Grow
The species here requires a sunny location, abundant water, and well-drained soil. It will grow well only in the warm region of zone 10. Propagate by seeds or by cuttings over bottom heat.

haematocephala *p. 94*
Red Powderpuff. A shrub, to 15 ft. (4.5 m). Leaves with 2 pairs of pinnae, each with 5–8 pairs of leaflets to 3½ in. (9 cm) long. Flower heads 2 in. (5 cm) in diameter, reddish. Also called *C. inaequilatera.* Bolivia. Blooms fall to winter. Zone 10.

Callicarpa

Verbena family
Verbenaceae

Kal′li-kar-pa. A large genus of shrubs, often called Beautyberry, the species described below grown especially for their beautiful clusters of fruit in fall.

Description
Leaves opposite, toothed, the teeth often bluntish. Flowers small, tubular, 4-lobed at the top, the 4 stamens protruding. Fruit nearly globe-shaped, berrylike.

How to Grow
Plant beautyberries in full sun in a rich soil. Propagate by seeds or by cuttings of mature wood. Since flowers appear on new growth, prune in the spring to within 6 in. (15 cm) of ground. If plants should winter-kill, they will usually come back from the base.

americana *p. 263*
French Mulberry. A shrub, 5–8 ft. (1.5–2.4 m) high. Leaves 4–6 in. (10–15 cm) long, bluntly toothed, green above, rusty beneath. Flowers ⅕ in. (5 mm) long in a compact, short-stalked cyme 1¼ in. (3 cm) long, bluish, white, purple, lilac, or even red. Fruit violet, but a white-fruited variety, *C. a. lactea,* is also offered. Md. to Tex. and Okla. and in the West Indies. Blooms in spring. Zone 7.

dichotoma *p. 262*
Purple Beautyberry. A shrub, 2–4 ft. (60–120 cm) high. Leaves 1–3 in. (2.5–7.5 cm) long, bluntly toothed toward the base, without teeth toward the tip. Flowers pink, ⅛ in. (3.2 mm) long, the cluster usually few-flowered. Fruit violet or lilac. Often sold as *C. purpurea.* Blooms in summer. Zone 5.

japonica *pp. 262, 263*
Japanese Beautyberry. Not over 6 ft. (1.8 m) high. Leaves 3–5 in. (7.5–12.5 cm) long, finely toothed. Flowers white or pink, ¼ in. (6 mm) long, the clusters 1¼ in. (3 cm) long, stalked and profuse. Fruit violet. A white-fruited cultivar, 'Leucocarpa', is also offered. Japan. Blooms summer to fall. Zones 6–8.

Callistemon
Myrtle family
Myrtaceae

Kal-lis-tee′mon. A genus of showy Australian shrubs and trees, popular for their handsome, spiky flowers which inspired the common name, bottle-brush.

Description
Many scattered or crowded small but stoutish leaves, narrow or pointed. Flowers in dense spikes, each flower minute, but the spike very showy with numerous, handsome, protruding stamens. Fruit a somewhat woody capsule.

How to Grow
Bottle-brushes are easy to grow in any soil. Propagate by cuttings of ripened wood or by seeds harvested in fall and sown in spring. Prune heavily every three years for best flowers and fruit.

citrinus *p. 95*
Crimson Bottle-brush. A shrub, 10–20 ft. (3–6 m) high. Leaves lance-shaped, 2½ in. (6 cm) long. Spikes 2–4 in. (5–10 cm) long, not dense, the bright red stamens 1 in. (2.5 cm) long. This is the most popular and dramatic bottle-brush. It performs best in acid soil, especially on beach fronts. It grows fast and is easily trained for use in espaliers. Se. Australia. Blooms spring to summer. Zone 9.

Calluna

Heath family
Ericaceae

Ka-loo′na. A single, remarkably variable species of low shrub found throughout Europe and in Asia Minor, widely cultivated in this country for its evergreen foliage and profusion of small, nodding flowers. Commonly called heather.

Description
Leaves small and opposite. Corolla bell-shaped, 4-parted above, ultimately becoming membranous and long-persisting, the bell-shaped, colored calyx extending beyond it. Stamens 8, included within the corolla. Fruit a small 4-valved capsule which is hidden by the persistent corolla.

How to Grow
Plant heather in poor soil, which prevents legginess, and full sun. The soil should be well-drained and acid. Since roots are near the surface, do not cultivate around the base of the plants. Prune in early spring, and propagate by softwood cuttings, treated with rooting hormone.

vulgaris *p. 152*
Scotch Heather. Usually grows in dense masses less than 18 in. (45 cm) high. Leaves minute, stalkless, keeled, mostly in 4 ranks, and so numerous that they completely clothe the twigs. Flowers in dense terminal spikes to 10 in. (25 cm) long. Many varieties are available in colors ranging from white to red. A splendid plant for sandy banks or slopes. Blooms summer to fall. Zone 5.

Calycanthus
Sweet-shrub family
Calycanthaceae

Kal-ee-kan'thus. Aromatic North American shrubs, variously called sweet-shrub, strawberry-shrub, and Carolina allspice.

Description
Leaves opposite and without teeth. Flowers fragrant, large, the sepals and petals similarly colored, either brown or brownish purple.

How to Grow
Though they have no special soil preferences, these shrubs do best in rich, well-drained soil with plenty of moisture. Propagate by layers, suckers, division, or seeds.

floridus *p. 92*
Carolina Allspice; Common Sweet-shrub. A densely hairy shrub, 4–8 ft. (1.2–2.4 m) high. Leaves oval or elliptic, 3–5 in. (7.5–12.5 cm) long, glossy, pale on the underside, aromatic when crushed or dried. Flowers dark purple-brown, generally fragrant, 2 in. (5 cm) wide. Va. to Fla. and Miss., mostly near the coast. Blooms in spring. Zone 4.

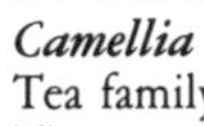

Camellia
Tea family
Theaceae

Ka-mee'li-a; also, in the South, Ka-mell'i-a. Asiatic evergreen shrubs or small trees, widely grown for their waxlike, very showy and lasting bloom. Favorites of Southern gardeners.

Description
Leaves alternate, toothed, usually solitary. Flowers nearly stalkless, red in the typical plant, but of other colors or even double in the many horticultural forms. Petals mostly 5. Sepals 5–7, often falling away. Fruit a woody capsule.

How to Grow
Easy to grow by transplanting from containers into moist, well-drained, acid soil. The root systems are shallow, so mulch areas around the plant. Camellias prefer partial shade for best flowering. Propagate by seeds or from cuttings of current season's growth.

japonica *p. 120*
Common Camellia; Japanese Camellia. A shrub or, rarely, a tree up to 20–25 ft. (6.0–7.5 m) high. Leaves ovalish, 3–4 in. (7.5–10.0 cm) long, shining dark green. Flowers 3–5 in (7.5–12.5 cm) wide, waxy, the petals roundish. Sometimes offered as *Thea japonica* or called merely Japonica. Several hundred varieties are grown in the U.S., with single or double flowers ranging from white to dark red. China and Japan. Blooms fall to spring. Zone 8.

sasanqua *p. 121*
Sasanqua Camellia. Similar to *C. japonica,* but lower, 6–10 ft. (1.8–3.0 m) high, and more hardy, often safe outdoors up to Zone 8. There are over 70 named forms, with white to rose flowers 2–3 in. (5.0–7.5 cm) wide. China and Japan. Blooms fall to winter, earlier than *C. japonica*. Zone 8.

Caragana
Pea family
Leguminosae

Ka-ra-gay′na. Decorative shrubs and trees comprising nearly 60 species, mostly native to cen. Asia.

Description
The species below is a shrub with pinnately compound leaves, without a terminal leaflet. Flowers typically pealike, yellow. Legumes narrow and nearly round.

How to Grow
The pea shrubs are hardy plants that are easy to grow in any garden soil, preferably in full sunlight. As hedge plants for windbreaks and snow traps, few plants are superior in regions of intense cold. Propagate by seeds, first soaked in hot water, or by cuttings.

arborescens *p. 178*
Siberian Pea Shrub. Not over 20 ft. (6 m) high, usually less, the spines often lacking. Leaves 1–3½ in. (2.5–9.0 cm) long, composed of 4–6 pairs of tiny leaflets, each ⅓ in. (8 mm) long. Flowers nearly ¾ in. (19 mm) long, borne singly, but several close together, hence showy when in bloom. Pod 1½–2 in. (4–5 cm) long, stalked. Tolerates drought, alkaline soils, and salt. Watch for leafhoppers in this species. There

are dwarf forms suitable for hedges and valuable in regions where privet is not hardy. Var. *pendula* has weeping branches. Siberia. Blooms in spring. Zone 2.

Carissa

Dogbane family
Apocynaceae

Ka-ris′sa. A genus of 30 species of spiny shrubs, chiefly South African, the one below grown for ornament or hedges, more rarely for its fruit.

Description
Leaves opposite, without marginal teeth. Flowers in stalked cymes, the corolla salver-shaped, white or pink. Stamens 5, inserted in the corolla tube. Fruit a fleshy berry.

How to Grow
Easy to grow in warm, moist climates in full sun. Propagate by seeds or cuttings.

grandiflora *p. 215*
Natal Plum or Amatungula. A very bushy shrub, to 15 ft. (4.5 m) high, the spines forked. Leaves ovalish, 1–2½ in. (2.5–6.0 cm) long. Flowers fragrant, white, nearly 2 in. (5 cm) wide. Berry egg-shaped, red, 1–2 in. (2.5–5.0 cm) long. The fruit, which can be eaten fresh or in a sauce, tastes somewhat like a cranberry. This species is useful as a screen or hedge because of its plentiful spines. South Africa. Blooms year-round. Zone 10.

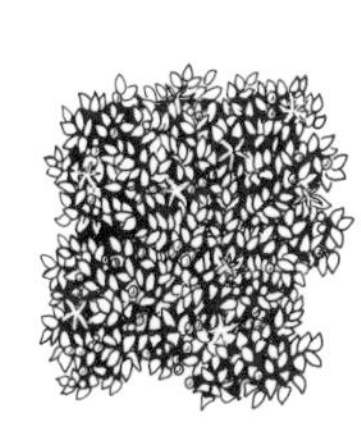

Caryopteris

Verbena family
Verbenaceae

Carry-op′ter-is. Attractive Asiatic shrubs grown for their showy bloom. Of the 6 species, only one and its hybrids are well known, usually as Bluebeard or Blue Spirea.

Description
Leaves opposite, short-stalked, and toothed. Flowers in profuse cymes, the corolla irregular, one of its 5 lobes larger than the others and fringed. Stamens 4, protruding.

Fruit dry, separating into 4 slightly winged nutlets.

How to Grow
These shrubs grow best in good loam soil in full sun. Give them moderate amounts of water. The stems should be cut back in winter since flowers grow on new wood.

× ***clandonensis*** *pp. 154, 155*
Bluebeard; Blue Spirea. A low, mounded shrub, to 2 ft. (60 cm) high. Leaves lance-shaped, to 3 in. (7.5 cm) long. Flowers blue, to ⅜ in. (9 mm) long. Hybrid derived from *C. incana* and *C. mongholica*. 'Kew Blue' and 'Blue Mist' are popular cultivars. Blooms in summer. Zone 5.

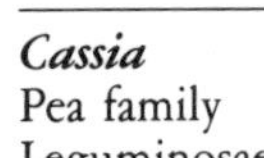

Cassia
Pea family
Leguminosae

Cash′i-a. The general term senna is used for immense genus of about 500 herbs, shrubs, and trees grown for their usually showy flowers.

Description
Leaves pinnately compound, without a terminal leaflet. Flowers very nearly regular, rather than pealike, but one of the clawed petals often a little larger than the other 4. Fruit a flattened or roundish pod, usually 4-angled or winged.

How to Grow
The Feathery Cassia is a drought-resistant shrub that performs best in sunny areas in a well-drained soil. It should be pruned lightly after flowering to prevent a heavy set of fruit, which is not attractive.

artemisioides *p. 182*
Feathery Cassia; Wormwood Senna. A compact shrub, to 4 ft. (120 cm) high, with silky-gray foliage. Leaflets 6–8, needle-like, 1 in. (2.5 cm) long. Flowers yellow, in racemes 2–6 in. (5–15 cm) long, arising in leaf axils. Australia. Blooms early spring to summer. Zone 9.

Ceanothus
Buckthorn family
Rhamnaceae

See-a-no′thus. A large genus of very handsome North American shrubs, only a few of which are cultivated because their hardiness is often restrictive. In Calif. they are generally called wild lilac or buckbrush.

Description
Leaves evergreen in some species, nearly always 3-veined at the base. Flowers small, blue or white, but showy because they are borne in dense, branched clusters. Sepals incurved and often colored. Petals hooded and with a narrow shank. Fruit dry, 3-lobed, and separating into 3 segments when ripe.

How to Grow
Ceanothus prefers open sunlight and a light, porous soil. It is best to keep it out of the path of the sprinkler system because too much water is deadly. These plants get rangy with age and are then best replaced. Propagate by seeds, cuttings, or layering.

***cyaneus* 'Sierra Blue'** *p. 76*
San Diego Ceanothus. An evergreen shrub, 10–12 ft. (3.0–3.5 m) high, sometimes trained on walls. Leaves 3-veined, alternately arranged, more or less oval, 1–2 in. (2.5–5.0 cm) long, the marginal teeth glandular. Flowers blue, in showy panicles that may be 2–5 in. (5.0–12.5 cm) long. Calif. Blooms in spring. Zone 8.

griseus* var. *horizontalis *p. 77*
Carmel Creeper. Low, spreading to prostrate evergreen shrub, 2–3 ft. (60–90 cm) high. Leaves alternate, ovalish, to 1¾ in. (4.5 cm) long, glossy, bright green. Flowers blue, in 2 in. (5 cm) panicles. Coastal, cen. Calif. Blooms in spring. Zone 8.

ovatus *p. 137*
Inland Ceanothus. 2–3 ft. (60–90 cm) high, with glossy bright green leaves, 2½ in. (6 cm) long, toothed. Flowers white, but not as ornamental as red fruit capsules in summer. Vt. to Colo. and Tex. Blooms in late spring. Zone 5.

Cephalanthus
Madder family
Rubiaceae

Sef-a-lan′thus. About 6 species of shrubs or small trees native to the temperate regions of Africa, Asia, and North America. The single American species grows naturally in swamps.

Description
Leaves are opposite or whorled, with stipules between them. Flowers small, tubular, borne in congested heads.

How to Grow
These shrubs will grow in any ordinary garden soil if it is kept moist. Propagate by seeds or cuttings.

occidentalis *p. 143*

Button Bush. A shrub, 5–12 ft. (1.5–3.5 m) high, with opposite or whorled leaves having no marginal teeth. It has ball-like clusters of small, white, tubular flowers 1 in. (2.5 cm) wide. Nova Scotia to Mexico and west to Calif. Blooms in summer. Zone 5.

Cercis
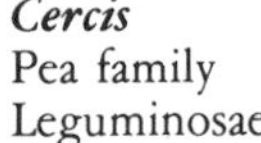
Pea family
Leguminosae

Sir′sis. Redbuds are very attractive shrubs or small trees. Four of the 7 known species are grown for their showy flowers, which bloom in early spring before the leaves expand.

Description
Leaves simple, not pealike, usually roundish or heart-shaped, stalked, with the veins arranged palmately. Flowers small, but usually numerous, pealike or nearly so, rose-pink or rose-purple in the cultivated sorts. Stamens 10, not united. Fruit flat, thin, and narrowly winged, its seeds flattened.

How to Grow
Easy to grow in open, rather sandy loam, but redbuds do not like heavy, moist sites and are hard to move when mature. They may be propagated by seeds, which should be scarified; by layers; or by softwood cuttings under glass.

chinensis *pp. 82, 83*
Chinese Redbud. A cultivated shrub or small

tree to 10 ft. (3 m). Leaves deeply heart-shaped at the base, 3–5 in. (7.5–12.5 cm) long. Rosy purple flowers, ¾ in. (19 mm) long, in numerous clusters of 4–8. Sometimes offered as *C. japonica*. Cen. China. Blooms in spring, earlier than many other plants. Zone 7.

Chaenomeles
Rose family
Rosaceae

Kee-nom'e-lees. All the known species of the flowering quince, which come from e. Asia, are popular garden shrubs because of their beautiful, early spring bloom. They also bear hard, aromatic, quincelike fruits that can be made into preserves.

Description
Leaves alternate. Flowers solitary or in small, close clusters, blooming before, or with, the unfolding of the leaves. Petals 5, showy. Stamens many. Fruit a pome, with numerous brown seeds.

How to Grow
Flowering quinces are easy to grow in any soil. Though they will not stand heavy clipping, they are widely used for hedges. Propagate by semi-hardwood cuttings, layering, or root cuttings.

japonica *p. 110*
Japanese Quince. Dwarf, scarcely more than 3 ft. (90 cm) high, the branches often spiny and hairy, at least when young. Leaves broadly oval, 1½–2 in. (4–5 cm) long, coarsely toothed. Flowers brick-red, 1 in. (2.5 cm) wide. Fruit yellow, 1½–2 in. (4 cm) long. Tolerates city conditions. Japan. Zone 5.

speciosa *pp. 110, 111*
Common Flowering Quince. A shrub, 6–10 ft. (1.8–3.0 m) high, the branches somewhat spiny and smooth. Leaves oval-oblong, 2–3 in. (5.0–7.5 cm) long, finely toothed. Flowers scarlet-red, 1–2 in. (2.5–5.0 cm) wide. Fruit yellowish green, nearly 2 in. (5 cm) long. There are varieties with pink or white flowers. This is the best of the flowering quinces to use for hedges. China. Zone 5.

× ***superba*** *p. 111*
Flowering Quince. A shrub with erect, spreading stems, to 5 ft. (1.5 m) high, the twigs tipped with slender spines, young shoots hairy. Flowers 1–2 in (2.5–5.0 cm) wide, red, white, pink, or orange. Fruit yellow when mature, and apple-shaped. Hybrid derived from *C. japonica* and *C. speciosa*. Zone 5.

Chimonanthus
Sweet-shrub family
Calycanthaceae

Ky'mo-nan-thus. A genus of deciduous or evergreen late-blooming Chinese shrubs comprising 4 species. The one below is cultivated for ornament and for the fragrance of its flowers.

Description
Leaves opposite, smooth, without marginal teeth. Flowers appearing before the leaves, the sepals numerous, overlapping, yellow. Petals none. Stamens 5–6.

How to Grow
Easy to grow in any soil if drainage is good. Consider planting this shrub alongside a walkway or under a bedroom window so its perfume can be enjoyed. Propagate by layering in fall or by sowing seeds in spring.

praecox *p. 165*
Fragrant Wintersweet. A shrub growing to 10 ft. (3 m) high. Leaves 4–6 in. (10–15 cm) long, ovalish, long-pointed. Flowers 1 in. (2.5 cm) across, the outer sepals yellow, the inner striped purplish brown. Often listed as *Meratia fragrans*. Blooms in winter. Zone 7.

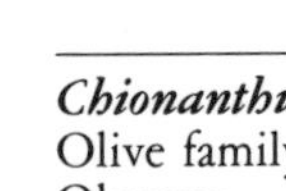

Chionanthus
Olive family
Oleaceae

Ki-o-nan'thus. Three or 4 handsome shrubs or small trees, one widely cultivated for its showy white flowers.

Description
Leaves opposite, without marginal teeth. Flowers in loose, often hanging, clusters. Petals 4, strap-shaped, slightly united at the

base. Male and female flowers on separate plants, the male flowers larger but producing no fruit. Fruit fleshy, 1-seeded, blue.

How to Grow
Easy to grow in moist, fertile soil in full sun. The Fringe Tree prefers a slightly acid soil. Propagate by layers or cuttings of plants forced for the purpose.

virginicus *pp. 88, 89*
Fringe Tree; Old-Man's-Beard. A shrub or tree, to 25 ft. (7.5 m) high. Leaves narrowly elliptic or oblongish, 6–8 in. (15–20 cm) long. Flower cluster 7 in. (17.5 cm) long, fragrant, from lateral buds at the end of old twigs. Petals 1 in. (2.5 cm) long. Fruit egg-shaped, 1 in. (2.5 cm) long. N.J. to Fla. and Tex. Blooms in spring. Zone 4.

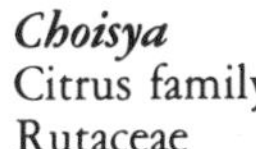

Choisya
Citrus family
Rutaceae

Shaw'si-a. Seven species of aromatic evergreen shrubs, one of which is grown for its fine foliage and the fragrant white flowers that appear in early spring.

Description
Leaves opposite, compound, the 3 leaflets nearly stalkless and without marginal teeth. Flowers in 3- to 6-flowered, slender-stalked cymes. Petals 5. Stamens 10. Fruit a 3–5-lobed capsule.

How to Grow
Plant the Mexican Orange in well-drained, acid soil,full sun to partial shade. You might place it near a window or walkway so that its fragrance will be noticed. Propagate by hardwood cuttings. Prune often to maintain full growth.

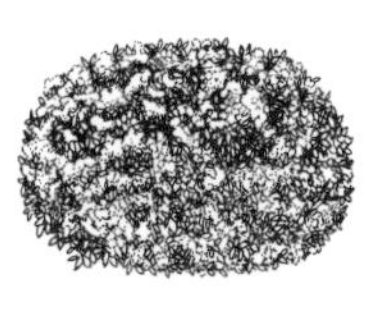

ternata *p. 136*
Mexican Orange. A shrub, 6–8 ft. (1.8–2.4 m) high. Leaflets 2–3 in. (5.0–7.5 cm) long. Flowers 1–1½ in. (2.5–4.0 cm) wide. A good plant for massing, hedging, or screening. Mexico. Zone 8.

Cistus
Rockrose family
Cistaceae

Sis′tus. Mediterranean shrubs, usually called rockroses, long known in Old World gardens. Because most are flame-retardant, they are valuable in dry areas of California. Rockroses are good plants for a rock garden.

Description
Leaves opposite, simple, without marginal teeth, evergreen or nearly so, generally soft-hairy. Flowers large, somewhat like a single rose, with 5 separate petals but many stamens. Fruit a 5–10 valved capsule.

How to Grow
The rockroses require partial to well-drained soils that are slightly alkaline. They must have open sunlight and will tolerate drought, but not wet, cold winters. They are easily grown in Calif. and the South. Propagate by seeds sown in pots. After planting seedlings outdoors, do not attempt further transplanting. Or take cuttings of nonflowering side shoots, preferably in late summer or fall.

× ***hybridus*** *p. 118*
White Rockrose. A hybrid shrub, 2–4 ft. (60–120 cm) high and more or less bushy, the twigs downy, as are the ovalish leaves. Flowers 1½ in. (4 cm) wide, white, with a yellow "eye." Also called *C. corbariensis.* Blooms spring to summer. Zone 8.

ladanifer *p. 117*
Crimson-spot Rockrose. A sticky-branched shrub, scarcely over 4 ft. (120 cm) high. Leaves slightly stalked, green and sticky above, densely white-hairy beneath, lance-shaped, 3–4 in. (7.5–10.0 cm) long. Flowers fragrant, solitary, white, but purple-blotched and with yellow center, nearly 3½ in. (9 cm) wide. Var. *maculatus* has a brownish-red-centered flower. W. Mediterranean. Blooms in summer. Zone 7.

× ***pulverulentus*** *p. 119*
To 2 ft. (60 cm), leaves ovalish. Flowers rose-red, 1 in. (2.5 cm) wide. Hybrid derived from *C. albidus* and *C. crispus.* Blooms in summer. Zone 8.

× ***purpureus*** *p. 116*
Orchid Rockrose. 3–4 ft. (90–120 cm) high,

the twigs sticky-hairy. Leaves oblongish, 1–2 in. (2.5–5.0 cm) long, nearly stalkless. Flowers showy, 2–3 in. (5.0–7.5 cm) wide, reddish purple, with a darker blotch on each petal and a yellow "eye." Hybrid derived from *C. ladanifer* and *C. villosus*. Tolerant of salt spray. Blooms in summer. Zone 8.

Clethra

Summer-sweet family
Clethraceae

Kleth′ra. Very fragrant, white-flowered shrubs, sometimes called white alder. Most of the approximately 30 species are common in North America and e. Asia.

Description
Leaves alternate, toothed, short-stalked. Flowers in terminal, spirelike racemes with 5 sepals and 5 petals, neither tubular. Stamens 10. Fruit a 3-valved, many-seeded capsule.

How to Grow
The species described below is easy to grow in moist, acid soil. Propagate by cuttings taken in summer.

alnifolia *p. 145*
Summer sweet Clethra; Sweet Pepperbush; Spiked Alder. A shrub, 3–8 ft. (0.9–2.4 m) high. Leaves oblongish, pointed, 2½–5 in. (6.0–12.5 cm) long. Flowers very fragrant, the clusters numerous, erect, and 5 in. (12.5 cm) long. There are pink-flowered varieties, 'Pink Spires' and 'Rosea'. Maine to Fla. and Tex. Blooms in summer. Zone 4.

Colutea

Pea family
Leguminosae

Ko-lew′tee-a. Eurasian shrubs of the pea family, the species below often grown for ornament.

Description
Leaves pinnate, with a terminal leaflet. Flowers pealike, in axillary clusters. Fruit an inflated, pealike legume.

How to Grow
The Common Bladder Senna is easy to grow

in any well-drained soil in full sun. To keep it looking neat, cut the stems back to the old wood after flowering.

arborescens *p. 179*
Common Bladder Senna. A shrub with erect stems, to 8 ft. (2.4 m) high. 9–13 leaflets, without teeth, 2 in. (5 cm) long. Flowers bright yellow, 1 in. (2.5 cm) long, in long-stalked racemes from the leaf axils. Pod papery, inflated and not splitting, 2½ in. (6 cm) long. S. Europe. Blooms spring to summer. Zone 6.

Comptonia

Wax-myrtle family
Myricaceae

Komp-to′ni-a. A single, highly aromatic shrub found in sandy or rocky soil throughout e. North America.

Description
Leaves alternate, stalked and narrow. Flowers small and inconspicuous, green, in catkins. Fruit a small nutlet, beneath which are narrow bracts, making the fruit look burrlike.

How to Grow
Plant Sweet Fern in a well-drained, sandy, acid soil in partial to full sun. Propagate by seeds sown in a container, and transplant carefully, keeping rootball intact.

peregrina *pp. 184, 185*
Sweet Fern or Shrubby Fern (not actually a fern); Sweetbush. A hairy shrub, to 5 ft. (1.5 m), but often much less. Leaves fragrant when crushed, 4–5 in. (10.0–12.5 cm) long, the margins obliquely cut into rounded lobes. Also known as *Myrica asplenifolia*. Zone 3.

Coprosma

Madder family
Rubiaceae

Ko-pros′ma. A large genus of shrubs or small trees from New Zealand, grown widely in Calif. and other warm regions for their foliage and fruit. They are useful as hedges or screens.

Description
Leaves opposite, persistent, or half-evergreen, thick and shining in the species described below. Male and female flowers on different plants, small, greenish white, in short, dense heads. Fruit fleshy.

How to Grow
Coprosmas grow best in partial shade and will tolerate drought. Without pruning, *C. repens* is an open, straggly shrub, so prune it twice a year for a neat shape. Male and female plants must be planted in order for the showy fruits to form.

repens *p. 280*

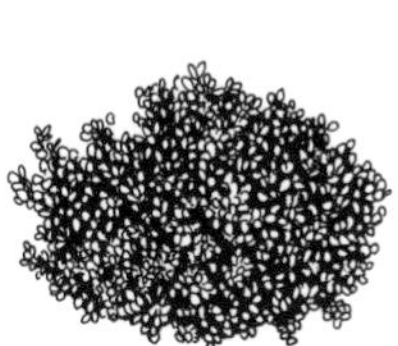

Mirror Plant. To 10 ft. (3 m) high. Leaves nearly evergreen, very glossy, oval or oblongish, 2–3 in. (5.0–7.5 cm) long, usually notched or blunt at the tip. Fruit on female plants only, orange-yellow, ⅓ in. (8 mm) long. The var. *variegata* has yellow-green blotched leaves. This is the commonest species in cultivation. New Zealand. Zone 9.

Cornus

Dogwood family
Cornaceae

Kor′nus. The dogwoods comprise an important group of garden shrubs and trees grown for their handsome spring flowers, brightly colored fruits, and, in some species, for the winter effect of their colored twigs. All the 45 known species are native to the north temperate zone.

Description
Leaves generally opposite, without marginal teeth. Flowers small, with 4 small petals and 4 stamens. In many species these flowers are white and grouped in flat-topped or rounded cymes, making them resemble viburnums, but the latter have 5 stamens and a united corolla. Cornelian Cherry has yellow flowers. Fruit fleshy.

How to Grow
Most of the dogwoods are easy to grow in any good garden soil. Propagate by cuttings of hardwood or by layering. Some choice varieties are occasionally grafted.

alba *p. 241*
Tartarian Dogwood. A showy shrub, 6–10 ft.

(1.8–3.0 m) high, its twigs bright red. Leaves ovalish, 3–5 in. (7.5–12.5 cm) long, bluish green beneath. Flowers white, the clusters numerous and 2 in. (5 cm) wide. Fruit whitish blue. There are forms with variegated leaves. Use especially for the winter effect of the twigs. E. Asia. Zone 3.

mas *pp. 242, 243*
Cornelian Cherry. A shrub or small tree, 20–25 ft. (6.0–7.5 m) high, the naked twigs of which are crowded with short-stalked, small, headlike clusters of minute yellow flowers in spring. Clusters ¾ in. (19 mm) wide. Leaves oval or elliptic, 3–4 in. (7.5–10.0 cm) long. Fruit edible, but acid, the size of a cherry; scarlet, ripening in late summer. Tolerates a city atmosphere better than most shrubs. Eurasia. Zone 5.

racemosa *pp. 240, 241*
Gray Dogwood. A shrub, 8–15 ft. (2.4–4.5 m) high, with gray twigs. Leaves elliptic or narrowly oval, 2–4 in. (5–10 cm) long, tapering at the tip, but wedge-shaped at the base. Flowers white, the cluster branched, not flat-topped, 2 in. (5 cm) wide. Fruit white on red pedicels. Most effective in summer, with its red-stalked white berries. Will tolerate shade and both wet and dry conditions. E. U.S. Zone 4.

sericea *p. 240*
Red Osier. A shrub, to 6 ft. (1.8 m) high, its red branches erect but spreading by underground, prostrate stems, thus producing large clumps. Leaves ovalish or narrower, 3–5 in. (7.5–12.5 cm) long. Flowers white, small, in flat-topped clusters that are often 2½ in. (6 cm) wide. Fruit white or bluish. Tolerates wet conditions and is often used for massing. Also known as *C. stolonifera*. 'Flaviramea' has yellow twigs. North America. Zone 3.

Corylopsis
Witch hazel family
Hamamelidaceae

Kor-ril-lop′sis. A small group of Asiatic shrubs flowering in late winter or early spring before the leaves unfold, hence sometimes called winter hazel.

Description
Leaves alternate, stalked, prominently veined and toothed. Flowers yellow, in nearly stalkless, nodding racemes. Petals 5, clawed. Stamens 5. Fruit a 2-beaked pod with 2 black seeds.

How to Grow
The species below prefer a somewhat acid, sandy soil, but can be grown in any ordinary garden soil that is not too heavy. Propagate by softwood cuttings in summer. After rooting, the cuttings should be left undisturbed until growth begins the following spring, when you can plant them outdoors.

glabrescens *p. 167*
Fragrant Winter Hazel. A shrub, 8–15 ft. (2.4–4.5 m) high. Leaves broadly egg-shaped, to 4 in. (10 cm) long, the margins toothed, smooth above and sparingly hairy below when young. Flowers to ½ in. (13 mm) long and fragrant. Japan. Zone 5.

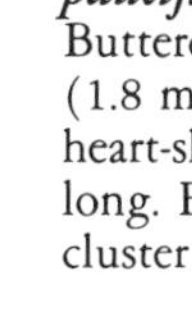

pauciflora *pp. 166, 167*
Buttercup Winter Hazel. A shrub, to 6 ft. (1.8 m) high. Leaves ovalish, obliquely heart-shaped at the base, 2–3 in. (5.0–7.5 cm) long. Flowers ¾ in. (19 mm) long, the cluster sparse. Japan. Zone 6.

Corylus
Birch family
Betulaceae

Kor′i-lus. About 10 species of trees and shrubs found throughout the north temperate zone. Some of them are cultivated commercially for their nutritious fruit, called hazelnuts or filberts.

Description
Leaves alternate, doubly toothed, stalked, and generally hairy. Male and female flowers in separate clusters on the same plant, both without petals. Fruit an egg-shaped, roundish or oblong nut with a hard, smooth shell, partly or wholly surrounded by a leafy, sometimes tubular, structure called the involucre.

How to Grow
The shrubby filberts grow best in well-drained, loam soil in sun or partial

shade. Prune regularly, thinning out the stems to maintain best shape. Propagate by cuttings and transplant as balled and burlapped or container plants.

avellana *p. 166*

European Filbert. A shrub, 10–15 ft. (3.0–4.5 m) high. Leaves roundish or broadest toward the tip, 3–4 in. (7.5–10.0 cm) long, heart-shaped at the base. Fruits 1–4, the leafy, deeply lobed involucre as long as, or shorter than, the nut, which is ¾ in. (19 mm) long. Commonly grown in Europe for the nuts, but in the U.S. mostly for ornament. 'Contorta,' commonly called Harry Lauder's Walking Stick, grows 8–10 ft. (2.4–3.0 m) high and has branches that are twisted and curled. Europe. Zone 4.

maxima *pp. 204, 205*

Giant Filbert. A shrub, 10–20 ft. (3–6 m) high, sometimes tree-like, the twigs and foliage sticky-hairy. Leaves roundish-oval, suddenly tapering at the tip, 3–5½ in. (7.5–14.0 cm) long. Fruits 1–3 in the cluster, the leafy, tubular, usually lobed involucre about twice as long as the nut, which is oblongish, its kernel with a red or whitish skin. Cultivar 'Purpurea' has dark-purple leaves. W. Asia and se. Europe. Zone 5.

Cotinus

Sumac family
Anacardiaceae

Ko-ty′nus. Three species of shrubs or small trees, the one below cultivated for ornament. The common name, smoke tree, comes from the soft look of the mass of fruiting panicles in summer.

Description

Leaves alternate, short-stalked, without marginal teeth. Flowers yellowish, not very showy, small, polygamous, in large-branching terminal clusters. Petals 5, longer than the sepals. Fruit fleshy, but somewhat dry, slightly lopsided. The fruiting cluster consists mostly of the lengthened stalks of the numerous sterile flowers, which are plumed and silky.

How to Grow

Common Smoke Trees are easy to grow in any ordinary garden soil that is not too rich or moist. They are also easy to raise from seed, but they start slowly in the garden, so provide plenty of water and attention after transplanting seedlings. Softwood cuttings may also be used.

coggygria *pp. 96, 97*
Common Smoke Tree or Smokebush. A Eurasian shrub, 10–15 ft. (3.0–4.5 m) high. Leaves ovalish, 2–3 in. (5.0–7.5 cm) long, abruptly narrowed at the base. Fruiting cluster much-branched, 7–10 in. (17.5–25.0 cm) long, covered with long, spreading, purplish-green hairs. The actual fruits few, kidney-shaped, scarcely ¼ in. (6 mm) wide. 'Purpureus' has purplish leaves and dark hairs. Often known as *Rhus cotinus*. Blooms in summer. Zone 5.

Cotoneaster
Rose family
Rosaceae

Ko-to′nee-as-ter. An important group of garden shrubs or small trees, comprising about 50 species, many of which are widely planted for their bloom and especially for their showy black or red berries in fall.

Description
Leaves alternate, stalked, without marginal teeth, in some species evergreen. Flowers small, white or pinkish, usually in small corymbs. Petals 5, upright or spreading. Stamens about 20. Fruit small, fleshy, apple-like, crowned by the persistent calyx, and with 2–5 seeds. All the species described below drop their leaves in the autumn unless noted as evergreen. All are spring-blooming.

How to Grow
Cotoneasters grow best in moist, well-drained soil in sunny locations, but they can tolerate almost any site. Propagate by seeds or by softwood cuttings with heat, grown in containers for successful transplanting. After plants are established they will tolerate drought, but do not attempt further transplanting. Watch for spider mites on plants grown in hot, dry areas.

adpressus *p. 244*
Creeping Cotoneaster. A prostrate shrub, 12–18 in. (30–45 cm) high, suited to the

rock garden. Leaves ½ in. (13 mm) long, wavy-margined. Flowers pinkish, the petals upright, ¼ in. (6 mm) wide. Fruit red. Var. *praecox* is a more vigorous form that is 3 ft. (90 cm) tall, with distinctly pink flowers and larger fruit. W. China. Zone 5.

apiculatus *p. 244*
Cranberry Cotoneaster. A semi-evergreen shrub, to 3 ft. (90 cm) high. Leaves nearly round, with a sharp tip, ¾ in. (19 mm) in diameter. Flowers mostly solitary, short-stalked, pink, ¼–⅜ in. (6–9 mm) wide. Fruit scarlet, nearly stalkless, and essentially round. W. China. Zone 5.

dammeri **'Skogsholm'** *p. 245*
Bearberry Cotoneaster. An evergreen, prostrate shrub to 18 in. (45 cm) high, its trailing branches often rooting at the joints, making it a valuable plant for the rock garden. Leaves 1 in. (2.5 cm) long, pale beneath. Flowers white, solitary, ⅜–½ in. (9–13 mm) wide, the petals spreading. Fruit red. Cen. China. Zone 6.

divaricatus *p. 246*
Spreading Cotoneaster. Upright shrub, 3–7 ft. (0.9–2.1 m) high, its branches wide-spreading. Leaves ¾ in. (19 mm) long, pale beneath, turning orange and red in fall. Flowers pinkish, the petals erect, ¼ in. (6 mm) wide. Fruit bright red, profuse and showy, ultimately becoming plum-red. One of the handsomest and easiest species to grow. China. Zone 5.

horizontalis *p. 245*
Rockspray Cotoneaster. A low shrub to 2 ft. (60 cm) high, its branches forked and almost trailing. Leaves semi-evergreen, or dropping in the northern edge of its hardiness range, nearly round, ½ in. (13 mm) long. Flowers pinkish, the petals upright, ¼ in. (6 mm) wide. Fruit red. Useful as a bank cover. W. China. Zone 5.

lacteus *p. 246*
Parney Cotoneaster. An evergreen shrub, to 12 ft. (3.5 m) high, with an arching habit. Leaves lanceolate to broadly elliptic, 1–3 in. (2.5–7.5 cm) long, hairy beneath. Flowers white, in clusters 2–3 in. (2.5–7.5 cm) across. Fruit red, ¼ in. (7 mm) long. Useful as a hedge. Zone 7.

multiflorus *p. 247*
Many-flowered Cotoneaster. A shrub, 8–10 ft. (2.4–3.0 m) high, its branches arching. Leaves thin, broadly oval, 1–2 in. (2.5–5.0 cm) long, ¾–1½ in. (2–4 cm) wide, obviously stalked. Flowers white, ½ in. (13 mm) wide, in a many-flowered, loose, smooth corymb. Fruit nearly round, red, ⅜ in. (9 mm) in diameter. One of the loveliest and easiest to grow of the flowering species. W. China. Zone 4.

salicifolius *p. 247*
Willowleaf Cotoneaster. An upright shrub, 7–12 ft. (2.1–3.5 m) high. Leaves evergreen southward, semi-evergreen northward, 1½–3 in. (4.0–7.5 cm) long, the veins and stalks sometimes reddish. Flowers white, the petals spreading, the clusters densely woolly and to 2 in. (5 cm) wide. Fruit red. Cultivar 'Scarlet Leader' is lower growing, 6–12 in. (15–30 cm), and excellent as a bank cover. 'Repens' is also low-growing, and 'Emerald Carpet' has smaller foliage and a more compact habit. W. China. Zone 6.

Cyrilla

Cyrilla family
Cyrillaceae

Sigh'rill-a. One species of shrub or small tree, native to the coastal plain from s.e. Va. to Tex.

Description
Leaves alternate, entire and simple. Flowers white, clustered in racemes at the terminal of previous year's growth. Fruit yellow.

How to Grow
Plant cyrillas in acid soil and propagate by root cuttings, by softwood cuttings taken in summer, or by seeds.

racemiflora *pp. 184, 185*
Swamp Cyrilla; Leatherwood. As a shrub, 10–15 ft. (3.0–4.5 m) high. Flowers very showy, especially in early summer. Racemes to 6 in. (15 cm) long. A good plant for naturalized areas. Beautiful foliage in fall. Blooms in summer. Zone 6.

Cytisus
Bean family
Leguminosae

Sigh′ti-sus. Fifty species of mostly s. European shrubs, many grown for their profuse blooms of pealike flowers. The species below are shrubs planted in the open border.

Description
Leaves compound, with 3 leaflets. Flowers yellow, purple, or white, solitary or in small clusters. Calyx irregular and 2-lipped. Fruit a flat pod.

How to Grow
The brooms are easy to grow in dry, infertile soil. Propagate by seeds or cuttings taken in summer. Grow young plants in containers to make transplanting easier.

× ***praecox*** *pp. 176, 177*
Warminster Broom. A handsome plant to 10 ft. (3 m) high, usually with simple leaves. Flowers yellowish white or yellow, 1 in. (2.5 cm) long. Hybrid derived from *C. multiflorus* and *C. purgans*. Cv. 'Allgold' has a dense, mounded habit and bright yellow flowers. 'Hollandia' has pale cream and purple-red flowers. Blooms in spring. Zone 7.

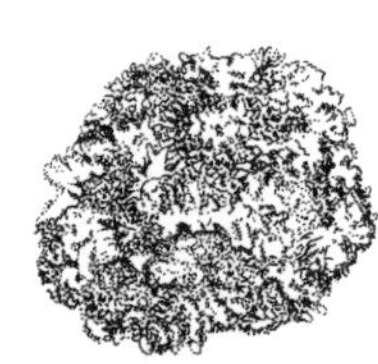

racemosus *pp. 176, 177*
Easter Broom. An evergreen shrub, 6–8 ft. (1.8–2.4 m) high. Leaflets ovate-lanceolate and silvery. Flowers bright yellow, in terminal racemes to 6 in. (15 cm) long. Blooms in spring. Zone 8.

scoparius *pp. 178, 179*
Scotch Broom. A shrub, 4–9 ft. (1.2–2.7 m) high, with green branches. Leaflets ⅓–½ in. (8–13 mm) long, sometimes reduced to only a single leaflet. Flowers profuse, usually 1 or 2 together in leaf axils, bright yellow, 1 in. (2.5 cm) long. Can become troublesome because of its rampant growth. A lower, more compact form, with sulfur-yellow flowers, is called Moonlight Broom. There are many other varieties with different colored flowers. Blooms in spring. Zone 6.

Daphne
Daphne family
Thymeliaceae

Daf′nee. Very popular Eurasian shrubs, some evergreen. A few species are widely grown as low borders or in rock gardens for their pretty, fragrant spring flowers, some of which bloom before the leaves unfold.

Description
Leaves generally alternate, without marginal teeth. Flowers in small clusters, without petals, the usually bell-shaped calyx corolla-like. Stamens 8 or 10, in 2 rows, not protruding. Fruit leathery or fleshy, a 1-seeded drupe.

How to Grow
Some daphnes will grow in ordinary garden soil, but a loose, sandy loam that is neutral or slightly alkaline is best. Hardiness varies with species. Propagate by layers, by hardwood cuttings, or by seeds sown immediately and stratified.

× ***burkwoodii*** *p. 135*
Burkwood Daphne. Semievergreen, erect shrub, to 4 ft. (120 cm) high. Leaves narrowly oblongish, to 2 in. (5 cm) long. Flowers 6–16 in terminal clusters 2 in. (5 cm) wide, white fading to pink. Hybrid derived from *D. caucasica* and *D. cneorum.* Does best in neutral soil. Popular cultivars are 'Somerset' and 'Carol Mackie'. Zone 4.

cneorum *p. 134*
Rose Daphne. Low-creeping evergreen shrub forming large mats, to 12 in. (30 cm) high, useful as a ground cover or in the rock garden. Leaves crowded, more or less oblong, 1 in. (2.5 cm) long, blunt at the tip, with a minute point. Flowers fragrant, pink, in terminal clusters 1½ in. (4 cm) wide. 'Eximea' has larger, deep pink flowers. Cover plants with pine boughs in winter to protect them from sun damage. Mts. of Europe. Zone 5.

mezereum *p. 134*
February Daphne. An upright shrub, to 5 ft. (1.5 m) high, the foliage not evergreen. Leaves oblongish, 2–3 in. (5.0–7.5 cm) long, wedge-shaped at the base. Flowers, in stalkless clusters of 3, 1½ in. (4 cm) wide, blooming before the leaves unfold, lilac-purple or rosy purple, and very fragrant. Fruit scarlet.

Prefers partial shade and moderately alkaline soil. Eurasia, sometimes in e. North America. Zone 6.

odora *p. 135*
Fragrant or Winter Daphne. An evergreen shrub, to 4 ft. (120 cm) high. Leaves oblongish or elliptic, 2–3 in. (5.0–7.5 cm) long, narrowed at both ends but bluntly pointed. Flowers rosy purple, very fragrant, in dense headlike terminal clusters 1 in. (2.5 cm) wide. Tolerates shade. Cultivar 'Aureo-marginata' has yellow-bordered leaves. Japan and China. Zone 7.

Deutzia

Saxifrage family
Saxifragaceae

Doot′zi-a. An important group of garden shrubs, comprising about 40 species, most Asiatic, and related to *Philadelphus*. They provide a fine display of bloom, mostly in the spring. There are many named garden forms, some of hybrid parentage.

Description
Usually hollow twigs and shreddy bark. Leaves opposite, short-stalked, and toothed. Flowers mostly in terminal cymes or panicles, generally white. Calyx with 5 teeth, petals usually 5, stamens 10. Fruit a 3- to 5-valved capsule with minute seeds.

How to Grow
Easy to grow in any ordinary garden soil. Propagate by cuttings of softwood, which root easily.

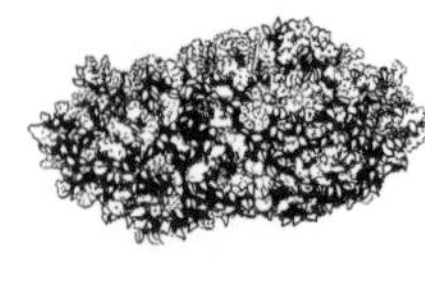

gracilis *p. 103*
Slender Deutzia. A shrub to 5 ft. (1.5 m) high, usually lower and bushy, its bark not very shreddy and yellowish gray. Leaves oblong or narrower, 1½–2½ in. (4–6 cm) long. Flowers very numerous, white, ¾ in. (19 mm) wide, the clusters loose. The best known of all the deutzias. Japan. Blooms in spring. Zone 5.

× ***lemoinei*** *p. 102*
Lemoine Deutzia. A shrub, to 7 ft. (2.1 m) high. Leaves elliptic or narrower, to 4 in. (10 cm) long, sharply toothed. Flowers pure white, ¾ in. (19 mm) wide, very numerous, in pyramidal or flattish clusters 2–4 in.

(5–10 cm) wide. Petals broadest toward the tip. Hybrid derived from *D. gracilis* and *D. parviflora*. The most popular of the taller deutzias. Blooms in spring. Zone 4.

scabra *pp. 102, 103*
Fuzzy Deutzia. A branching, more or less arching, shrub, to 8 ft. (2.4 m) high, the shreddy bark reddish brown. Leaves ovalish, to 3 in. (7.5 cm) long, hairy both sides. Flowers white, or pinkish outside, nearly 1¼ in. (3 cm) wide, the clusters spirelike and 3–5 in. (7.5–12.5 cm) long. A widely cultivated shrub, in forms such as Pride-of-Rochester, a double-flowered variety, and 'Candidissima', with pure white flowers. Can tolerate city conditions. E. Asia. Blooms spring to summer. Zone 5.

Diervilla

Honeysuckle family
Caprifoliaceae

Dy-er-vil′la. A small genus of low shrubs, mostly North American, usually called bush honeysuckle. They are useful in partial shade or in the wild garden, where their underground stems spread, making rather extensive patches.

Description
Leaves opposite, short-stalked, and toothed. Flowers yellow, funnel-shaped, mostly in small, leafless clusters, from the leaf axils. Corolla irregular, slightly 2-lipped. Stamens 5. Fruit a 2-valved capsule crowned with the narrow lobes of the calyx.

How to Grow
The species described below is easy to grow. It does best in full sun, but tolerates partial shade well. It grows freely from suckers or may be increased by cuttings.

sessilifolia *p. 174*
Southern Bush Honeysuckle. Stems to 5 ft. (1.5 m) high. Flowers usually 3–7 to a cluster; cluster 2–3 in. (5.0–7.5 cm) wide. Useful to prevent erosion and as background plantings. In mountain woods N.C. to Tenn., Ga., and Ala. Blooms in summer. Zone 4.

Dirca
Daphne family
Thymelaeaceae

Der'ka. A small genus of North American shrubs with attractive dark foliage.

Description
Leaves alternate, with no marginal teeth. Flowers yellowish, in clusters of 2–4 on old wood. Fruit a drupe, red or green.

How to Grow
Easy to grow in moist soil in shady areas. In drier sites, amend the soil with organic matter. Shade is important to keep the foliage dark.

palustris *pp. 164, 165*
Leatherwood; Wicopy; Rope Bark. A tough-wooded but pliable shrub, 3–5 ft. (0.9–1.5 m) high, the leaves elliptic, 2–3 in. (5.0–7.5 cm) long, short-stalked. Flowers blooming before the leaves unfold, without petals but the calyx petal-like, grouped in small, nearly stalkless clusters, 1 in. (2.5 cm) wide, in the axils of last year's wood. E. North America. Blooms in spring. Zone 5.

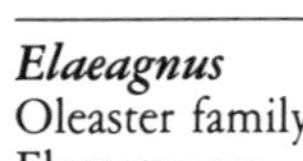

Elaeagnus
Oleaster family
Elaeagnaceae

Eel-ee-ag'nus. A genus of handsome shrubs or trees, comprising about 40 species, of the north temperate zone. Several are cultivated for their ornamental foliage and their decorative or edible fruits.

Description
Leaves alternate, short-stalked, more or less dotted with silvery or scurfy scales. Flowers not showy, without petals, the calyx tubular or bell-shaped, 4-lobed. Stamens 4. Fruit berrylike.

How to Grow
Easy to grow in a variety of dry sites. These are hardy shrubs, useful as windbreaks or hedges. Easy to propagate by root cuttings or layers or by grafting. Stratified seeds will also yield new plants the second season.

angustifolia *pp. 260*
Russian Olive. A Eurasian, sometimes spiny,

small tree or shrub, to 20 ft. (6 m) high. Leaves silvery beneath, oblongish, 2–3 in. (5.0–7.5 cm) long. Flowers fragrant, silvery or whitish outside, yellow inside. Fruit egg-shaped, ½ in. (13 mm) long, yellow but silvery-scaled, the flesh sweet but mealy. Blooms in spring. Zone 3.

multiflora *p. 261*
Cherry Elaeagnus. A spreading shrub, to 6 ft. (1.8 m) high. Leaves more or less elliptic, 1–3 in. (2.5–7.5 cm) long, silvery beneath. Flowers fragrant, yellowish white, silvery and brown-scaly on the outside. Fruit red, scaly, with a pleasant acid flavor. Also offered as *E. longipes*. Tolerates city conditions. E. Asia. Blooms in spring. Zone 5.

pungens *pp. 258, 259*
Thorny Elaeagnus. A usually spiny, spreading shrub, to 15 ft. (4.5 m) high, the foliage evergreen. Leaves wavy-margined, silvery beneath, oblongish, to 5 in. (12.5 cm) long, stalked. Flowers 1–3, hanging, silvery white, and very fragrant. Fruit brown at first, then red. Good for hedges. Tolerates shade. 'Aurea' has yellow-margined leaves; 'Maculata' has yellow-blotched leaves; 'Variegata' has white or yellowish-white-margined leaves; and 'Simonii' and 'Fruitlandii' have somewhat larger leaves, scarcely scaly beneath. Japan. Blooms in fall. Zone 7.

umbellata *p. 260, 261*
Autumn Elaeagnus. A branching shrub, to 18 ft. (5.5 m) high, the branches brown-scaly. Leaves elliptic to oval-oblong, to 3½ in. (9 cm) long, silvery beneath, the margins often crisped. Flowers fragrant, yellowish white, scaly on the outside, about ¾ in. (19 mm) long. Fruit brown, then red in fall. 'Cardinal' is 12 ft. (3.5 m) tall, especially tolerant of drought, and bears heavy fruit. E. Asia. Blooms in spring. Zone 4.

Enkianthus
Heath family
Ericaceae

En-ki-an′thus. Asiatic shrubs, 3 of the 10 known species cultivated for ornament. They are handsome shrubs for the border, with their yellow-orange flowers and fine red color in the fall.

Description
Leaves alternate, mostly clustered at the ends of the twigs, stalked and finely toothed. Flowers usually nodding, in terminal umbels or racemes. Corolla bell- or urn-shaped, the 10 stamens not protruding. Fruit a 5-valved capsule.

How to Grow
Plant these shrubs in full sun to partial shade, in a well-drained, moderately acid soil like that needed for rhododendrons. They do not stand moving very well and should be left in place when established. Propagate by seeds or cuttings.

campanulatus *pp. 98, 99*
Redvein Enkianthus. A shrub, 8–12 ft. (2.4–3.5 m); can grow to 30 ft. (9 m) high. Leaves elliptic or somewhat 4-sided, 1–3 in. (2.5–7.5 cm) long, the small marginal teeth minutely bristly. Flowers ½ in. (13 mm) long, yellow to pale orange but veined with red. Pod oblongish or egg-shaped, ¼ in. (6 mm) long, green at first, ultimately rusty brown. Japan. Blooms in spring. Zone 5.

Erica
Heath family
Ericaceae

E′ri-ka. The true heaths comprise a genus of over 500 species, largely from South Africa and the Mediterranean region. They are most often low shrubs, some nearly prostrate.

Description
Leaves small, narrow, and needle-like, usually in clusters of 3–6, but densely crowded, prevailingly evergreen. Flowers sometimes solitary, more often in small umbels or spikes, often nodding. Corolla urn- or bell-shaped, never large, with 4 small lobes. Stamens 8. Fruit a many-seeded capsule.

How to Grow
Plant in acid, sandy, organic soil that is moist and well-drained. Provide full sun or partial shade for abundant flowering. Shelter plants from sweeping winds and water them during dry periods. Erica needs very little fertilizer; in fact, its high fertility often leads

to rank, open growth. Prune in spring before growth commences. Propagate by seeds, which will germinate in 2 or 3 weeks. Softwood also roots easily.

× ***darleyensis*** *p. 153*
Darley Heath. To 2 ft. (60 cm) high, the minute leaves in fours, their edges rolled. Flowers pink, scarcely ¼ in. (6 mm) long, urn-shaped, in showy racemes that are 3–6 in. (7.5–15.0 cm) long. Hybrid derived from *E. carnea* and *E. mediterranea*. Blooms fall to spring. Zone 6.

Escallonia
Saxifrage family
Saxifragaceae

Es-ka-low′ni-a. Handsome, chiefly evergreen, shrubs and trees, unfortunately not hardy in the North, but very popular especially in California, where their late fall or winter bloom is most welcome.

Description
Leaves alternate, toothed. Flowers white, red, or pink, in terminal racemes or panicles or, occasionally, in clusters in the leaf axils. Sepals 5, the tube turban-shaped. Petals with a long claw. Stamens 5. Fruit a 2- to 3-valved capsule.

How to Grow
Easy to grow in most soils and tolerant of wind and salt. Propagate by cuttings made in fall, rooted in a cold frame, and planted out the following spring, a procedure possible only in mild climates.

rubra *p. 131*
Red Escallonia. An evergreen shrub, 10–15 ft. (3.0–4.5 m) high, its foliage sticky, the twigs reddish. Leaves broadly lance-shaped, tapering at both ends, 1–3 in. (2.5–7.5 cm) long. Flowers red, ⅓ in. (8 mm) wide, in loose panicles that are up to 3 in. (7.5 cm) long. Shorter cultivars are 'C.F. Ball', 3 ft. (90 cm) and 'William Watson', 4 ft. (120 cm). Chile. Blooms spring to summer. Zone 8.

Euonymus
Spindle tree family
Celastraceae

You-on′i-mus. Shrubs, vines, or trees of great garden importance. Of the 170 known species, sometimes called spindle trees, over a dozen are grown for their showy fruits, evergreen foliage, or both. All are spring-flowering and bear fruits from midsummer to frost.

Description
Leaves opposite, stalked, nearly always smooth. Flowers small, greenish, white, or yellowish, in small cymes in the leaf axils. Sepals and petals 4–5. Fruit a capsule, often lobed.

How to Grow
Spindle trees grow well in any soil or exposure. Propagate by stratified seeds or by semi-hardwood cuttings.

alata *p. 194*
Winged Euonymus. A stiff, spreading shrub, 12–15 ft. (3.5–4.5 m) high, the twigs corky-winged. Leaves elliptic to ovalish, to 2 in. (5 cm) long. Flowers yellowish. Fruit red, ½ in. (13 mm) long. Grown for its brilliant red autumn coloring. 'Compactus' is a smaller, globe-shaped cultivar, to 10 ft. (3 m). E. Asia. Zone 4.

japonica *p. 195*

Japanese Euonymus. An evergreen shrub, to 15 ft. (4.5 m) high or more, the twigs a little angled. Leaves narrowly elliptic or broadest toward the tip, 1–3 in. (2.5–7.5 cm) long, bluntly toothed. Flowers greenish white. Fruit nearly round, pinkish, the aril orange. Tolerates shade. There are many cultivars available. S. Japan. Zone 7.

kiautschovica *p. 194*
Spreading Euonymus. Evergreen or half-evergreen shrub, 6–10 ft. (1.8–3.0 m) high, the lower branches sometimes prostrate and rooting. Leaves oblongish, 2½–4 in. (6–10 cm) long, bluntly fine-toothed. Flowers greenish white. Fruit nearly round, ⅝ in. (16 mm) wide, pinkish, the aril orange-red. A good plant to use in hedges. 'Manhattan' has dark, glossy leaves. China. Zone 6.

Exochorda
Rose family
Rosaceae

Ecks-o-kor′da. A small but important genus of Asiatic shrubs, often called pearlbushes, valued for their white bloom at lilac time.

Description
Leaves alternate; flower parts in fives. The fruit a woody, 5-lobed capsule.

How to Grow
Grow pearlbushes in full sun or partial shade in any well-drained soil. They will adapt to your soil's acidity. Propagate by seeds, layers, or softwood cuttings.

× ***macrantha* 'The Bride'** *p. 101*
A dense, compact shrub, to 4 ft. (120 cm) high. The flowers are larger and more numerous than in *E. racemosa*. The 3–4 in. (7.5–10.0 cm) flowering racemes appear on buds of the past year's growth. Cultivar of the hybrid *E. racemosa* and *E. korolkowii*. Zone 5.

racemosa *p. 100*
Common Pearlbush. A shrub, to 15 ft. (4.5 m) high. Leaves elliptic, to 2½ in. (6 cm) long. Flowers in racemes of 6–10, to 2 in. (5 cm) across, stamens 15. Prune after flowering for best shape. China. Zone 5.

× ***Fatshedera***
Aralia family
Araliaceae

Fats-hed′e-ra. A hybrid between two species belonging to different genera, derived from crossing an English Ivy or Hedera and a Japanese Fatsia.

Description
The plants have large leaves shaped like the ivy's, colored bright green like those of fatsia.

How to Grow
Fatshedera grows best in full or partial shade. It is tolerant of full sun in only the coolest summer climates. Give the plant plenty of moisture, and protect it from hot, drying winds. It is easy to root from cuttings.

× ***lizei*** *p. 136*
Fatshedera. A shrub with rusty-hairy twigs in youth, to 6 ft. (1.8 m) high, its evergreen leaves often 5–10 in. (12.5–25.0 cm) wide. Flowers small, light green, in dense umbels grouped in large, showy, branched panicles that may be 8–10 in. (20–25 cm) long and half as wide. Blooms in fall. Zone 8.

Fatsia
Aralia family
Araliaceae

Fat′si-a. A single evergreen Japanese shrub or small tree, often planted in the South for its tropical-looking foliage.

Description
Leaves alternate, cut into 5–9 ovalish, broad, toothed lobes, shiny and stiff. Flowers small, in umbels, many of which are grouped in large, very showy, branched clusters. Fruit berrylike.

How to Grow
This plant grows well in nearly every type of soil but prefers rich, sandy ones that are slightly acid. It does best in full shade, with generous doses of fertilizer and water. Protect from winter sun and wind, which can cause marginal leaf burn. Propagate by semi-hardwood cuttings.

japonica *p. 137*
Japanese Aralia. An unarmed, bushy shrub or small tree, 10–12 ft. (3.0–3.5 m) high. Leafstalks 8–12 in. (20–30 cm) long, the blades nearly round in outline, 9–15 in. (22.5–38.0 cm) wide. Flowers whitish, in clusters to 18 in. (45 cm) long. Fruit black, ¼ in. (6 mm) in diameter. Often offered as *Aralia japonica.* There is a form with variegated leaves. Blooms in fall. Zone 8.

Feijoa
Myrtle family
Myrtaceae

Fa-jo′a. A small genus of evergreen South American shrubs or small trees. The species below is grown in the Southeast and California for its delicious, white-fleshed fruit, which ripens in late summer, but its flowers and foliage are also attractive. *Feijoa* are considered the hardiest of the "subtropical fruits."

Description
Leaves opposite, oval-oblong. Flowers solitary; fruit a berry.

How to Grow
Pineapple Guava grows well in sandy, rich loam. If more than one plant is used, leave 15–20 ft. (4.5–6.0 m) between them. This plant can be pruned to almost any shape. Propagate by seeds, which germinate 2–3 weeks after sowing, or by cuttings made in July or August.

sellowiana *p. 93*
Pineapple Guava. A shrub, to 20 ft. (6 m) high. Leaves 2–3 in. 5.0–7.5 cm) long, white-felty beneath. Flowers ¾–1½ in. (2–4 cm) long, white-felty outside, purplish inside, long-stalked. Petals 4. Stamens many, red, protruding, and showy. Fruit a greenish-red berry, 2–3 in. (5.0–7.5 cm) long. Blooms in spring. Zone 8.

Forsythia
Olive family
Oleaceae

For-sith′i-a; also for-sy′thi-a. Very handsome, spring-blooming, Asiatic shrubs, widely planted for their profuse, usually yellow, flowers that bloom before or with the unfolding of the leaves. They are inclined to be arching or spreading, and some cultivars root at the ends of their pendulous branches.

Description
Leaves opposite, stalked. Flowers in clusters of 1–6 in the leaf axils, practically stalkless, and so numerous as nearly to cover the stems in some varieties. Calyx 4-lobed and persistent. Corolla bell-shaped below, but split into 4 strap-shaped lobes that look like 4 separate petals. Stamens 2. Fruit a 2-celled capsule.

How to Grow
Forsythias are easy to grow in any garden soil. They are extremely effective when planted in large masses, especially against an evergreen background. Although the plants are very hardy, the flower buds of most

cannot survive temperatures below −10° to −20° F (−23.5° to −29.0° C). Most tolerate city conditions better than other decorative shrubs. Prune them after flowering, by cutting to the ground or removing older, weak-growing, or dead wood. They root easily from cuttings of the stems or from suckers.

× ***intermedia*** *pp. 172, 173*
Border Forsythia. A shrub, to 10 ft. (3 m) high, with arching or spreading pithy branches. Leaves oblong or ovalish, 3–5 in. (7.5–12.5 cm) long, sometimes 3-parted, but usually merely toothed. Flowers yellow, usually several at each cluster, 1½ in. (4 cm) long, the clusters very numerous. Cultivar 'Beatrix Farrand' has many large, yellow flowers and an upright habit. 'Spectabilis' has profuse flowers at each axil and is one of the finer forsythia in cultivation. It is useful for forcing. 'Arnold Dwarf' is low-growing and useful as a ground cover. Hybrid derived from *F. suspensa* and *F. viridissima.* Zone 5.

suspensa* var. *sieboldii *p. 173*
Weeping Forsythia. An upright shrub, to 12 ft. (3.5 m) high, the tips of the long, arching, hollow branches often pendulous and, in age, rooting at the tip. Leaves oval-oblong, toothed, 3–5 in. (7.5–12.5 cm) long. Flowers golden yellow, 1 in. (2.5 cm) long, mostly 1–3 at each cluster. If left unpruned, this species may sometimes climb like a vine. Var. *fortunei* is chiefly erect and has few or no pendulous branches. China. Zone 5.

***viridissima* 'Bronxensis'** *p. 172*
Bronx Greenstem Forsythia. A dwarf shrub, 12–18 in. (30–45 cm) high, the branches pithy. Leaves serrated, 1–1½ in. (2.5–4.0 cm) long. Flowers greenish yellow, usually only 1–3 at each cluster, not as showy as those of *F.* × *intermedia.* Valued for its compact habit. China. Zone 5.

Fothergilla
Witch hazel family
Hamamelidaceae

Foth-er-gil′la. A small genus of North American shrubs, sometimes called witch alder, related to the witch hazel. They have lovely, fragrant, brushy blooms in spring and orange to red foliage in fall.

Description
Leaves coarse, toothed, alternate. Flowers small, white, in small terminal heads or spikes, without petals, the showy feature being the numerous white stamens. Fruit a beaked capsule.

How to Grow
Fothergillas prefer acid, sandy loam, well-drained soils, but are otherwise very adaptable and pest free. Propagate by softwood cuttings in the summer.

gardenii *pp. 198, 199*
Dwarf Fothergilla. A low shrub, to 3 ft. (90 cm) high, the broadly wedge-shaped leaves 1–2 in. (2.5–5.0 cm) long, dark green, bluish white and hairy on the underside. Flowers white, the spikes oblongish and 1 in. (2.5 cm) long, blooming before the leaves unfold. Va. to Ga. Zone 5.

major *pp. 198, 199*
Large Fothergilla. A shrub, 4–10 ft. (1.2–3.0 m) high, the nearly round or ovalish leaves 2–5 in. (5.0–12.5 cm) long, pale and a little hairy on the underside. Flowers white, the clusters 1½–4 in. (4–10 cm) long, blooming with the unfolding of the leaves. N.C. to Ala. Zone 5.

Fremontodendron
Chocolate family
Sterculiaceae

Free-mont-o-den′dron. A small genus of chiefly Californian evergreen shrubs with showy flowers.

Description
Leaves alternate, unlobed or palmately lobed. Flowers solitary, on short stalks, showy, consisting of petal-like sepals; there are no true petals.

How to Grow
Flannel bushes require well-drained soil and full sun. They are completely drought tolerant and an excellent plant to combine with *Ceanothus.* Their roots are shallow, so young plants need staking as they become

established. Propagate by seeds or by softwood cuttings with bottom-heat.

californicum *p. 162*
Common Flannel Bush; Leatherwood; Mountain Leatherwood; Slippery Elm. A shrub, 10–25 ft. (3.0–7.5 m) high, with lobed leaves 1–2 in. (2.5–5.0 cm) long and felty-hairy beneath. Flowers yellow, nearly 1½ in. (4 cm) wide, solitary in the leaf axils. Blooms in spring. Zone 8.

Gardenia

Coffee family
Rubiaceae

Gar-den′i-a. A genus of 200 species of tropical Old World shrubs and trees with fragrant white flowers and glossy evergreen leaves.

Description
Leaves opposite, some found in threes at a single joint. Flowers large, white, usually solitary in the leaf axils. Calyx tubular. Corolla salver-shaped or short-tubular, its limb with 5–11 spreading, more or less twisted, waxy, petal-like lobes. Stamens 5–9. Fruit stalkless, leathery, or fleshy.

How to Grow
Plant gardenias high in moisture-retentive, acid soil, to which peat or other organic matter has been added. Mulch to help retain moisture and keep roots safe from damage done by cultivation. A partially shady location is best. Propagate by softwood cuttings 6–8 in. (15–20 cm) long.

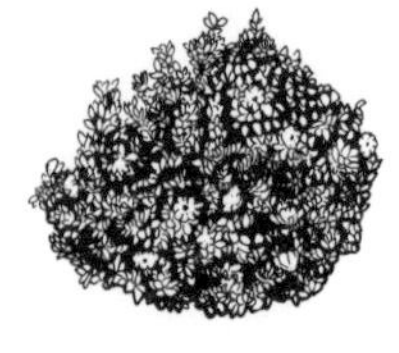

jasminoides *p. 123*
Gardenia; Cape Jasmine. A shrub, 2–5 ft. (0.6–1.5 m) high. Leaves generally lance-shaped or broader toward the tip, 3–4 in. (7.5–10.0 cm) long, thick, leathery, and occasionally variegated. Flowers 2–3½ in. (5–9 cm) wide, single or double, very fragrant. Blooms spring to summer. Some popular cultivars are 'August Beauty', 4–6 ft. (1.2–1.8 m) high, with double flowers, blooming spring to fall; 'Mystery', 6–8 ft. (1.8–2.4 m) high, also with double flowers; 'Radicans', a 12 in. (30 cm) high miniature; and 'Veitchii', 3–4 ft. (90–120 cm) high, a very good bloomer from spring to fall. China. Zone 8.

Gaylussacia
Blueberry family
Ericaceae

Gay-loo-say′she-a. About 40 species of fruit-bearing or ornamental, sometimes evergreen, North and South American shrubs commonly known as huckleberries. The species below is a nearly prostrate evergreen grown as a ground cover.

Description
Leaves alternate, usually without teeth, evergreen in *G. brachycera,* but falling in other species. Flowers in small racemes mostly in the leaf axils. Corolla bell- or urn-shaped, the 5 shallow lobes usually bent backward. Stamens 10. Fruit fleshy, edible, with 10 seedlike nuts.

How to Grow
Box Huckleberry requires a well-drained, but moist, acid soil. It grows best in partial shade but will tolerate full sun. Propagate by seeds, layers, division, or cuttings of semi-hardwood under glass.

brachycera *p. 153*
Box Huckleberry; Juniper Berry. A shrub, 8–16 in. (20.0–40.5 cm) high, the stems subterranean, with ascending aerial branches. Leaves many, elliptic, to 1½ in. (4 cm) long, smooth. Flowers white or pink, ¼ in. (6 mm) long. Fruit blue. Del. to Tenn. Blooms in spring. Zone 6.

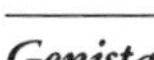

Genista
Pea family
Leguminosae

Je-niss′ta. The brooms comprise over 75 species of low, handsome, often evergreen or nearly leafless shrubs, all from temperate or mild regions of the Old World.

Description
Sometimes spiny, usually green-barked shrubs with compound leaves, the leaflets often reduced to 1 and without teeth. Flowers typically pea-like, yellow or white, usually borne in terminal racemes, rarely in the leaf axils. Fruit a longish, flattened pod, usually several-seeded.

How to Grow
Brooms are easy to grow in alkaline or acid soil that is dry and infertile. Prune them back after flowering to promote sporadic blooms later in the summer. These shrubs do not transplant easily, so do not move them once they have become established. Propagate by seeds or by layering.

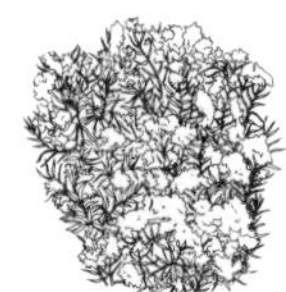

lydia *p. 180*
Lydia Woadwaxen. A dwarf, spreading shrub, to 2 ft. (60 cm) high with numerous, pendulous branches and yellow flowers ¼ in. (6 mm) wide. Useful as a ground cover. Blooms in summer. Zone 7.

tinctoria *p. 181*
Woadwaxen; Dyer's Greenweed. An upright shrub to 3 ft. (90 cm) high, with 1 leaflet to each leaf. Leaflets oblongish, ½–1 in. (1.3–2.5 cm) long, smooth, but fringed with hair on the margin. Flowers yellow, in profuse clusters. 1–3 in. (2.5–7.5 cm) wide. Pod narrow-oblong, often slightly hairy. The best-known species in cultivation. The cultivar 'Plena' has double flowers. Eurasia. Blooms in spring. Zone 5.

Grevillea
Australian oak family
Proteaceae

Gre-vil′lee-a. Australasian shrubs or trees comprising about 250 species, the shrubs often grown as specimens. An attractive feature is their long, showy styles, which rise much above the general level of the flower cluster.

Description
Leaves alternate, either small and heathlike or much larger and divided or deeply parted, feather-fashion, into 5 segments. Flowers in close racemes, without petals, but the calyx more or less tubular, the 4 lobes joined even after the flower has opened. Stamens 4. Fruit a woody follicle.

How to Grow
The 3 species or cultivars here are all drought tolerant. They perform very well in full sun in infertile, rocky, dry soil, but will grow in most any garden soil. Propagate easily from seed sown as soon as it is ripe in warm, moist sand.

'Canberra' *p. 157*
Canberra Grevillea. An open-branched shrub to 8 ft. (2.4 m) high, with slender branches and bright green, needlelike leaves 1 in. (2.5 cm) long. The red flowers, 2 in. (5 cm) long, are at their peak in spring but appear intermittently during the summer. Zone 8.

'Constance' *p. 156*
Constance Grevillea. Similar to 'Canberra' but with a wider spread and orange-red flowers, 2 in. (5 cm) long. Blooms in spring. Zone 8.

rosmarinifolia *p. 156*
Rosemary Grevillea. A shrub, to 6 ft. (1.8 m) high, its foliage resembling that of rosemary, the leaves 1½ in. (4 cm) long, practically stalkless, and silvery beneath. Flowers crowded in dense, short terminal racemes, 2 in. (5 cm) long, the styles red. Commonly planted in s. Calif. New South Wales. Blooms in summer. Zone 8.

Grewia
Linden family
Tiliaceae

Grew'ee-a. About 150 Old World trees and shrubs native to warm regions. They are sprawling, fast-growing evergreens with small, star-shaped flowers.

Description
Leaves alternate, simple, serrate. Flowers axillary or terminal, with 5 sepals that are longer than the petals.

How to Grow
Plant in full sun in a well-drained soil. Grewia can be trained as a bank cover if the upright, open growth is pruned out. It will make an espalier if you provide support. Propagate by seed or softwood cuttings.

occidentalis *p. 130*
Lavender Starflower. A sprawling shrub, to 10 ft. (3 m) high, smooth or hairy. Leaves dark green, lance-shaped, to 3 in. (7.5 cm) long. Flowers lavender, to 1 in. (2.5 cm) wide. Africa. Blooms in spring and may flower sporadically year-round. Zone 9.

Hamamelis
Witch Hazel family
Hamamelidaceae

Ha-ma-mell′is. A small genus of shrubs, confined to North America and e. Asia, usually called witch hazel or winter bloom, the latter in allusion to their blooming season. They are valuable in the shrub border and as screens or backgrounds, and their autumn colors are outstanding.

Description
Leaves alternate, short-stalked, oblique at the base, more or less wavy-toothed. Flowers yellow or reddish, crumpled in the bud, the 4 petals strap-shaped. Stamens 4. Fruit a 2-valved, explosively splitting capsule, which shoots its 2 black, shining seeds a considerable distance.

How to Grow
The witch hazels are very easy to grow and will thrive in any ordinary garden soil, although they prefer moist sites. Propagate by seeds, which will take two years to germinate, or by softwood cuttings.

× ***intermedia*** *p. 170*
Hybrid Witch Hazel. A shrub or small tree, to 20 ft. (6 m) high. Leaves roundish or broadly oval, 3–4 in. (7.5–10.0 cm) long, slightly hairy beneath, turning yellow to red in fall. Flowers yellow, ¾ in. (19 mm) long. Hybrids derived from *H. japonica* and *H. mollis* and usually sold by selected cultivar names. 'Arnold Promise' has fragrant, yellow flowers; 'Jelena' has copper-colored flowers and orange-red fall color; and 'Ruby Glow' has coppery-red flowers and orange and red fall colors. Blooms winter to spring. Zone 5.

mollis *p. 171*
Chinese Witch Hazel. A shrub or small tree, to 15 ft. (4.5 m) high. Leaves roundish or broadest toward the tip, 3–6 in. (7.5–15.0 cm) long, finely toothed, and grayish-hairy beneath. Flowers fragrant, golden yellow, but reddish at the base, ¾ in. (19 mm) long. China. Blooms in winter. Zone 6.

vernalis *p. 171*
Vernal Witch Hazel. A shrub, often with many stems, to 10 ft. (3 m) high. Leaves oblongish, or broadest toward the tip, 3–5 in. (7.5–12.5 cm) long, coarsely toothed above

the middle, turning yellow in fall. Flowers very fragrant, ½ in. (13 mm) long, dark yellow, or reddish toward the base. A useful shrub for forcing. Cen. U.S. to La. Blooms in winter. Zone 5.

virginiana *p. 170*
Common Witch Hazel, a coarsely-textured shrub, to 20 ft. (6 m) high. Leaves elliptic or broadest toward the tip, 4–6 in. (10–15 cm) long, coarsely toothed, yellow in fall. Flowers fragrant, bright yellow, ¾ in. (19 mm) long. E. North America. Blooms in fall. Zone 4.

Hibiscus

Mallow family
Malvaceae

Hy-bis′kus. An important genus of over 250 species of herbs, shrubs, and trees. The shrub species have been favorites of gardeners for many years for their showy flowers.

Description
Leaves alternate, always with the veins arranged palmately, sometimes lobed or parted. Flowers usually large, generally bell-shaped, with 5 petals and sepals, or sometimes with the sepals united to form a 5-toothed calyx. Stamens united into a tubular structure that surrounds the style. Fruit a dry 5-valved capsule.

How to Grow
Both species listed here need good drainage. Plant Rose-of-China in full sun where temperatures will be high, and protect it from wind and frost. Rose-of-Sharon is easier to grow: It will tolerate partial shade and lower temperatures. Vigorous growth can be promoted by pruning ⅓ of the stems out each spring. Pinching stem tips in spring and summer promotes flower production. Propagate by seeds or softwood cuttings made in summer.

rosa-sinensis *p. 121*

Rose-of-China. A gorgeous tropical Asiatic shrub, 8–15 ft. (2.4–4.5 m) high. Leaves broadly oval, 3–4 in. (7.5–10.0 cm) long, tapering at the tip, unlobed but often toothed. Flowers usually solitary in upper leaf axils, 4–6 in. (10–15 cm) wide, typically rose-red, flaring and spectacularly showy, due to their petals and long column of stamens.

A few of the many cultivars are: 'Agnes Gault', with single, rose-pink flowers; 'Lemon Chiffon', with yellow flowers; 'Bride', with large, single, crepe-textured white flowers with a pink flush; and 'Brilliant', with single red flowers. Blooms in summer. Zone 10.

syriacus *p. 120*
Rose-of-Sharon; Shrub Althea. A shrub, 5–15 ft. (1.5–4.5 m) high, with ovalish leaves 2–5 in. (5.0–12.5 cm) long, sharply toothed, some 3-lobed and some unlobed, often on the same plant. Flowers solitary, short-stalked, 3–5 in. (7.5–12.5 cm) wide, red, purple, violet, or white, broadly bell-shaped and most showy on dark days. The only really hardy shrub of the genus and a valuable garden subject because of its late bloom. Some popular cultivars are 'Diana', with large white flowers; 'Helene', whose white flowers have a reddish-purple base; 'Blushing Bride', with double pink flowers; and 'Collie Mullens', with double lavender flowers. China. Blooms summer to fall. Zone 5.

Hippophae

Oleaster family
Elaeagnaceae

Hip-po′fee. Eurasian spiny shrubs or small trees with willowlike leaves.

Description
Leaves narrow, covered with silvery scale-like hairs. Flowers unisexual, male and female borne on separate plants, appearing before leaves. Fruit fleshy, drupelike.

How to Grow
Easy to grow in any soil. To ensure fruit, which is one of the most attractive features, plant both male and female plants in close proximity. Propagate by seeds, which should be stratified, or by root cuttings or layers.

rhamnoides *p. 256*
Sea Buckthorn. A hardy shrub, sometimes treelike, 10–25 ft. (3.0–7.5 m) high. Leaves alternate, lance-shaped or narrower, 1–3 in. (2.5–7.5 cm) long, and more or less silvery in youth, later greenish on the upper surface. Flowers yellowish, inconspicuous, without petals. Fruit fleshy, edible but somewhat

hard, not quite egg-shaped, ¼ in. (6 mm) long, orange-yellow and persistent for most of the winter. This shrub is tolerant of salt spray. Eurasia. Zone 4.

Holodiscus

Rose family
Rosaceae

Ho-lo-dis′kus. American, mostly hairy shrubs, planted as ornamentals.

Description
Leaves alternate, stalked, usually toothed, sometimes slightly lobed. Flowers white, very small, but numerous, in a branching panicle. Calyx tube cup-shaped, the sepals 5. Petals scarcely longer than the sepals. Stamens numerous, a little protruding.

How to Grow
The species below prefers open, dry, sandy loam and full sunlight. It is especially handsome in bloom, with its gracefully arching branches a mass of creamy white, spirea-like trusses. Propagate by seeds or by layers.

discolor *p. 175*
Cream Bush. A spreading shrub, 3–20 ft. (0.9–6.0 m) high. Leaves oval, 2–4 in. (5–10 cm) long, white-felty beneath. Flower cluster 9 in. (22.5 cm) long, very showy. British Columbia to Calif. and Mont. Blooms in summer. Zone 4.

Hydrangea

Saxifrage family
Saxifragaceae

Hy-dran′jee-a. Important garden shrubs and woody vines, many of the 23 species cultivated for their showy flower clusters in summer. Most of the garden sorts are Asiatic or North American, but the genus ranges to South America and Java.

Description
Leaves opposite, stalked, usually toothed. Flowers small, prevailingly white, blue, or pink, arranged in dense, flat-topped or globe-shaped clusters, the outer flowers of the cluster often without stamens or pistils

and with larger petals than the inner, fertile flowers. Petals usually 5. Stamens mostly 10. Fruit a 2- to 5-valved capsule splitting at the top.

How to Grow
Hydrangeas need rich, well-drained, moist soil and full sun or partial shade. It is important to provide moisture during dry periods. Propagate by softwood cuttings in summer. *H. quercifolia* is easiest to propagate by suckers.

arborescens *p. 140*
Smooth Hydrangea. An upright but open, straggling shrub, 3–5 ft. (0.9–1.5 m) high. Leaves ovalish, more or less rounded or heart-shaped at the base, 3–6 in. (7.5–15.0 cm) long. Flowers white, the cluster 2–5 in. (5.0–12.5 cm) wide, flattish or a little rounded; both fertile and sterile flowers present. The stems can be cut to the ground each spring without sacrificing flowering. The cultivar 'Grandiflora', Hills of Snow, is a form with all the flowers sterile and in a ball-like cluster. N.Y. to Iowa, south to Tenn. and Ark. Blooms in summer. Zone 4.

macrophylla *p. 141*
Bigleaf Hydrangea; Hortensia. A shrub, to 6 ft. (1.8 m). Leaves broadly oval, shortly tapering at the tip, 3–9 in. (7.5–22.5 cm) long, coarsely toothed, shining green above, lighter beneath. This is the common forcing hydrangea of the florists, often grown in pots or tubs for spring bloom. It usually has 6–10 in. (15–25 cm) globe-shaped clusters of blue or pink flowers, all of which are sterile, although an occasional white-flowered form is found. For pink flowers, grow the plants in a neutral or slightly alkaline soil and use a fertilizer high in phosphorus. For blue flowers, use soil that has an acid pH, a fertilizer without phosphorus, and an aluminum sulfate addition. Flowers appear on buds formed on the previous year's growth, so prune immediately after flowering. Japan. Blooms in summer. Zone 7.

paniculata *pp. 140, 141*
Panicle Hydrangea. A treelike shrub, 8–30 ft. (2.4–9.0 m) high, the leaves elliptic or ovalish, rounded or wedge-shaped at the base, 3–6 in. (7.5–15.0 cm) long. Flower cluster 8–12 in. (20–30 cm) long, dense,

white, later changing to pink and purple, long-persistent, nearly all the flowers sterile. The commonest hardy hydrangea, almost universally grown in its cultivated form 'Grandiflora', which is a Peegee hybrid. E. Asia. Blooms in summer. Zone 4.

quercifolia *pp. 138, 139*
Oakleaf Hydrangea. A shrub, to 6 ft. (1.8 m) high, the twigs reddish and hairy. Leaves 3- to 7-lobed, almost oak-fashion, the lobes toothed, white-felty beneath, attractive in fall. Flowers on old wood in panicles to 10 in. (25 cm) long, many of its flowers sterile, white, later turning purple. Not as hardy as *H. paniculata.* Ga. to Fla. and Miss. Blooms in summer. Zone 5.

Hypericum

St. Johnswort family
Hypericaceae

Hy-per′i-cum. The St. Johnsworts constitute a useful group of herbs or shrubs. Although most of the 300 known species, nearly all from the north temperate zone, are somewhat weedy, those described below are popular for the border or rock garden.

Description
Leaves generally opposite, mostly resinous-dotted, without marginal teeth or lobes. Flowers yellow, in cymes or solitary. Petals 5, somewhat oblique. Stamens many, usually conspicuous. Fruit a capsule.

How to Grow
The St. Johnsworts are easy to grow. Some do best in partial shade. Propagate by division or softwood or hardwood cuttings, or by seeds.

calycinum *p. 159*

Aaronsbeard St. Johnswort. A semi-evergreen subshrub, 12–18 in. (30–45 cm) high. Leaves oblongish, 3–4 in. (7.5–10.0 cm) long, pale beneath. Flowers few or solitary, 2 in. (5 cm) wide. A good ground cover for sandy soil, this species tolerates alkalinity. Se. Europe and Asia Minor. Blooms in summer. Zone 6.

frondosum *p. 160*
Golden St. Johnswort. A shrub, to 4 ft. (120 cm) high, the bark reddish and peeling. Leaves oblongish, bluish green, 2–3 in.

(5.0–7.5 cm) long. Flowers nearly 2 in. (5 cm) wide, solitary or few. 'Sunburst' is a 2 ft. (60 cm) high cultivar. This species is drought tolerant. Se. U.S. Blooms in summer. Zone 6.

kalmianum *p. 161*
Kalm St. Johnswort. An evergreen subshrub, to 3 ft. (90 cm) high, the stems 4-angled. Leaves narrowly oblong, 1½–2½ in. (4–6 cm) long. Flowers few, 1 in. (2.5 cm) across. Quebec to Ill. Blooms in summer. Zone 5.

patulum **'Hidcote'** *p. 160*
Hidcote Goldencup St. Johnswort. An evergreen shrub, to 18 in. (45 cm) high. Leaves ovalish or oblong, 2½ in. (6.8 cm) long. Flowers fragrant, 2 in. (5.0 cm) wide, solitary or in sparse cymes. Tolerates drought. In northern areas, handled as an herbaceous perennial. E. Asia. Blooms in summer. Zone 7.

prolificum *p. 161*
Shrubby St. Johnswort. An evergreen shrub, 2–3 ft. (0.6–0.9 m) up to 5 ft. (1.5 m) high, the branches 2-edged, the bark peeling. Leaves oblongish or narrower, 2–3 in. (5.0–7.5 cm) long. Flowers ¾ in. (19 mm) wide, in terminal cymes. N.Y. to Iowa and southward. Blooms in summer. Zone 4.

Ilex
Holly family
Aquifoliaceae

Eye'lecks. Extremely valuable, mostly evergreen trees and shrubs. There are about 400 species, widely scattered in temperate and tropical regions, grown for their attractive leaves, showy fruits, and pleasing shapes.

Description
Leaves alternate, sometimes spiny-toothed. Flowers inconspicuous, white or greenish, usually in small clusters in the leaf axils. Sepals 3–6, and petals 4–5, both small. Fruit only on female plants, berrylike, often showy, actually a drupe with 2-5 stones.

How to Grow
Deciduous hollies are easy to grow in any good garden soil and present no difficulties

in transplanting. The evergreen kinds are more valuable but slower-growing and more difficult to establish. Nurseries sell plants with their root-balls wrapped in burlap or in containers. Keep them moist until planting and water them freely the first year or so. Since the sexes of most hollies are borne on separate plants, you must have male and female plants growing close together in order to ensure a crop of berries. Many hollies are useful as hedges. Be sure to begin pruning quite early in order to force the plants to put out extra stems. Hollies can be propagated by seeds, but they must be stratified and usually take 18 months to germinate. A quicker method is to take cuttings, dip them in a plant hormone, and plant them in sand in a cool greenhouse. They should root in a few weeks.

× ***altaclarensis* 'Wilsonii'** *p. 252*
Wilson Altaclara Holly. To 30 ft. (9 m), but usually kept 10–15 ft. (3.0–4.5 m) as a shrub. Resembles English Holly, but the leaves are flatter at the margin, 5 in. (12.5 cm) long and 3 in. (7.5 cm) wide. Very vigorous grower. Zone 8.

aquifolium *pp. 248, 249*
English Holly. An evergreen tree, to 50 ft. (15 m) high, usually 10–15 ft. (3.0–4.5 m) when maintained as a shrub. Leaves short-stalked, dark lustrous-green above, ovalish or oblong, 1–2 in. (2.5–5.0 cm) long, the margin wavy and with large, triangular, spiny teeth, sometimes lacking in age. Fruit nearly round, pea-sized, bright red, usually in clusters. Does poorly in hot, dry summers. This species has been long cultivated and is found in over 100 varieties. To be sure you get plants that will produce fruit, select a named form. Eurasia and n. Africa. Zone 7.

× ***attenuata* 'Fosteri'** *p. 250*
Foster Holly. Small evergreen tree, 10–15 ft. (3.0–4.5 m) high when maintained as a shrub, with small, light green, few-toothed narrow leaves. Fruit small, scarlet. There are many forms with different habits in this hybrid group. Zone 6.

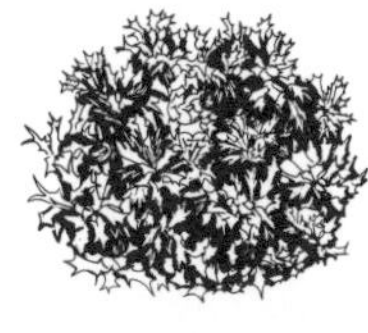

cornuta *pp. 248, 249, 252, 253*
Chinese Holly. Dense-branched evergreen shrub, usually 8–15 ft. (2.4–4.5 m) high, the oblongish, angular, lustrous leaves with 3 spines at the tip and 1 or 2 along the sides.

Fruit globe-shaped, red, stalked, nearly ½ in. (13 mm) in diameter. Fruit is produced without fertilization, so it is not necessary to have a male tree nearby. The female cultivar 'Burfordii' usually grows to 10 ft. (3 m) and has bright green wedge-shaped leaves with only a few spines at the tip; it is also grown in a compact form. There are several other forms of *I. cornuta,* which tolerates heat and dryness. 'Rotunda' is a dwarf male form to 6 ft. (1.8 m). E. China. Zone 7.

crenata *pp. 264, 265*
Japanese Holly. An extremely handsome evergreen shrub 5–10 ft. (1.5–3.0 m) high, with box-like habit. Leaves generally oblong, but broadest toward the tip, 1 in. (2.5 cm) long, more or less wedge-shaped at the base, dark green, and very finely toothed. Fruit black but inconspicuous. Performs best in slightly acid soil. Tolerates shade. The cultivar 'Convexa' has convex leaves; 'Helleri' is a female compact dwarf. Japan. Zone 6.

decidua *pp. 254, 255*
Possum Haw. A deciduous shrub, 10–30 ft. (3–9 m) high, its leaves ovalish, 1–3 in. (2.5–7.5 cm) long, wedge-shaped at the base, blunt at the tip, with many small, rounded teeth; generally hairy on the upper surface. Fruit orange, becoming red, ¼ in. (6 mm) in diameter. Se. U.S. Zone 5.

glabra *p. 265*
Inkberry. Evergreen shrub, to 6 ft. (1.8 m) high, but usually 3–5 ft. (0.9–1.5 m). Leaves oblongish, broadest toward the tip, wedge-shaped at the base, 1–2½ in. (2.5–6.0 cm) long. Fruit pea-sized, stalked, black, not showy. Grows best in moist, acid soil and is easily pruned. Tolerates wet soils. E. North America. Zone 5.

× ***meserveae*** *p. 253*
Meserve Holly. An evergreen shrub, 8–12 ft. (2.4–3.5 m) high, resembling *I. aquifolium* but the twigs deep purple and the leaves purplish green. 'Blue Princess' has dark, blue-green leaves and numerous berries; 'Blue Prince' has a compact, pyramidal shape and no berries. 'Blue Maid' is hardy and fast-growing; and 'Blue Angel' has small, crinkled, shiny leaves and dark red berries. Meserve Holly is probably the best evergreen holly for northern areas. Zone 5.

opaca *pp. 250, 251*
American Holly. A spreading tree or shrub to 50 ft. (15 m) but usually 15–30 ft. (4.5–9.0 m) high. Leaves evergreen, elliptic, 1½–4 in. (4–10 cm) long, dull green above, yellowish green beneath, the marginal teeth remote and spiny. Fruit usually solitary, pea-sized, red. Grows best in acid soil and is difficult to transplant. Now found in hundreds of named forms. Mass. to Fla., west to Mo. and Tex. Zone 6.

pendunculosa *p. 251*
Longstalk Holly. An evergreen shrub or small tree, to 20 ft. (6 m) high, the ovalish or elliptic leaves 1½–3 in. (4.0–7.5 cm) long, without marginal teeth, shining green above. Fruit nearly round, pea-size, scarlet, solitary or in sparse hanging clusters, rather persistent through late fall. Japan. Zone 5.

verticillata *pp. 254, 255*
Common Winterberry. A deciduous, usually spreading shrub 5–15 ft. (1.5–4.5 m) high, grown mostly for its bright red fruits, which are more profuse than in any other holly and persist over most of the early winter. Leaves ovalish or narrower, wedge-shaped at the base, 1½–3 in. (4.0–7.5 cm) long, very finely toothed. Prefers acid soil and is tolerant of poor drainage. 'Chrysocarpa' has yellow fruit. E. North America. Zone 4.

vomitoria *p. 264*
Yaupon; Cassena. An evergreen shrub or small tree, 15–25 ft. (4.5–7.5 m) high, with short-stalked, elliptic or oblongish leaves 1½ in. (4 cm) long, the margins wavy-toothed. Fruit scarlet, borne on the old wood. There are many different cultivars. Va. to Fla. and Tex. Tolerates salt spray and alkaline soils. Zone 7.

Illicium

Anise family
Illiciaceae

Il′li-sum. A genus of 40 species of shrubs and trees mostly native to Asia, with aromatic, evergreen leaves. Two are found in the se. U.S.

Description
Leaves alternate, usually short-stalked and without marginal teeth. Flowers yellowish or

purplish red, solitary or in few-flowered clusters in the leaf axils. Sepals, which soon fall away, 3–6. Petals 9 or more. Stamens numerous.

How to Grow
Anise trees perform best in moist, even wet, soils with high amounts of organic matter added. They can be grown in sun or shade. Propagate by semi-hardwood cuttings.

floridanum *p. 92*
Florida Anise Tree. To 10 ft. (3 m) high. Leaves elliptic, to 6 in. (15 cm) long, resin-scented. Flowers dark purple-red, to 1½ in. (4 cm) across, malodorous. Fruit to 1¼ in. (3 cm) across. Fla. to La. Blooms in spring. Zone 8.

Itea
Saxifrage family
Saxifragaceae

It′ee-a. A small genus of shrubs or trees cultivated for their showy flowers. One species is native to North America.

Description
Leaves alternate, rather narrow. Flowers in racemes, white, with 5 narrow petals and 5 persistent sepals. Fruit a 2-valved capsule.

How to Grow
Itea is an easily-grown landscape plant that performs best in a well-drained, moist soil. It will grow in sun or shade. Propagate by cuttings taken in June.

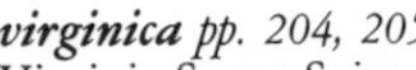

virginica *pp. 204, 205*
Virginia Sweet Spire. A shrub, 5–10 ft. (1.5–3.0 m) high. Branches slender, upright, reddish when young. Leaves oval, 2–4 in. (5–10 cm) long, turning red in fall. Flowers fragrant, showy, 6 in. (15 cm) long. N.J. to Fla., Mo., and Tex. Blooms in summer. Zone 5.

Jasminum
Olive family
Oleaceae

Jas′mi-num. The jasmines comprise 200 species of climbing or spreading shrubs or vines widely cultivated for their attractive, fragrant flowers. Chiefly tropical and subtropical, they are found in Eurasia and Africa. Only one species is found in the New World.

Description
Leaves compound, opposite or alternate, often green, with angled stems. Flowers generally 1 in. (2.5 cm) across, in many-flowered clusters, yellow or white in cultivated species. Calyx bell-shaped. Corolla tubular, but with 4-9 spreading lobes. Fruit a small berry.

How to Grow
Jasmines are easy to grow, preferring a sunny position and loamy soil. Propagate by layers and cuttings of nearly hardwood.

nudiflorum *p. 163*
Winter Jasmine. Upright deciduous shrub 4–5 ft. (1.2–1.5 m) high, with stiff, arching 4-angled branches. Leaves opposite, dark green, with 3 oval leaflets 1 in. (2.5 cm) long. Flowers yellow, ¾–1 in. (2.0–2.5 cm) across, solitary along branches of previous season, appearing in winter or spring before the leaves. Branches can be trained to fall over a wall. Tolerates shade. China. Blooms winter to spring. Zone 7.

Kalmia
Heath family
Ericaceae

Kal′mi-a. Shrubs, known as laurels, mostly evergreen, from North America. Mountain Laurel is an exceptionally handsome plant when in bloom and is splendid for massing or as a single specimen. Sheep Laurel is useful in wild plantings or mixed with other evergreens.

Description
Leaves entire and may be opposite, alternate, or whorled. Flowers purple, pink, or white, usually showy and borne in terminal or lateral clusters, flat or cup-shaped, 5-lobed, with 10 slender stamens that are caught in the corolla and spring up when touched or disturbed, discharging their pollen. Fruit a round 5-celled capsule.

How to Grow
Kalmias prefer a somewhat shady position in moist, peaty, acid soil. They can grow well in rather dry, exposed places, but they need a permanent mulch of oak or beech leaves. Propagate by seeds.

angustifolia *p. 114*
Sheep Laurel; Lambkill; Dwarf Laurel. Evergreen shrub of thin, open habit, 2–3 ft. (60–90 cm) high. Leaves opposite or in threes, oblong, 1–2 in. (2.5–5.0 cm) long, to ½ in. (13 mm) across. Flowers lavender-rose in lateral clusters 2–3 in. (5.0–7.5 cm) wide. Labrador to Ga. and westward. Blooms in spring. Zone 3.

latifolia *pp. 114, 115*
Mountain Laurel; Calico-Bush. Round-topped shrub, usually growing 7–15 ft. (2.1–4.5 m) high, though occasionally becoming a small tree. Leaves evergreen, oval, alternate or sometimes whorled, 2–4 in. (5–10 cm) long. Flowers rose to white, ¾ in. (19 mm) across, in large terminal clusters 4–6 in. (10–15 cm) wide. An excellent shrub for wild or formal plantings. New England to Fla. and La. Blooms in spring. Zone 5.

Kerria
Rose family
Rosaceae

Ker′ri-a. A genus of shrubs with only one species. Commonly cultivated for its attractive flowers and bright green stems, it is useful in borders and foundation plantings.

Description
Leaves alternate and simple, deciduous. Flowers solitary, borne on old wood.

How to Grow
Kerrias thrive in any ordinary garden soil. They are very tolerant of shade and of poor but well-drained soil. Thin out the old stems every few years and prune right after blooming. Propagate by division and cuttings.

japonica *pp. 162, 163*
Japanese Kerria. Shrub with slender green branches, growing 4–6 ft. (1.2–1.8 m) high.

Leaves tapered-oval, 1½–4 in. (4–10 cm) long, toothed. Flowers at the end of short, lateral branches, yellow, 5-petaled, ¾–1½ in. (2–4 cm) across. The cultivar 'Pleniflora', or Japanese Rose, is a taller, more vigorous form, with large double flowers. China. Blooms in spring. Zone 5.

Kolkwitzia
Honeysuckle family
Caprifoliaceae

Kolk-wit′zi-a. A single species of Chinese shrub much cultivated for its showy bloom under the name Beauty Bush.

Description
Leaves are opposite and simple. The flowers are borne in pairs in terminal corymbs. Stems develop peeling brown bark at maturity.

How to Grow
Beauty Bush is easy to grow in full sun in any type of soil. Plant it where it will have room to spread out, although transplanting is not difficult. Prune out old stems every year. Propagate by cuttings of softwood.

amabilis *p. 97*
Beauty Bush. A shrub, 6–12 ft. (1.8–3.5 m) high with upright, arching habit. Leaves ovalish, 2–3 in. (5.0–7.5 cm) long. Flowers in flattish corymbs, on old wood, the corolla bell-shaped, pink, but with a yellow throat, ½ in. (13 mm) long, the stalks and sepals bristly. Fruit dry, both it and the stalk covered with bristly hairs. Branches may be forced inside weeks before outdoor flowering is due. Blooms in spring. Zone 5.

Lantana
Verbena family
Verbenaceae

Lan-ta′na. A genus of 155 tropical or subtropical shrubs, one of which is often grown outdoors in the South and in Calif., as a houseplant elsewhere, or for summer bedding. It is a profuse bloomer.

Description
Leaves generally opposite, stems usually hairy, sometimes prickly. Flowers small, borne in dense spikes or heads that may be terminal or in the leaf axils. Calyx minute. Corolla tubular, 4- to 5-parted, slightly irregular, but not 2-lipped. Stamens 4. Fruit fleshy, with 2 hard seeds.

How to Grow
Red Sage grows easily and quickly in any sort of soil in full sun. Prune back in spring to prevent legginess. Propagate by cuttings of softwood.

camara *p. 158*

Red, or Yellow, Sage. To 4 ft. (120 cm) high, occasionally prickly. Leaves ovalish or heart-shaped, 2–6 in. (5–15 cm) long, with rounded teeth, roughish above and hairy beneath. Flower clusters 1–2 in. (2.5–5.0 cm) wide, flat-topped, usually on stalks longer than the leafstalks. Flowers ⅓ in. (8 mm) wide, yellow at first, then orange or red, sometimes all three colors simultaneously in a single cluster. The foliage has a scent unpleasant to some. Tropical America, north to Tex. and Fla. Blooms year-round. Zone 9.

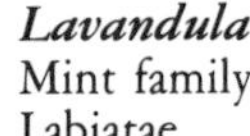

Lavandula
Mint family
Labiatae

La-van′dew-la. Lavender. Aromatic Old World perennial herbs or shrubs, grown for their oil and, in some species, their attractive flowers.

Description
Leaves opposite, without marginal teeth, and narrow. Flowers lavender or dark purple, crowded into dense clusters in the leaf axils. Corolla irregular, the upper lip 2-cleft, the lower one 3-cleft. Stamens 4, not protruding. Fruit a collection of dry nutlets.

How to Grow
Plant lavender in full sun in a very well-drained soil. Use it alone or as a hedge or edging. It grows well with little water or fertilizer added. Prune just after flowering for best shape. Propagate by cuttings taken in spring or fall.

dentata *p. 151*
French Lavender. A shrub, 1–3 ft. (30–90 cm) high, densely gray-hairy. Leaves linear-oblong, to 1½ in. (4 cm) long, deeply toothed. Flowers lavender purple, in dense spikes 1½–2½ in. (4–6 cm) long, among which are conspicuous purple bracts. Corolla dark purple. S. Spain and the Balearic Islands. Blooms in summer, and through the winter in mild climates. Zone 9.

Leptospermum

Myrtle family
Myrtaceae

Lep-to-sper′mum. Tea Tree. Australasian shrubs and trees comprising over 40 species, several of which are widely cultivated in mild climates for their long branches of white, pink, or red flowers.

Description
Leaves alternate, small, rigid, often almost prickle-like. Flowers numerous, but solitary or 2 or 3 together in the leaf axils. Calyx more or less bell-shaped, its lobes 5. Petals 5. Stamens many, not protruding. Fruit a leathery capsule.

How to Grow
Tea trees are easy to grow in well-drained soil and in full sun. Water them generously when newly-planted; they are fairly drought tolerant after establishment. Propagate by seeds or cuttings.

scoparium *p. 157*
New Zealand Tea Tree. A tall shrub or small tree 10–25 ft. (3.0–7.5 m) high, or occasionally dwarf and only 1–2 ft. (30–60 cm) high, the foliage silky when young. Leaves very numerous, to ½ in. (13 mm) long, almost prickle-tipped. Flowers ½ in. (13 mm) wide, white or pink. Several varieties are cultivated and are more valuable as landscape plants than the species, since they are smaller and more compact. New Zealand and Tasmania. Blooms spring to summer. Zone 9.

Leucophyllum
Figwort family
Scrophulariaceae

Loo-ko-fill′um. A small genus of showy, evergreen shrubs from Tex., N. Mex., and adjacent Mexico, used often for hedges.

Description
Leaves alternate, without marginal teeth. Flowers bell-shaped, only slightly irregular, solitary at the leaf joints. Fruit a dry capsule.

How to Grow
Leucophyllum grows well in hot, dry, windy areas. It will tolerate alkalinity if your soil is well-drained.

frutescens *p. 202*
Texas Ranger; Barometer Bush. A compact shrub, 6–8 ft. (1.8–2.4 m) high. Leaves gray, oblongish, 1 in. (2.5 cm) long, white-woolly on the underside. Flowers 1 in. (2.5 cm) long, violet-purple, hairy on the inside. Tex. to Mexico. Blooms in summer. Zone 9.

Leucothoe
Heath family
Ericaceae

Lew-koth′o-ee. Ornamental shrubs grown for their handsome, dark foliage and attractive, fragrant flowers. The evergreen species are of low habit, with graceful, arching branches and thick leaves that turn red or bronze in winter. They are valuable for use with other evergreens, or in foundation plantings or borders. They grow well in light woods, and the sprays make beautiful winter bouquets.

Description
Leaves alternate, deciduous or evergreen. Flowers white, occasionally tinged pink, urn-shaped with 5 little teeth at the top, and borne in clusters along, or at the tip of, the branches. The fruit is a dry, round, 5-celled capsule.

How to Grow
Leucothoes need moist, acid, peaty soil or sandy loam with plenty of humus added. They prefer full shade, but will grow in full sun if kept constantly moist. Propagate by division, cuttings, or seeds.

axillaris *p. 203*
Coast Leucothoe. Evergreen shrub with minutely hairy, arching branches, growing 4 ft. (120 cm) high. Leaves leathery, ovoid lance-shaped, 2–4 in. (5–10 cm) long, usually short-pointed and with a stalk of ¼–⅓ in. (6–8 mm). Flowers white, in clusters 1–2 in. (2.5–5.0 cm) long borne in leaf axils. Va. to Fla. and Miss. Blooms in spring. Zone 6.

fontanesiana *pp. 202, 203*
Drooping Leucothoe; Fetter Bush. Evergreen shrub, to 6 ft. (1.8 m) high, with slender, arching branches. Flowers white, in drooping clusters 3 in. (7.5 cm) long along the branches. This is the hardiest of the evergreen leucothoes. It resembles *L. axillaris,* but has smooth stems and long-tipped leaves, with petioles ⅓–⅗ in. (8–15 mm) long. 'Scarletta' is a reddish-purple-leaved cultivar. Va. to Ga. and Tenn. Blooms in spring. Zone 5.

Ligustrum
Olive family
Oleaceae

Ly-gus′trum. The privets are best known as hedge plants. Most species are hardy and very tolerant of pruning, pollution, wind, and drought.

Description
Leaves opposite, generally ovalish, often persistent, semi-evergreen or evergreen, without marginal teeth. Flowers small, white, sometimes malodorous, mostly in terminal panicles, often not produced on clipped hedge specimens. Corolla short-tubular, its 4-lobed limb spreading. Stamens 2. Fruit a small berrylike drupe, usually black or bluish, 1- to 4-seeded.

How to Grow
Privet is easy to grow and will adapt to any soil condition except constant wetness. Plant shrubs in full sun to partial shade. They will grow fast and are not difficult to transplant. If you do not want flowers to form, prune in early spring. Softwood cuttings root easily and are the best way to propagate.

amurense *p. 276*
Amur Privet. A shrub, 10–15 ft. (3.0–4.5 m) high, its branches erect. Leaves semi-evergreen, 1½–2½ in. (4–6 cm) long, hairy

on the midrib beneath. Flower cluster almo[st] 2 in. (5 cm) long, the corolla with a tube longer than the lobes. N. China. Blooms in spring. Zone 4.

japonicum *p. 124*
Japanese Privet. An evergreen shrub, 7–10 ft (2.1–3.0 m) high. Leaves oblong-oval, leathery, 3–4 in. (7.5–10.0 cm) long, smooth. Flower clusters 4–6 in. (10–15 cm) long, the tube of the corolla only slightly longer than the lobes. Often used for topiary or in containers. 'Rotundifolium', sometimes offered as *L. coriaceum,* is a lower, more compact shrub, with lustrous, dark green, more numerous leaves that are nearly circul[ar] in outline. Japan and Korea. Blooms in spring. Zone 7.

lucidum *p. 277*
Glossy Privet. An evergreen shrub or small tree, to 30 ft. (9 m) high. Leaves pointed, 4–6 in. (10–15 cm) long, shining and smooth. Flower cluster nearly 10 in. (25 cm) long, the tube and lobes of the corolla abou[t] of equal length. Japan and China. Blooms in spring. Zone 8.

obtusifolium *pp. 124, 125*
Border Privet. A spreading or arching deciduous shrub, 8–12 ft. (2.4–3.5 m)high. Leaves elliptic or oblongish, 1½–2½ in. (4–6 cm) long, hairy beneath. Flower clusters nodding, not over 1½ in. (4 cm) long, the corolla tube three times longer than its lobes. A widely cultivated shrub with profuse flowers and black, slightly bloomy fruit. The var. *regelianum,* Regel's Privet, is lower and has horizontally spreadin[g] branches. Japan. Blooms in spring. Zone 4.

× ***vicaryi*** *p. 277*
Golden Vicary Privet; Golden Privet. A deciduous shrub, to 10–12 ft. (3.0–3.5 m) high. Leaves oblongish, to 2½ in. (6 cm) long and bright yellow. Flowers white, in 2–3 in. (5.0–7.5 cm) clusters. Popular for its foliage, which will be greenish if not in full sun. Blooms in spring. Zone 5.

vulgare *pp. 125, 276*
European Privet. A shrub, 5–15 ft. (1.5–4.5 m) high. Leaves oblong-oval, 1½–2½ in. (4–6 cm) long. Flower cluster not over 3 in. (8 cm) long, the corolla tube shorter than, or about the length of, its lobes. One of the most widely grown of all

hedge privets, its leaves are sometimes semi-evergreen southward. Europe and n. Africa, sometimes naturalized in U.S. Blooms in late spring. Zone 4.

Lindera

Laurel family
Lauraceae

Lin-der′a. A group of 100 species of aromatic shrubs and trees, most of them tropical. The species described below, the well-known Spicebush, is native to American swamps and woods. It has a mass of yellow bloom in early spring and bright red berries later.

Description
Leaves without marginal teeth, alternate. Flowers small, yellow, blooming long before the leaves unfold, unisexual. Sepals 6, colored. Petals none. Male flowers with 9 stamens. Fruit fleshy, nearly round, bright red.

How to Grow
The Spicebush is easy to grow in most garden soil. If it has any preference, it is for partial shade and a moist site. Propagate by seeds, layers, or softwood cuttings under glass.

benzoin *pp. 242, 243*
Spicebush; Spicewood; Benjamin-Bush. A shrub, 6–12 ft. (1.8–3.5 m) high. Leaves more or less oblong, but wedge-shaped at the base, 3–5 in. (7.5–12.5 cm) long, turning yellow in fall. Flowers small, crowded in small, nearly stalkless clusters that are ⅓ in. (8 mm) long. Fruit scarlet, ellipsoidal, to ½ in. (13 mm) in diameter. Tolerates drought. Ontario to Fla. and westward. Zone 4.

Lonicera

Honeysuckle family
Caprifoliaceae

Lon-iss′er-ra. The honeysuckles comprise a group of 150 or more species of shrubs and woody climbers found throughout the northern hemisphere. The tall forms are useful in shrub borders; some of the lower ones are grown in rock gardens. The often showy flowers are abundant and sometimes sweetly scented. The fruits, which are white, yellow, orange, red, blue, or black, are quite ornamental and a favorite food for birds.

Description
Leaves opposite, usually entire, rarely evergreen. The flowers are tubular or bell-shaped, equally 5-lobed or (more often) 2-lipped, the upper lip composed of 4 lobes and the lower of 1. They are borne in pairs in the leaf axils or in clusters at the ends of the branches. Fruit a fleshy berry.

How to Grow
Honeysuckles are easy to grow, thriving in almost any location, although a loamy, reasonably moist soil is best. Prune just after flowering. Propagate by seeds or cuttings.

fragrantissima *p. 282*
Winter Honeysuckle. A shrub, 5–10 ft. (1.5–3.0 m) high, with spreading, somewhat recurved branches that form a rounded mass. Leaves oval, thick, 1–2 in. (2.5–5.0 cm) long, dark green above, paler beneath, evergreen in mild climates. Flowers creamy white, ½ in. (13 mm) long, very fragrant. Fruit red. Valued for its lovely foliage and early flowers. China. Blooms winter to spring. Zone 5.

maackii *p. 237*
Amur Honeysuckle. A vigorous, wide-spreading shrub, often 10–15 ft. (3.0–4.5 m) high. Leaves ovate, with long, slender points, 1½–3 in. (4.0–7.5 cm) long, sometimes hairy. Flowers ⅔ in. (17 mm) long, white, turning yellow in age. Fruit red. One of the handsomest and largest honeysuckles, conspicuous in bloom and with its bright red berries in the fall. Tolerates drought. Manchuria (China), Korea. Blooms in spring. Zone 3.

nitida *p. 283*
Boxleaf Honeysuckle. An evergreen or half-evergreen shrub, rather low, though sometimes to 6 ft. (1.8 m), with slender branches. Leaves small, thick, glossy, oval to rounded, ¼–½ in. (6–13 mm) long. Flowers ¼ in. (6 mm) long, fragrant. Fruit purple. An unusually neat-looking species, useful for hedges; there are cultivars with different leaf shapes and colors. China. Blooms in spring. Zone 7.

tatarica *p. 236*
Tatarian Honeysuckle. An upright, vigorous shrub of arching habit, growing 8–10 ft. (2.4–3.0 m) high. Leaves oblong-ovate, pointed, 1–2½ in. (2.5–6.0 cm) long, pale beneath. Flowers white to pink, ¾–1 in. (2.0–2.5 cm) long, 2-lipped. Fruit red. The commonest of the bush honeysuckles; ornamental and easy to grow, although it tends to become leggy. U.S.S.R. Blooms in spring. Zone 4.

xylosteum *p. 282*
European Fly Honeysuckle. A bushy shrub, growing to 12 ft. (3.5 m) high. Leaves oval to obovate, to 2½ in. (6 cm) long, pointed at tip, rounded or wedge-shaped at base, paler and hairy beneath. Flowers yellow, often tinged red, ½ in. (13 mm) across, tube swollen at base. Fruit red. Tolerates drought and is useful as hedge. 'Claveyi' is a smaller form. Eurasia. Blooms in spring. Zone 5.

Loropetalum
Witch hazel family
Hamamelidaceae

Lor-o-pet′a-lum. A single Chinese evergreen shrub closely related to the witch hazel, but evergreen.

Description
Leaves alternate, without marginal teeth. Flowers resembling the witch hazel, *Hamamelis,* but white and much more showy.

How to Grow
Loropetalum needs a moist, well-drained acid soil that is rich in organic matter. It can be grown in sun or shade and can withstand severe pruning, although it's probably at its best when allowed to take its own rounded shape. Propagate by cuttings taken in July and treated with rooting hormone.

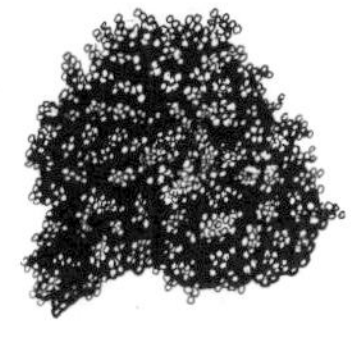

chinense *pp. 174, 175*
A shrub, 6–12 ft. (1.8–3.5 m) high, with ovalish leaves 1–2 in. (2.5–5.0 cm) long. Flowers fragrant, petals strap-shaped, 1 in. (2.5 cm) long. Fruit a woody capsule. Blooms in spring. Zone 7.

Magnolia
Magnolia family
Magnoliaceae

Mag-no′li-a. A genus of North American, West Indian, Mexican, and Asiatic evergreen or deciduous trees or shrubs. There are about 85 species, many of which are prized for their showy flowers, which appear from early spring to summer, depending on the species.

Description
Leaves alternate, without marginal teeth, large. Flowers regular, solitary, usually large and showy, commonly white, yellow, rose, or purple, appearing with or before the leaves on the species that are not evergreen. Petals 6-20. Sepals 3, often petal-like, the stamens numerous. The fruit is a conelike brown or scarlet body, the seeds of which, when ripe, hang by threadlike cords.

How to Grow
Magnolias do best in acid soils amended with organic matter like peat moss or leaf compost. They require a deep, well-drained soil. Magnolias are usually grown in full sun but will tolerate partial shade. They have a fleshy root system that is close to the surface, so be careful when cultivating around them. Move plants carefully, with roots balled and burlapped. Pruning is not necessary except to remove dead wood. Propagate by softwood cuttings taken in June or July.

× ***loebneri*** *pp. 90, 91*
Loebner Magnolia. A plant similar in habit to *M. stellata,* but larger in all its parts, maturing at 30 ft. (9 m) high. These plants are very vigorous. Blooms in spring. Zone 4.

quinquepeta *pp. 90, 91*
Lily Magnolia. A large, spreading shrub, to 12 ft. (3.5 m) high, the branchlets smooth except near the tips; buds soft-hairy. Leaves somewhat oval, 3–7 in. (7.5–17.5 cm) long, light green and soft-hairy beneath when young, narrowing to a short point. Flowers lily-shaped, slightly fragrant, white inside, purple outside, on short stout stalks, blooming before leaves appear. Petals 6, to 4 in. (10 cm) long. Sepals 3, shorter than the petals, soon falling. Fruit brown, oblong. China. Blooms in spring. Zone 5.

stellata *pp. 88, 89*
Star Magnolia. A much-branched, spreading

shrub or small tree, to 15 ft. (4.5 m) high, the young growth densely soft-hairy. Leaves broadly oval to oblong, 1½–5 in. (4.0–12.5 cm) long, smooth, dark green above, light green beneath. Flowers appearing before leaves, white, fragrant, 3 in. (7.5 cm) across. Petals and sepals, 12-18 in number, look alike: narrow, strap-shaped, 1½ in. (4 cm) long, at first spreading and horizontal, becoming reflexed with age. Fruit 2 in. (5 cm) long, red. Flowers so early that bloom can be destroyed by late frosts, so plant in a protected area. Japan. Blooms in spring. Zone 4.

Mahonia

Barberry family
Berberidaceae

Ma-ho′ni-a. A genus of American and Asian evergreen, thornless shrubs, comprising about 100 species. Their low-growing habits and attractive foliage make them valuable in the border and as foundation plantings.

Description
Leaves alternate, pinnately compound, or, rarely, in threes, spiny, often turning purplish in autumn. Flowers yellow, fragrant, in terminal racemes or panicles. Petals 6. Sepals 9. Fruit a dark blue berry, usually covered with a powdery bloom.

How to Grow
Plant mahonias in sheltered positions where they are protected from wind and sun in winter. *M. aquifolium* does well as far north as Canada, where it is protected by a heavy covering of snow all winter. Propagate by seeds and softwood and hardwood cuttings under glass.

aquifolium *p. 188*
Oregon Grape Holly. A shrub, 3–6 ft. (0.9–1.8 m) high. Leaflets 5–9, shiny, ovalish or oblong, stiff, leathery, the marginal teeth spiny. Flowers yellow, fragrant, in dense, erect terminal racemes 3 in. (7.5 cm) high. Fruit a small bluish berry, edible. Individual cultivars vary in height and in the glossiness of their upper leaf surfaces. British Columbia to Oreg. Blooms in spring. Zone 5.

bealei *p. 189*
Leatherleaf Mahonia. A shrub with stout,

upright stems, to 12 ft. (3.5 m) high. Leaflets 9–15, round-oval, with a few large teeth on the margins, the end leaflets larger, bluish green, with a slight bloom beneath, stiff, and leathery. Flowers lemon-yellow, fragrant, in close-growing, upright terminal racemes that grow 4–6 in. (10–15 cm) high. Fruit bluish black. The upright stems and stiff leaves give this a striking silhouette. China. Blooms in spring. Zone 7.

lomariifolia *pp. 188, 189*
A shrub, to 12 ft. (3.5 m) high. The evergreen, compound leaves have 10-24 pairs of leaflets, which are 2–3 in. (5.0–7.5 cm) long and nearly ¾ in. (19 mm) wide, blunt at the base, the margins with 2-6 teeth, the tip almost spine-like. Yellow flower raceme 3–7 in. (7.5–17.5 cm) long. Fruit ovalish, black with blue bloom. China. Blooms winter to spring. Zone 9.

Michelia

Magnolia family
Magnoliaceae

Me-chel′i-a. A genus of Asiatic trees or shrubs, comprising nearly 50 species. The one below is popular in Calif. and along the Gulf Coast for its dense habit and abundant flowers.

Description
Michelias resemble *Magnolia,* but the flowers come from the axils of the leaves rather than at ends of branches. Flowers solitary, sepals and petals similar, 9-15, or more. Fruit a long spike of leathery carpels.

How to Grow
Plant Banana Shrubs in fertile, well-drained soil in sun or partial shade in a very hot area. Keep the soil moist. Consider planting them near a patio or entryway so the sweet fragrance can be enjoyed. Propagate by seeds sown when ripe or by hardwood cuttings, bearing 1 or 2 leaves, started under glass with bottom-heat.

figo *p. 164*
Banana Shrub. A shrub to 10–15 ft. (3.0–4.5 m) high. Young growth covered with a brownish wool. Leaves elliptic or narrower, smooth in maturity. Flowers 1–1½ in. (2.5–4.0 cm) across, brownish

yellow, edged with light carmine, and having a strong banana fragrance. China. Blooms in spring. Zone 9.

Myrica

Bayberry family
Myricaceae

Mir-i′ka. Shrubs or trees, often pleasantly aromatic, comprising about 50 species. Those below are attractive, useful shrubs for dry, sandy soils, since both grow naturally in such places.

Description
Leaves alternate and small. Flowers greenish, inconspicuous, without sepals or petals, the male and female separate and often on different plants, mostly in catkins. Fruit fleshy or nut-like, covered with an aromatic wax or resin.

How to Grow
The species below prefer poor, sandy soil and full sun to partial shade. Use them in a shrub border, for massing, or in combination with broadleaf evergreens. Prune old, leggy plants to the ground to renew them. Propagate by seeds.

cerifera *pp. 268, 269*
Wax Myrtle; Southern Wax Myrtle. A tall shrub or small tree, to 10–20 ft. (3–6 m) high. Leaves evergreen or very persistent, more or less lance-shaped, 1–3 in. (2.5–7.5 cm) long. Fruit grayish-waxy, aromatic. Tolerates salt. S. N.J. to Fla. and Ark. Zone 7.

pensylvanica *pp. 268, 269*
Northern Bayberry. A shrub, 3–10 ft. (0.9–3.0 m) high, the leaves ultimately falling but often holding on until early winter. Leaves very aromatic, more or less elliptic or broadest toward the tip, 3–4 in. (7.5–10.0 cm) long. Fruit conspicuously grayish-waxy, very aromatic, and used in making bayberry candles. Tolerates salt. E. North America, mostly along the coast. Zone 3.

Myrtus

Myrtle family
Myrtaceae

Mir′tus. Myrtle. Tropical or subtropical shrubs or trees comprising about 16 species, from the Old and New World, one of them widely grown for its handsome evergreen foliage, which is easily trained for hedges.

Description
Leaves opposite, simple, without marginal teeth, very aromatic in some species. Flowers white or pink, solitary in the leaf axils or in few-flowered clusters, neither large nor showy. Petals 4. Stamens numerous, longer than the petals but not conspicuously protruding. Fruit a berry, crowned with the persistent calyx lobes.

How to Grow
Myrtle grows well in sun or partial shade in well-drained soil. It tolerates heat and drought. Propagate by cuttings of semi-hardwood under glass, or by seeds.

communis *p. 279*
True Myrtle. An aromatic evergreen shrub, 3–15 ft. (0.9–4.5 m) high. Leaves ovalish to lance-shaped, 1–2 in. (2.5–5.0 cm) long, shining green, almost stalkless. Flowers to ¾ in. (19 mm) wide, white or pinkish. Fruit ½ in. (13 mm) long, bluish black or white. 'Compacta' is a small, slower growing form, 2–3 ft. (60–90 cm), useful for edgings, and 'Microphylla' is a dense dwarf. Mediterranean region and w. Asia. Blooms in summer. Zone 9.

Nandina

Barberry family
Berberidaceae

Nan-dy′na. A single species of evergreen shrub, native to China and Japan, grown often in the South for its columnar form, bright red berries, and brilliant fall foliage.

Description
Leaves alternate, 2-3 pinnately compound. Flowers small, in panicles. Fruit a berry.

How to Grow
Nandina grows well in any soil but prefers a reasonably moist site: it will die if not

watered regularly. It may be planted north of zone 7 in protected places, where, if the top should be winter-killed, the roots may survive, especially if they are well mulched. It will tolerate shade. Propagate by seeds.

domestica *pp. 238, 239*
Nandina; Heavenly Bamboo. An attractive shrub, 6–8 ft. (1.8–2.4 m) high. Leaflets narrow, 1–2 in. (2.5–5.0 cm) long. Flowers white, not showy, but the panicles nearly 1 ft. (30 cm) long and handsome. Sepals numerous, in series of 3, gradually passing into the white petals. Stamens as many as the petals. Fruit a red, 2-seeded berry ½ in. (13 mm) in diameter, very handsome when ripe, and the chief attraction of the plant. 'Nana' and 'Harbour Dwarf' are excellent dwarf cultivars; 'Alba' has white fruit. Blooms in spring. Zone 7.

Nerium
Dogbane family
Apocynaceae

Neer′i-um. Oleanders are widely-cultivated, ornamental evergreen shrubs or small trees. They are especially useful in the South and West because they tolerate heat, drought, and salt.

Description
Leaves opposite or, more usually, in whorls of 3, rather thick and leathery, without teeth. Flowers in showy terminal cymes. Corolla funnel-shaped, its limb bell-shaped, and with 5 fringed or broad teeth, slightly twisted to the right. Stamens not protruding. Fruit a cluster of 2 long cylindrical follicles.

How to Grow
Plant oleanders in any well-drained soil in a hot, sunny location. Prune in early spring for best shape. All parts of this plant are poisonous, so keep children and pets from ingesting them and do not burn clippings. Propagate by cuttings of softwood taken in summer.

oleander *pp. 122, 123*
Common Oleander; Rose-Bay. A shrub or small tree, 8–20 ft. (2.4–6.0 m) high, leaves narrowly oblong, 4–10 in. (10–25 cm) long, dark green above, paler and with a prominent midrib beneath. Flowers are

yellowish, red, white, pink, or purple, 2½ in. (6 cm) wide, 4–5 in a cluster; double in some cultivars, sometimes fragrant. Useful for borders, screens, or along roads or walks. Recommended cultivars include 'Calypso', cherry-red; 'Hardy Pink'; 'Hawaii', salmon-pink with yellow throats; 'Jannoch', large red flowers; and 'Mrs. Roeding', double, salmon-pink flowers. S. Europe and n. Africa to Japan. Blooms in summer. Zones 8–10.

Ochna

Ochna family
Ochnaceae

Ok′na. Ninety species of Tropical Old World shrubs and trees, one of which is grown in s. Calif., often as a tub plant or espalier.

Description
Leaves entire, toothed, alternate. Flowers large, yellow, borne in clusters. The stamens are numerous and the fruits are attached to an expanded receptacle.

How to Grow
Bird's-Eye Bush does best in sun to partial shade in a well-drained, slightly acid soil. After establishment, it is fairly drought tolerant. Propagate by softwood cuttings taken in summer or fall or by seeds.

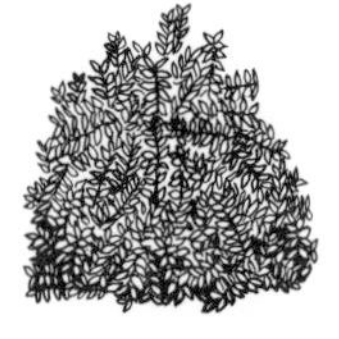

serrulata *p. 93*
Bird's-Eye Bush; Mickey Mouse Plant. A shrub, to 10 ft. (3 m), with leathery, oblongish leaves 3–6 in. (7.5–15.0 cm) long, with prominent veins. Flowers in clusters of 12–20, regular, yellow, the calyx of 5 separate, petal-like sepals; petals 5, to ⅜ in. (9 mm) long, slightly twisted. Fruit a kidney-shaped fleshy drupe, green, turning glossy black with red sepals below it. Also known as *O. multiflora.* Tropical Africa. Blooms in summer. Zone 9.

Osmanthus

Olive family
Oleaceae

Oz-man′thus. Evergreen shrubs or small trees, all of the 30-40 known species Asiatic or Polynesian, except Devilwood, a native of the se. U.S.

Description
Leaves opposite, spiny-toothed or toothless. Flowers often very fragrant, not showy, usually unisexual or polygamous, in cymes or panicles at ends of branches or in the leaf axils. Calyx short and 4-lobed. Corolla tubular, but short, 4-lobed at the summit. Stamens mostly 2, not protruding. Fruit fleshy, egg-shaped, a drupe with a single stone.

How to Grow
Easy to grow in acid soil in partial shade. Use for hedges, espaliers, or in containers. Propagate by late-summer cuttings of semi-hardwood, rooted under glass.

americanus *pp. 270, 273*
Devilwood. A large shrub or small tree, 20–30 ft. (6–9 m) high. Leaves elliptic or narrower, 4–6 in. (10–15 cm) long, without marginal teeth, shining green above. Flowers fragrant, greenish. Va. to Fla. and Miss. Blooms in spring. Zone 7.

× ***fortunei*** *p. 272*
Fortune's Osmanthus. A fragrant shrub, 10–20 ft. (3–6 m) high. Leaves ovalish, 3–4 in. (7.5–10.0 cm) long, spiny-toothed on the margin. Hybrid derived from *O. fragrans* and *O. heterophyllus*. Blooms in fall. Zone 7.

fragrans *p. 273*
Fragrant Tea Olive. Shrub or small tree, to 25 ft. (7.5 m) high. Leaves ovalish or oblong, 2–4 in. (5–10 cm) long, slightly toothed or without any teeth. Flowers white, very fragrant, the corolla ¼ in. (6 mm) long, divided nearly to the base. Se. Asia. The most common species in cultivation. Blooms fall to winter. Zone 8.

heterophyllus *pp. 270, 271, 272*
Holly Osmanthus. A shrub, 15–20 ft. (4.5–6.0 m) high. Leaves oblong to ovalish, 1½–2½ in. (4–6 cm) long, the margins with a few spiny teeth, similar to holly leaves but opposite. Flowers fragrant, white, in clusters 1–1½ in. (2.5–4.0 cm) wide, the corolla divided almost to the base. Tolerates shade. Japan. Blooms in fall. Zone 7.

Parrotia

Witch hazel family
Hamamelidaceae

Par-ro′ti-a. A single species of shrub or small tree native to Persia, prized most for its fall foliage.

Description
Leaves resemble those of witch hazel. Flowers borne without petals and clustered in dense heads. Fruit is a woody capsule with 2 cells.

How to Grow
Parrotia performs well in slightly acid soil that is well drained. It will tolerate partial shade. Pruning should be done in the spring. Propagate by seeds, layers, or cuttings.

persica *pp. 212, 213*

Persian Parrotia. 20–40 ft. (6–12 m) high, the leaves alternate, ovalish, or oblong, 3–4 in. (7.5–10.0 cm) long, coarsely toothed toward the tip, turning scarlet, orange, or yellow in the fall and long-persistent. Flowers in dense heads nearly ½ in. (13 mm) in diameter, blooming before the leaves unfold, the head surrounded by brown-hairy bracts. Petals none. Fruit an egg-shaped, beaked capsule. Bark on older branches and trunk flakes off, creating interesting green, gray, brown, and white patches. Blooms in spring. Zone 5.

Paxistima

Spindle-tree family
Celastraceae

Pax-is′ti-ma. A genus comprising 2 North American species of low evergreen shrubs, grown mostly in the Northeast and the Pacific Northwest. The one below forms neat evergreen tufts, and is useful in the rock garden or as a ground cover.

Description
Leaves small, opposite. Inconspicuous flowers borne in the leaf axils. Fruit a 2-valved capsule.

How to Grow
Plant in sandy, somewhat peaty soil that is well drained. Paxistima will grow well in full sun or partial shade with little care. Propagate by seeds, cuttings, or layers.

canbyi *p. 280*

Canby Paxistima. Low shrub, growing 12 in. (30 cm) high, with trailing, rooting branches. Leaves ½–1 in. (1.3–2.5 cm) long, linear or narrowly oblong, toothed toward the tip, the margins turned under. Flowers tiny, reddish, on slender stems from leaf axils. Open rocky slopes of the mts. in Va. and W.Va. to Ky. and Ohio. Tolerates alkaline soil. Zone 4.

Philadelphus

Saxifrage family
Saxifragaceae

Fill-a-del′fus. The mock-oranges are a genus of about 60 North American and Eurasian deciduous shrubs, mostly erect, but with curved or drooping branches and close or flaky bark. They are widely grown for their fragrant, late spring flowers.

Description
Leaves opposite, with or without marginal teeth. Flowers white or, rarely, purple near the base, solitary or in small clusters, often fragrant. Sepals and petals 4. Stamens numerous. Fruit a capsule with small seeds.

How to Grow
Easy to grow in any soil, in sun or partial shade. Plants tend to become leggy, so prune yearly—immediately after blossoming, since flowers appear on wood of the previous year. Propagate by cuttings, seeds, layers, and suckers. Cuttings are usually made from semi-hardwood, in June and July.

coronarius *pp. 126, 127*
Common Mock-Orange; Sweet Mock-Orange. A shrub, to 10 ft. (3 m) high. Bark dark brown and peeling off on last year's growth. Leaves ovalish to oblong, pointed, 1½–4 in. (4–10 cm) long. Flowers creamy white, very fragrant, to 1½ in. (4 cm) across, in 5-to-7-flowered terminal racemes. Europe and sw. Asia. Zone 5.

× ***lemoinei*** *p. 126*
Lemoine Mock-Orange. An upright, spreading shrub, 4–6 ft. (1.2–1.8 m) high. Leaves ovalish to narrower, to 2 in. (5 cm) long, pointed, smooth above, stiff-hairy beneath. Flowers in 3-to-7-flowered terminal

racemes, 1½ in. (4 cm) across, very fragrant. Zone 5.

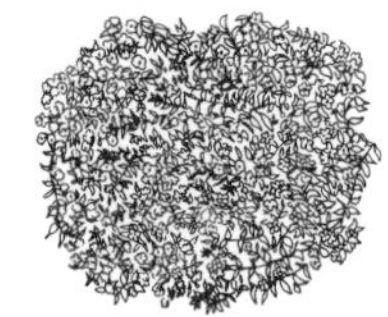

× ***virginalis*** *p. 127*
Virginal Mock-Orange. A shrub, 5–10 ft. (1.5–3.0 m) high. Bark brown and peeling or gray-brown and slightly peeling. Leaves ovalish, 2½–3 in. (6.0–7.5 cm) long, slightly toothed, soft-hairy beneath. Flowers semidouble or double, in 3-to-7-flowered racemes 3–5 in. (7.5–12.5 cm) wide, not as fragrant as some other species. Useful for forcing. Blooms in spring. Zone 5.

Phlomis

Mint family
Labiatae

Flo′mis. Jerusalem Sage. Strong-growing perennial herbs or subshrubs comprising about 100 species, found in the Mediterranean region and as far east as China. Their coarse appearance makes them especially suited to informal gardens.

Description
A shrub with coarse, square stems, 1½–6 ft. (0.5–1.8 m) high. Leaves large, ovalish or heart-shaped, opposite. Flowers yellow, purple, or white, in whorls in the axils. Corolla 2-lipped, the upper lip hairy. Stamens 4, two long and two short. Fruit 2-celled.

How to Grow
Jerusalem Sage grows best in full sun and will readily adapt to infertile, dry soils. If you prune off the spent flowers, new ones will grow in their place. Cut the plant back by ⅓ in fall to maintain its shape. This subshrub is easy to propagate by seeds, cuttings, or division of tubers.

fruticosa *p. 181*
Jerusalem Sage. A many-branched subshrub, 2–4 ft. (60–120 cm) high and covered with yellowish matted hairs. Leaves ovalish, to 4 in. (10 cm) long, wrinkled. Flowers yellow, to 1 in. (2.5 cm) long, numerous in whorls. S. Europe. Blooms in early summer. Zone 7.

Photinia
Rose family
Rosaceae

Fo-tin′i-a. 40 species of deciduous or evergreen shrubs or trees from n. Asia with attractive white flowers and red fruit. The deciduous species' leaves turn red and scarlet in the fall; the evergreens have handsome, shiny foliage that is red at first.

Description
Leaves alternate, often leathery. Flowers white, with 5 petals, borne in corymbs or panicles. Fruit a round or oval pome, red, ¼ in. (6 mm) long.

How to Grow
Photinias like a sunny location and well-drained, loamy soil. Water them often. Propagate by seeds or cuttings.

× ***fraseri*** *p. 206*
Fraser Photinia. Evergreen shrub, to 15 ft. (4.5 m) high. Leaves elliptic, 3–5 in. (7.5–12.5 cm) long. New growth red. Flowers in 3–5 in. (7.5–12.5 cm) clusters. Useful as a hedge. Mildew resistant. Hybrid derived from *P. glabra* and *P. serrulata.* Blooms in spring. Zone 8.

glabra *p. 207*
Japanese Photinia. Evergreen shrub, to 12 ft. (3.5 m) high. Leaves elliptic to oblong-obovate, 2–3 in. (5.0–7.5 cm) long, wedge-shaped at base, finely toothed. New growth red. Flowers in panicles 2–4 in. (5–10 cm) across. Fruit red. Good for hedges. Japan. Blooms in spring. Zone 8.

serrulata *p. 206*
Chinese Photinia. An evergreen shrub, 10–30 ft. (3–9 m) high. Leaves oblong, shiny, reddish when young, finely toothed, 4–8 in. (10–20 cm) long. Flowers in clusters 4–6 in. (10–15 cm) across. Fruit red and profuse. China. Blooms in spring. Zone 8.

villosa *p. 207*
Oriental Photinia. Deciduous shrub or small tree, to 15 ft. (4.5 m) high, hairy on new growth. Leaves obovate to oblong-obovate, 1–3 in. (2.5–7.5 cm) long, pointed at tip, finely toothed, hairy beneath, yellowish-red to scarlet in fall. Flowers in clusters 1–2 in. (2.5–5.0 cm) across, stems warty. Fruit red.

Japan, China, and Korea. Blooms in spring. Zone 5.

Physocarpus

Rose family
Rosaceae

Fy-so-kar′pus. Ninebark. Attractive white-flowered, spirea-like shrubs, all the 10 species North American except for one that is Asiatic. Their shreddy or peeling bark gives them their common name.

Description
Leaves alternate, stalked, toothed, and often 3-lobed. Flowers small, white, crowded in dense terminal corymbs, the sepals and petals 5 each. Stamens 20-40. Fruit a collection of inflated follicles, the seeds shining and yellowish.

How to Grow
The ninebarks are easy to grow in any ordinary garden soil and will tolerate drought. Propagate by seeds or softwood cuttings.

opulifolius *p. 142*
Common Ninebark. An erect or arching shrub, 5–10 ft. (1.5–3.0 m) high. Leaves ovalish or rounded, 2–3 in. (5.0–7.5 cm) long. Flower cluster profuse, nearly 2 in. (5 cm) wide. Fruits usually 5 to a cluster, smooth. 'Luteus', or Goldleaf Ninebark, is similar except the leaves are first yellow, fading nearly green in summer. E. North America. Blooms in spring. Zone 3.

Pieris

Heath family
Ericaceae

Py-ear′is. Eight species of valuable broad-leaved evergreen shrubs or small trees, which are very widely planted for their clusters of flowers in early spring and their dark green foliage, which is reddish when it first appears.

Description
Leaves generally alternate, stalked, toothed. Flowers in terminal, narrow panicles, the buds very obvious all winter before

blooming. Corolla white, urn-shaped, its 5 lobes short. Stamens 10. Fruit a dry capsule.

How to Grow
Plant pieris in peaty, somewhat sandy, moderately acid soil mulched with leaves. These are slow-growing plants, useful for gateway plantings, as accent plants, and for the rock garden. Propagate by seeds or layers.

floribunda *p. 200*
Mountain Pieris. An erect shrub, 3–6 ft. (0.9–1.8 m) high. Leaves elliptic or ovalish, 1½–3½ in. (4–9 cm) long, pointed, minutely hairy on the margin. Flowers fragrant, nodding, the cluster upright, 2–4 in. (5–10 cm) long. Sometimes known as *Andromeda floribunda.* Va. to Ga. Zone 5.

forrestii *p. 200*
Chinese Pieris. A shrub or tree, to 10 ft. (3 m) high, with shoots and leaves bright red at first. Leaves elliptic or lance-shaped, to 4½ in. (11.5 cm) long. Flower clusters pendulous to erect, 4–6 in. (10–15 cm) long, flowers white or pink. Himalayas. Zone 7.

japonica *p. 201*
Japanese Pieris. A splendid evergreen shrub, 3–10 ft. (0.9–3.0 m) high, or even more in age. Leaves oblongish, 1½–3½ in. (4–9 cm) long, dark shiny-green. Flowers slightly fragrant, the clusters hanging, 3–5 in. (7.5–12.5 cm) long, the corolla ½ in. (13 mm) long. Cultivars 'Forest Flame' and 'Mountain Fire' have especially vivid new growth. 'Wada', 'Dorothy Wycoff', 'Flamingo', and 'Valley Rose' have pink flowers. Often sold as *Andromeda japonica.* Japan. Zone 5.

Pittosporum
Tobira family
Pittosporaceae

Pit-toss′por-um. Australian laurel. Chiefly Australasian evergreen shrubs and trees comprising over 100 species, several of which are grown often in s. Calif. and along the Gulf Coast.

Description
Leaves alternate, or on young twigs apparently whorled, wavy-margined and faintly toothed or without teeth. Flowers in

clusters or solitary, usually terminal, but sometimes in the leaf axils. Sepals 5, usually distinct. Petals 5, mostly clawed and more or less joined at the base, free above. Fruit a capsule, its seed sticky.

How to Grow
The Australian laurels are easy to grow in a variety of soils. They adapt especially well to sandy soils and hot, dry locations but can also stand shade. *P. tobira* is often grown as a container plant. Propagate by seeds, or cuttings of semi-hardwood.

tobira *pp. 274, 275*
Japanese Pittosporum. A shrub, 6–18 ft. (1.8–5.5 m) high, useful for informal hedges. Leaves thick and leathery, ovalish but blunt toward the tip, 3–4 in. (7.5–10.0 cm) long. Flower clusters terminal, 2–3 in. (5.0–7.5 cm) wide, the corolla fragrant, greenish white to lemon yellow, ½ in. (13 mm) long. Fruit densely hairy, ½ in. (13 mm) long. 'Variegatum' has white-marked leaves and is more compact. Both are hardier than other species, have lemon-scented foliage and brittle twigs. China and Japan. Blooms in spring. Zone 9.

tobira **'Wheeler's Dwarf'** *p. 274*
Wheeler's Dwarf Pittosporum. Dense-growing, compact form of the species, to 3 ft. (90 cm) high. Flowers in clusters 1–2 in. (2.5-5.0 cm) wide. A good plant for foreground plantings and as ground cover. Blooms in spring. Zone 9.

Podocarpus
Podocarpus family
Podocarpaceae

Po-do-kar′pus. Handsome evergreen trees or shrubs, mostly from the southern hemisphere northward to the West Indies and Japan, and chiefly from mountainous areas. Of the 75 known species, only a few are in cultivation in the U.S., mostly in Calif., along the Gulf Coast, and in Fla. In the South they are commonly, but incorrectly, called Japanese yew.

Description
Leaves alternate, mostly narrow or ovalish. Male and female flowers consisting of naked, catkinlike masses of anthers, the female a

solitary naked ovule between 1 or 2 small bracts. Fruit fleshy-stalked, mostly plumlike, or berrylike.

How to Grow
The species below grows in a variety of soils and presents no difficulties except that it will not stand severe frosts. Do not use it in areas north of zone 9. Plant in sun or partial shade and keep relatively moist. The Maki Podocarpus is an excellent container plant. Propagate by hardwood cuttings.

macrophyllus* var. *maki *pp. 286, 287*
Maki or Chinese Podocarpus. A variety of the commonest species in cultivation in the U.S., a shrub that grows to 6-8 ft. (1.8–2.4 m) high in the first 10 years and can grow to 35 ft. (11 m) eventually. Leaves narrowly lance-shaped, 3 in. (7.5 cm) long, dark green above, paler beneath. Fruit egg-shaped, ½ in. (13 mm) long, greenish purple, the fleshy stalk purple. Useful as a hedge. China. Zone 9.

Polygala
Milkwort family
Polygalaceae

Pol-lig′a-la. Milkwort. A genus of over 500 species of hardy or tender annual and perennial herbs or subshrubs, a few treelike, about 60 of which are North American.

Description
Leaves alternate, lance-shaped. Flowers in terminal clusters, or spikes, showy in some species. Calyx of 5 sepals, 3 small, 2 large, sometimes colored. Petals 4–5. Fruit a 2-celled capsule, sometimes winged.

How to Grow
Plant Sweet-Pea shrubs in sun or light shade. Since it is leggy, you may want to place lower growing plants in front of it, or prune frequently to keep the plant compact. Propagate by seeds sown in fall or early spring in sandy soil in a cold frame and transplanted to a permanent position when large enough to handle; or by cuttings made in early fall and inserted in sandy peat in a cool greenhouse or cold frame.

× ***dalmaisiana*** *p. 129*
Sweet-Pea Shrub. Tender evergreen shrub,

3–6 ft. (0.9–1.8 m) high. Leaves ovalish, to 1 in. (2.5 cm) long, not stalked. Flowers in terminal racemes, purplish red, the lower petal whitish. Long flowering period. Blooms in spring. Zone 9.

Poncirus
Citrus family
Rutaceae

Pon-sy′rus. A single, spiny, deciduous species of Chinese shrub useful as an impenetrable, defensive hedge. It is also used as grafting stock for the more tender citrus fruits.

Description
Closely related to *Citrus,* with which it has been hybridized, but with 3 leaflets.

How to Grow
Poncirus grows best in well-drained, acid soil. Its fruit is showy but inedible. It is easy to propagate from seeds.

trifoliata *pp. 86, 87*
Trifoliate Orange. Rarely over 20 ft. (6 m) high, its spines mostly ¾ in. (19 mm) long. Leaves alternate, compound, its 3 leaflets oval or oblong, 2–3 in. (5.0–7.5 cm) long, the stalk winged. Flowers white, usually fragrant, nearly 2 in. (5 cm) wide, flattish, the 5 petals oblongish and longer than the sepals. Stamens 8-10. Fruit orange-like, but scarcely over 2 in. (5 cm) in diameter, its flesh dryish, very acid, but fragrant. China. Blooms in spring. Zone 6.

Potentilla
Rose family
Rosaceae

Po-ten-till′a. Cinquefoil. Perennial—rarely, annual—herbs or small shrubs comprising over 500 species, found in temperate and arctic regions mostly in the North. Grown for its dense, rounded shape and long-blooming flowers.

Description
Stems creeping or erect, the creeping species rooting at the joints. Leaves compound; leaflets 3 or many, more or less hairy. Flowers in numerous small, loose clusters,

yellow, white, or red. Calyx of 5 sepals, joined at the base, forming a cup. Corolla of 5 petals growing on the calyx rim. Stamens numerous. Fruits several, dry, one-seeded.

How to Grow
The cinquefoils grow well in fertile, dry soils in sunny locations. They tolerate alkalinity and are suitable for clay loam soils. Prune plants if you do not want them open and sparse. Renewal pruning should be done in the winter by removing ⅓ of the stems. Propagate by softwood cuttings.

fruticosa *p. 158*
Shrubby Cinquefoil. Small, much-branched shrub, 1–4 ft. (30–120 cm) high. Leaves small. Leaflets 3–7, lance-shaped, to 1 in. (2.5 cm) long, covered with short silky hairs, the margins slightly rolled. Flowers numerous, showy, bright yellow, in 1–1½-in. (2.5–4.0-cm) clusters. This species and its varieties make some of the finest flowering shrubs for the garden and are useful as hedges. Europe, Asia, and North America. Blooms in summer. Zone 3.

Prunus

Rose family
Rosaceae

A large, important genus of shrubs and trees, nearly all from the north temperate zone. Besides fruit trees such as the plums and cherries, it contains many superb flowering shrubs.

Description
Nearly all deciduous, with alternate leaves that are nearly always sharply toothed. Flowers in corymbs or racemes, or sometimes few or only one; white, pink, or red, typically with 5 sepals, 5 petals, and many stamens. In some cultivars there is much doubling of the petals and sometimes no functional stamens and no fruit. Fruit usually fleshy with a single stone.

How to Grow
Plant shrubs in full sun in a well-drained soil. Prune them, if necessary, after flowering. Most species are relatively short lived, usually about 20 years for a healthy plant. Propagate by cuttings.

besseyi *p. 147*
Sand Cherry. A low shrub, 4–6 ft. (1.2–1.8 m) high, with often prostrate stems. Leaves elliptic or ovalish, 1–2 in. (2.5–5.0 cm) long. Flowers 2–4 in a cluster, white, ⅓ in. (8 mm) wide. Fruit nearly round, ½ in. (13 mm) in diameter, black, edible, and sweet. Cen. North America. Tolerates drought. Blooms in spring. Zone 4.

× ***cistena*** *p. 85*
Purple-leaf Sand Cherry. Small shrub, 8–10 ft. (2.4–3.0 m) high. Leaves intense purple, remaining so all summer, 1–2 in. (2.5–5.0 cm) long and lanceolate. Flowers fragrant, single, pinkish, 2–3 in a cluster, very numerous, ½ in. (13 mm) wide. Fruit blackish-purple, maturing in summer. Blooms in spring. Zone 3.

glandulosa *p. 84*
Dwarf Flowering Almond. A very showy shrub, to 5 ft. (1.5 m) high. Leaves ovalish-oblong, or narrower, 1½–4 in. (4–10 cm) long. Flowers very numerous, but in clusters of 1 or 2, blooming before the leaves unfold, white or pinkish, ½ in. (13 mm) wide. Fruit is red and ⅓ in. (8 mm) in diameter, not produced in all forms. China and Japan. Blooms in spring. Zone 5.

'Hally Jolivette' *p. 84*
Hally Jolivette Cherry. A large shrub or small tree, 8–15 ft. (2.4–4.5 m) high, with bushy upright habit. Leaves obovate to lanceolate. Flowers pink in bud, opening white, double, 1–1½ in. (2.5–4.0 cm) wide. Blooms in spring. Zone 5.

laurocerasus *pp. 145, 146, 147*
Cherry Laurel; English Laurel. An evergreen shrub or small tree, up to 20 ft. (6 m) high. Leaves oblongish, 2–7 in. (5.0–17.5 cm) long, remotely or not at all toothed, short-stalked. Flowers fragrant, white, ⅓ in. (8 mm) wide, the cluster shorter than the leaves. Fruit dark purple, ½ in. (13 mm) long. Tolerates shade. There are many cultivars, differing in leaf and plant shape and in hardiness. 'Otto Luyken' has a compact habit, 4 ft. (120 cm) high with a spread of 6–8 ft. (1.8–2.4 m) and tolerates deep shade. 'Schipkaensis' has narrow, dark green leaves and usually grows 4–5 ft. (1.2–1.5 m) high with a wider spread. It is probably hardier than the species. Se. Europe to Iran. Blooms in spring. Zone 7.

***tenella* 'Fire Hill'** *p. 85*
Dwarf Russian Almond. A dwarf, suckering shrub, 2–5 ft. (0.6–1.5 m) high. Leaves narrow, 1–3 in. (2.5–7.5 cm) long, sharply toothed, dark green above, paler beneath. Flowers in clusters of 1-3, rose red, ½ in. (13 mm) wide. Fruit hairy-skinned, egg-shaped, ¾ in. (19 mm) long. Eurasia. Blooms in spring. Zone 3.

Punica

Pomegranate family
Punicaceae

Pew′ni-ka. Pomegranate. Two species of deciduous shrubs or trees. One is widely grown in tropical or sub-tropical climates for the ornamental effect of its bright orange flowers, its vivid fall color, and its edible fruit.

Description
Leaves mostly opposite. Flowers bisexual, in small clusters. Fruit a many-seeded berry surrounded by juicy, edible pulp.

How to Grow
Plant pomegranates in deep, fertile, loam soil and in full sun for most flowers and fruit. Prune, if necessary, before flowering since blossoms form on new growth. Propagate by cuttings or seeds.

granatum *pp. 94, 95*
Pomegranate. An Asiatic shrub or small tree, 10–20 ft. (3–6 m) high. It often has spiny-tipped branches and short-stalked, oblongish or oval-oblong, shining leaves, 1½–3 in. (4.0–7.5 cm) long, turning bright yellow in fall. Flowers in clusters of 1–5 at the ends of short shoots borne in leaf axils. Calyx leathery, partly tubular, the 5–7 lobes persistent on the fruit. Corolla of 5–7 separate, wrinkled, orange-red petals, the flowers 1½ in. (4 cm) wide. Stamens numerous. Fruit several-chambered, white, brownish-yellow, pink, or red, 2–5 in. (5.0–12.5 cm) in diameter, the flesh crimson and slightly acid. Useful for hedges. Blooms in spring. Zone 8.

Pyracantha
Rose family
Rosaceae

Py-ra-kan′tha. Fire Thorn. A small genus of Asiatic evergreen, thorny shrubs closely related to *Cotoneaster.* Most are grown for their fine foliage and bright red or orange fruits that persist in winter.

Description
Leaves short-stalked; flowers spring-blooming, small, white, in compound corymbs. Petals 5, nearly round. Stamens 20, the anthers yellow. Fruit fleshy, red or orange, usually crowned with the persistent calyx.

How to Grow
Plant fire thorns in full sun in a well-drained soil for best fruiting. Their long thorns make these shrubs useful as hedges but painful to prune, so place them where they will have room to spread out. If pruning is necessary, you can do it at any time. The species listed below are resistant to scab and fireblight. Propagate by seeds, hardwood cuttings under glass, or layering.

coccinea *p. 234*
Scarlet Fire Thorn. A shrub 10–15 ft. (3.0–4.5 m) high. Leaves ovalish, 1–1½ in. (2.5–4.0 cm) long, toothed, ultimately without hairs. Flower cluster hairy, 5⁄16 in. (8 mm) wide. Fruit bright red, ⅓ in. (8 mm) in diameter. The best-known species in cultivation. 'Lalandei' has less deeply-toothed leaves and bears orange-red fruit. It is hardier and more vigorous than the typical form and does well when trained against a wall. Eurasia. Zone 6.

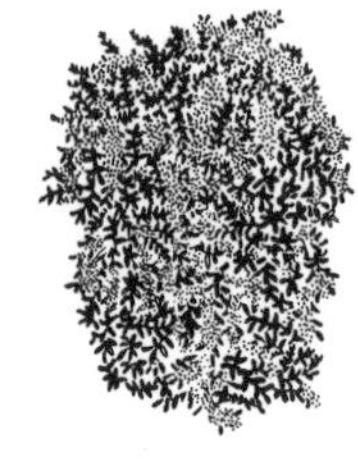

fortuneana **'Graberi'** *p. 234*
Graberi Fire Thorn. A handsome shrub, 10–15 ft. (3.0–4.5 m) high, its young twigs rusty-hairy. Leaves broadest toward the tip, 1–3 in. (2.5–7.5 cm) long, the margins wavy but not toothed. Flowers ½ in. (13 mm) wide, the clusters 1–2 in. (2.5–5.0 cm) wide. Fruit nearly round, ½ in. (13 mm) thick, brick-red. China. Zone 7.

'Navaho' *p. 235*
Navaho Fire Thorn. A shrub, to 6 ft. (1.8 m), with dense, mounded habit and orange-red fruit. Another hybrid, 'Mohave', grows to 10 ft. (3 m) and is more upright. Zone 7.

'Teton' *p. 235*
Teton Fire Thorn. An upright shrub, almost twice as tall as it is wide, to 15 ft. (4.5 m), with yellow-orange fruit. Zone 7.

Raphiolepis
Rose family
Rosaceae

Ra-fi-ol′e-pis. Handsome Asiatic evergreen shrubs widely planted in warm areas for their leathery green foliage, showy flower clusters, and usefulness as borders, hedges, and large ground covers.

Description
Leaves alternate, thick, fleshy, short-stalked. Flowers white or pink in rather showy terminal panicles or racemes. Petals 5. Stamens 15–20. Fruit a bluish black or purplish black, generally round berry with 1-2 seeds.

How to Grow
All the species are easy to grow in a variety of soils in full sun or partial shade. Though they will stand some frost, they cannot be grown safely north of zone 8. Propagate by seeds or hardwood cuttings under glass.

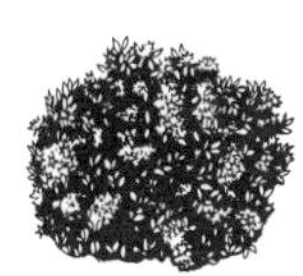

indica *pp. 132, 133*
Indian Hawthorn. Not over 5 ft. (1.5 m) high. Leaves oblongish, or narrower, 2–3 in. (5.0–7.5 cm) long, bluntly toothed, pointed at the tip. Flowers pinkish white, ½ in. (13 mm) wide, the clusters loose and without hairs. Tolerates drought. There are a number of widely-grown cultivars. S. China. Blooms in spring. Zone 8.

umbellata *pp. 132, 133*
Yeddo Raphiolepis. A shrub, often low and spreading, 4–6 ft. (1.2–1.8 m), but occasionally to 10 ft. (3 m) high. Leaves very thick, 2–3 in. (5.0–7.5 cm) long, slightly toothed, the margins rolled. Flowers white, ¾ in. (19 mm) wide, fragrant, the clusters dense and hairy. Fruit black, pear-shaped, ¼ in. (6.5 mm) long. Tolerates drought. 'Springtime' has pink flowers from January to April. Japan. Blooms in spring. Zone 8.

Rhamnus

Buckthorn family
Rhamnaceae

Ram′nus. Buckthorn. A large group of medicinally significant, mostly deciduous shrubs or trees, most of the 150 known species from the north temperate zone, a few from Brazil and South Africa. The cultivated species are chiefly shrubs grown for their lustrous foliage.

Description
Often somewhat thorny, with alternate or opposite leaves. Flowers small, greenish, often without petals and never showy. Fruit nearly round, berry-like.

How to Grow
Plant buckthorns in sun or partial shade in a well-drained soil. Tallhedge Buckthorn especially needs good drainage, but all species are easy to grow.

***frangula* 'Asplenifolia'** *pp. 286, 287*
Feathery Buckthorn. A shrub or small tree 10–12 ft. (3.0–3.5 m) high. Leaves narrow, wavy-margined, giving a feathery look. Flowers and fruit as in *R. f.* 'Columnaris'. Species from Eurasia and n. Africa. Zone 3.

***frangula* 'Columnaris'** *p. 284*
Tallhedge Buckthorn. A narrow shrub 10–15 ft. (3.0–4.5 m) high. Leaves ovalish, or broadest toward the tip, 1½–2½ in. (4–6 cm) long, bright yellow in fall. Flowers in umbels of 2–10. Fruit red at first, ultimately black. Makes a good, dense screen. Zone 3.

Rhododendron

Heath family
Ericaceae

Ro-doe-den′dron. A very large genus of evergreen or deciduous shrubs, chiefly from the north temperate zone, which includes the plants commonly called azaleas. Although their technical characteristics do not warrant separation into 2 genera, rhododendrons and azaleas are usually considered by gardeners and nurseries to be two different groups. Azaleas are mostly deciduous and have funnel-shaped flowers, while rhododendrons are usually evergreen with larger, bell-shaped flowers borne in terminal clusters. These distinctions are not always reliable, so it is best to know the scientific and cultivar name of the plant you want to grow. The common names given here will tell you which species are considered azaleas; otherwise, the genus name is used to refer to all the plants.

Description
Leaves alternate, mostly stalked, always without marginal teeth. Flowers very showy, mostly tubular or funnel-shaped, the 5-lobed limb slightly irregular. Stamens 5–10.

How to Grow
Plant rhododendrons in well-drained soil containing ample amounts of organic matter. If your soil does not drain well, plant high or use raised beds. Almost all rhododendron species require acid soil. Use mulch to conserve moisture and to reduce the need for cultivation around the plants, which could cause damage to the shallow roots. Full to partial sun is fine; deep shade will restrict flowering, but is tolerated well by some evergreen species. Protect evergreen species from drying winds and direct winter sun. Prune, if necessary, just after flowering. Propagate by seed, layers or, for evergreens, semi-hardwood cuttings rooted in sand.

catawbiense *p. 107*
Catawba Rhododendron. A magnificent evergreen shrub, 6–10 ft. (1.8–3.0 m), high. Leaves 3–6 in. (7.5–15.0 cm) long, shining green above, paler beneath. Flowers lilac-purple, the cluster 6–10 in. (15–25 cm) wide. Catawba is one of the most reliable and cold tolerant species. Mts. from Va. to Ga. Blooms in spring. Zone 5.

Dexter hybrids
Dexter Hybrid Rhododendrons. Evergreen shrubs developed for dense foliage and large, colorful, often fragrant flowers. To 8 ft. (2.4 m), clusters 10 in. (25 cm) wide. 'Scintillation' has pale pink flowers with gold dots. Blooms in spring. Zone 5.

Exbury hybrids *pp. 104, 105*
Exbury Hybrid Azaleas. Deciduous, upright-growing azaleas, to 4 ft. (120 cm) high, with leaves yellow, orange, and red in fall. Flowers, borne in 3 in. (7.5 cm) diameter trusses, can be yellow, pink, cream, orange, rose, or red. Blooms in spring. Zone 5.

Gable hybrids *p. 112*
Gable Hybrid Azaleas. Evergreen, 3–4 ft. (90–120 cm) high. Leaves shiny dark green, 1 in. (2.5 cm) long. Flowers about 2 in. (5 cm) across. Considered the hardiest of the evergreen azaleas. Cultivars offer flower colors of red, salmon pink, white, and rosy-pink. Blooms in spring. Zone 6.

kaempferi *p. 109*
Torch Azalea. Deciduous to semievergreen shrub, to 8 ft. (2.4 m) high. Leaves elliptic to egg-shaped, hairy on both surfaces, to 2½ in. (6 cm) long. Flowers pink, orange-red to bright red, funnel-shaped, to 2 in. (5 cm) wide. Leaves turn reddish in fall. Japan. Blooms in spring. Zone 5.

× ***kosteranum*** *p. 104*
Mollis Hybrid Azalea. Deciduous azalea, upright growing, 6–8 ft. (1.8–2.4 m) high. Leaves entire, 1½–4 in. (4–10 cm) long, oblong-ovate, with bristly stems and leaf margins. Flowers yellow, red, orange, or white, 2½–3½ in. (6–9 cm) wide. Blooms in spring. Zone 6.

Kurume hybrids *pp. 112, 113*
Kurume Azaleas. Evergreen Japanese shrubs, 4–6 ft. (1.2–1.8 m) high, and much-branched. Leaves shining dark green above, hairy on the midrib beneath, more or less elliptic, ¾–1 in. (2.0–2.5 cm) long. Flowers 2-3 in a cluster, 1½ in. (4 cm) wide and available in white to pink, lavender, scarlet, and salmon. Blooms in spring. Zone 7.

mucronulatum *p. 108*
Korean Rhododendron. To 8 ft. (2.4 m) high, the branches upright. Leaves deciduous, narrowly lance-shaped, 1–3 in. (2.5–7.5 cm) long, somewhat scaly. Flowers slightly hairy on the outside, funnel-shaped or bell-shaped, 1½ in. (4 cm) wide, rosy purple, appearing before the leaves unfold. Clusters 6–10 in. (15–25 cm) wide. A profuse bloomer with handsome yellow-bronze fall foliage. One of the easiest, hardiest, and earliest species, flowering with the forsythias. 'Cornell Pink' is a popular cultivar. E. Asia. Blooms in spring. Zone 5.

PJM hybrids *p. 106*
PJM Rhododendrons. Evergreen, rounded shrubs, 3–6 ft. (0.9–1.8 m) high. Leaves turn purplish in fall. Flowers vivid lavender pink

in 3–5-in. (7.5–12.5-cm) cluster. One of the hardiest broadleaf rhododendrons. Blooms in spring. Zone 4.

schlippenbachii *pp. 108, 109*
Royal Azalea. A deciduous shrub, 6–10 ft. (1.8–3.0 m) high. Leaves clustered at the ends of the twigs, green above, pale beneath, ovalish but broader toward the short-pointed tip, 3–5 in. (7.5–12.5 cm) long, turning bright yellow to orange or red in fall. Flowers pink, brown-spotted, 3-6 in a cluster, 2½ in. (6 cm) wide. E. Asia. Blooms in spring. Zone 5.

yakusimanum *pp. 106, 107*
Yako Rhododendron. Evergreen shrub, to 3 ft. (90 cm) high, rounded and compact. Leaves oblongish, to 3 in. (7.5 cm) long, densely white-hairy beneath. Flowers bell-shaped, white or pink, to 2½ in. (6 cm) wide. Clusters 6–10 in. (15–25 cm) wide. Japan. Blooms in spring. Zone 5.

Rhodotypos
Rose family
Rosaceae

Ro-doe-ty′pos. A single species of hardy Asiatic shrubs related to *Kerria* and grown for its white flowers, shiny black berries, and usefulness as a border or foreground shrub.

Description
Leaves opposite and serrated. Flowers white, composed of 4 petals and numerous stamens. Fruit black, usually arranged in multiples of 4, persisting in winter.

How to Grow
Easy to grow in any garden soil, Jetbead will tolerate pollution and sun or heavy shade. Propagate by seeds or cuttings.

scandens *p. 122*
Jetbead; White Kerria. A handsome shrub, 4–6 ft. (1.2–1.8 m) high, with opposite, short-stalked, doubly toothed leaves that are more or less oblongish, 3–4 in. (7.5–10.0 cm) long. Flowers pure white, nearly 2 in. (5 cm) wide, the 4 petals suggesting a single rose. Sepals 4, toothed, alternating with 4 small bracts. Fruit a collection of 4 shining, black, dry drupes set in the persistent calyx. China and Japan. Blooms in spring. Zone 5.

Rhus

Sumac family
Anacardiaceae

Rus. Sumac. A large genus of shrubs and trees, the 150 species scattered very widely. The cultivated sumacs are of great decorative value in fall, when their foliage turns a more brilliant red than that of almost any other shrubs or trees. Their fruits are also handsome.

Description
Leaves usually compound, the leaflets arranged pinnately. Flowers small, greenish, perfect or polygamous, the petals, sepals, and stamens each 5. Fruit small, berrylike, clustered, red and hairy in all the cultivated sumacs.

How to Grow
Easy to grow in any garden soil, or even in dry sand or on rocky hillsides. Transplanting is not difficult, nor is raising plants from seeds or root cuttings.

aromatica *pp. 210, 211*
Fragrant Sumac. A sprawling shrub, 2–6 ft. (0.6–1.8 m) high. Leaflets 3, ovalish, 2–3 in. (5.0–7.5 cm) long, coarsely toothed, the foliage aromatic. Flowers greenish yellow, borne in small, 1-in. (2.5 cm) spikes and blooming before the leaves expand. Fruit appearing in early summer. Also known as *R. canadensis*. 'Gro-low' is a low, spreading form, 1½–2 ft. (45–60 cm) tall and 6–8 ft. (1.8–2.4 m) wide. E. North America. Blooms in spring. Zone 3.

integrifolia *p. 285*
Lemonade Sumac. A shrub or small tree, usually 5–10 ft. (1.5–3.0 m) high, from s. Calif. and hardy only in similar climates, with evergreen foliage and simple leaves, without teeth or with a few. Flowers pinkish white in hairy clusters, followed by deep red and hairy, acid fruits, which have been used to flavor drinks. Can be espaliered or used as a ground cover on rocky slopes. Blooms in spring. Zone 9.

ovata *p. 284*
Sugar Bush. A smooth, evergreen shrub from the desert regions of sw. U.S., 5–10 ft. (1.5–3.0 m) high, with simple ovalish leaves, 1–3 in. (2.5–7.5 cm) long. Flowers greenish

white, in short, dense spikes. Fruit hairy, dark red. Blooms in spring. Zone 9.

typhina *pp. 210, 211*
Staghorn Sumac. A shrub or small tree 10–30 ft. (3–9 m) high, the twigs densely brown-hairy. Leaflets 11-31, oblong lance-shaped, 4–5 in. (10.0–12.5 cm) long, toothed. Flowers greenish, in a large terminal panicle. The cultivar 'Laciniata' has the leaflets attractively and finely cut into narrow segments. The Staghorn Sumac is by far the best species from the horticultural standpoint for both its showy fruiting cluster and its gorgeous fall foliage. It was long known as *R. hirta.* N. North America. Blooms in summer. Zone 4.

Ribes

Saxifrage family
Saxifragaceae

Ry'beez. A large genus of sometimes prickly shrubs, mostly from temperate regions, and of great horticultural importance because it includes currants, the gooseberry, and several related shrubs grown for ornament. There are over 140 species, but most of them are not in general cultivation.

Description

Leaves alternate, simple, but usually lobed pinnately. Flowers prevailingly greenish, yellowish, or reddish, the sepals usually colored and larger than the petals, which are sometimes very small or lacking. Stamens 5. Fruit a juicy berry. The individual flower-stalks are jointed in the currants.

How to Grow

The ornamental species are easy to grow in sun or shade in any soil. Prune at any time. Propagate by layering, cuttings, or seeds. All bloom early in the spring and fruit in midsummer.

alpinum *p. 81*
Alpine Currant. An ornamental shrub, 5–8 ft. (1.5–2.4 m) high. Lobes of the leaf toothed. Flowers small, in upright racemes, 1 in. (2.5 cm) long, greenish yellow, the male and female on different plants. Fruit scarlet, smooth. Good for hedges and massing in shaded areas. Europe. Zone 3.

odoratum *p. 80*
Clove Currant. An ornamental, unarmed shrub 4–6 ft. (1.2–1.8 m) high. Lobes of the leaf coarsely toothed. Flowers yellow, fragrant, the clusters 1½–2 in. (4–5 cm) long, showy and drooping. Fruit black, smooth, and edible. One of the finest ornamental currants. Cen. U.S. Blooms in spring. Zone 5.

sanguineum *pp. 80, 81*
Flowering Currant. A very ornamental and widely cultivated shrub, 5–12 ft. (1.5–3.5 m) high. Lobes of the leaf irregularly toothed. Flowers red, the sticky, drooping, many-flowered racemes very showy, 2–4 in. (5–10 cm) long. Fruit bluish black, with a powdery bloom. An extremely popular shrub, useful for the red garden, but found in many horticultural forms, with pink, white, deep red, or double flowers. Nw. North America. Zones 6–8.

Romneya
Poppy family
Papaveraceae

Rom′nee-a. Tender perennial herbs or subshrubs, comprising 1 species from Calif. and Mex. grown in warm regions for its grayish-green foliage and large, yellow-centered, white flowers.

Description
Leaves in pairs, stalked, broadly lance-shaped, deeply lobed, to 4 in. (10 cm) long. Flowers solitary, at the ends of the branches, white, to 6 in. (15 cm) across. Calyx of 3 sepals. Corolla of 6 petals, all alike. Stamens numerous. Fruit a many-seeded capsule.

How to Grow
Plant Matilija Poppies in full sun in a well-drained soil. The soil can be infertile and dry. In fact, better conditions encourage invasive growth of roots, which can damage weaker plants close by, so give this shrub plenty of room. Use it especially on hillsides or in mass plantings. Propagate by root cuttings in fall.

coulteri *p. 117*
Matilija Poppy; California Tree Poppy. Grows to 8 ft. (2.4 m), much-branched above, with spreading rootstocks and

branching stems. Leaves thin, paperlike. Flowers white, to 6 in. (15 cm) across, solitary. Calif. and Mexico. Blooms in summer. Zone 7.

Rosa
Rose family
Rosaceae

Ro′za. Rose. A genus of shrubs or vines comprising all the true roses, from species roses, which are naturally-occurring, to the miniature hybrids that are often grown in containers or indoors.

Description
Leaves alternate, compound, the leaflets arranged pinnately. The prickles may be hooked or straight. Flowers solitary or in small clusters, typically with 5 petals in wild, single roses, but much doubled in most of the horticultural forms; nearly always fragrant. Stamens numerous. Pistils numerous, enclosed at the base in a cup-shaped receptacle that enlarges in fruit and becomes fleshy and berrylike (the rose hip), enclosing the mature pistils that become bony seeds.

How to Grow
The species below are easy to grow in full sun and well-drained soils. Prune out the oldest canes each year to shape the plant and promote maximum bloom. Consider using the first two plants as informal hedges. Propagate species roses by softwood cuttings taken in summer or hardwood cuttings taken in fall or winter. Cultivars should be purchased as young plants.

hugonis *p. 159*
Hugo Rose; often called Father Hugo's Rose. A handsome free-flowering shrub, 6–8 ft. (1.8–2.4 m) high, the branches drooping, beset with flattened, straight prickles and bristles. Leaflets 5-13, ovalish or elliptic, ½–¾ in. (13–19 mm) long. Flowers slightly fragrant, solitary, 2 in. (5 cm) wide, yellow. Fruit scarlet, turning darker, ½ in. (13 mm) wide. One of the best single yellow roses in cultivation and one of the few that thrive in poor soil. China. Blooms in spring. Zone 5.

rugosa *p. 119*
Rugosa Rose; Saltspray Rose. An upright shrub, 4–6 ft. (1.2–1.8 m) high, ultimately making large patches 10–20 ft. (3–6 m) in diameter. Stems densely bristly and prickly, the prickles straight. Leaflets 5-9, more or less elliptic, 1–2 in. (2.5–5.0 cm) long, very rough and veiny on upper surface, shining. Flowers usually solitary, nearly 3½ in. (9 cm) wide, red to white. Rose hip brick red, 1 in. (2.5 cm) wide. Prefers slightly acid soil. Tolerates salt. There are many horticultural varieties, some with double flowers. Japan and China. Blooms in summer. Zone 3 and in sand along seashore in e. U.S.

wichuraiana *p. 118*
Memorial Rose. A prostrate or trailing semi-evergreen rose, to 1½ ft. (45 cm) high, the strong prickles hooked. Leaflets 7-9, roundish, blunt, shining, ¾–1 in. (2.0–2.5 cm) long. Flowers nearly 2 in. (5 cm) wide, white, fragrant, mostly in corymbs. Fruit egg-shaped, red, ½ in. (13 mm) long. The origin of many valuable roses useful for covering walls and banks, among them 'Dorothy Perkins', 'Dr. Walter Van Fleet', 'New Dawn', and 'May Queen', as well as the Kordesii Hybrids (*R. wichuraiana* × *R. rugosa*). E. Asia. Blooms in summer. Zone 6.

Rosmarinus
Mint family
Labiatae

Ros-ma-ry′nus. Rosemary. Three species of evergreen shrubs, native to the Mediterranean region, the one below widely cultivated as a culinary and sweet herb and also valuable as a shrub, especially in warm areas.

Description
Stems mostly square; leaves opposite, simple. Flowers in clusters; fruit a 4-part nutlet.

How to Grow
Rosemary tolerates dry soil and must have good drainage. It is easy to prune and can be used as a hedge. Excess fertilizing and watering only cause open, rank growth. In northern areas, plant in a sheltered position. Propagate by seeds, or by cuttings made in

early fall from young shoots and treated with a rooting hormone.

officinalis *pp. 154, 155*

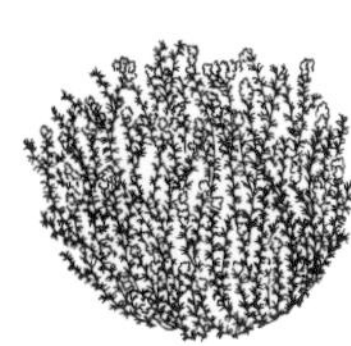

Rosemary. To 6 ft. (1.8 m), and of upright habit, much-branched. Leaves small, lance-shaped, to 1 in. (2.5 cm) long, grayish green on the upper side, covered with short white hairs on underside. Flowers pale blue, ½ in. (13 mm) long, in clusters growing from axils of the leaves. Calyx of 5 sepals. Corolla tubular, 2-lipped, upper lip consisting of 2 lobes, lower lip of 3 lobes. Stamens 4, in pairs, 2 long, 2 short. Fruit 2-celled when young, splitting into 4 parts when ripe. 'Collingwood Ingram' has curving branches; 'Albus' has white flowers. Mediterranean region. Blooms fall to winter. Zone 7.

Ruscus

Lily family
Liliaceae

Rus′kus. A small genus of low shrubs, found from Madeira to the Caucasus and grown outdoors in the South for their foliage and berries and for use, dried and dyed, as winter decorations.

Description
Leaves actually leaflike twigs, minute and scale-like. Flowers unisexual or bisexual, borne on the midrib of the twig. Fruit a red or yellow berry.

How to Grow
Plant Butcher's Broom in moist, well-drained soil. They prefer shade. Be sure to have both male and female plants, or there will be no berries.

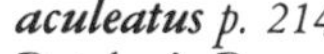

aculeatus *p. 214*

Butcher's Broom; Jew's Myrtle. A prickly, stiff, evergreen shrub, 2–3 ft. (60–90 cm) high, its leaflike branches ovalish, ¾–1½ in. (2–4 cm) long, thick, leathery, and prickle-tipped. Male and female flowers on different plants, small, greenish, inconspicuous, borne in the middle of the leaflike branches. Fruit a bright red (rarely, yellow) berry ½ in. (13 mm) in diameter. Useful for winter decoration, since the leaflike branches do not fall as would true leaves. Europe. Zone 8.

Salix
Willow family
Salicaceae

Say'licks. Willow. A huge group of quick-growing, often brittle-wooded shrubs and trees. About 300 species are known, chiefly from the cooler parts of the north temperate zone, but a few appear in the southern hemisphere.

Description
Leaves alternate, usually narrow, mostly lance-shaped and tapering at both ends. Male and female flowers on separate plants, both in catkins that bloom before or when the leaves expand. Petals and sepals none, the flowers thus naked, but each flower borne in the axil of a bract, the collection of which forms the catkin (the female is the familiar Pussy Willow). Fruit a 2-valved capsule.

How to Grow
Although willows usually grow best in moist places, most of them will do well in any ordinary garden soil. They are fast growing and may be pruned at any time of the year. Willows are probably the easiest of all plants to propagate. Cuttings will root almost anywhere, but are best placed in moist sand.

discolor *p. 169*
Common Pussy Willow. A shrub or small tree, 10–20 ft. (3–6 m) high. Leaves elliptic or oblongish, 3–4 in. (7.5–10.0 cm) long, finely wavy-toothed or without teeth, bluish green beneath. The 1 in. (2.5 cm) female catkins can be forced easily by bringing them into a warm room in midwinter.
E. North America. Blooms in spring.
Zone 3.

gracilistyla *p. 169*
Rosegold Pussy Willow. A shrub, 4–10 ft. (1.2–3.0 m) high, the twigs grayish-hairy. Leaves narrow, 2–4 in. (5–10 cm) long, one-quarter as wide, faintly toothed, bluish green and softly hairy beneath. Male catkins pinkish or reddish, showy, 1¼ in. (3 cm) long, the anthers orange. Japan and Korea. Blooms in spring. Zone 6.

'Melanostachys' *p. 168*
Black Pussy Willow. A shrub, 6–10 ft. (1.8–3.0 m) high, unusual for the purple-black color of the winter stems. The flowers are also purple-black, with red

anthers that turn to yellow. Japan. Blooms in spring. Zone 5.

***sachalinensis* 'Sekka'** *p. 168*
Japanese Fantail Willow. A shrub or small tree, 10–15 ft. (3.0–4.5 m) high. Leaves lance-shaped, to 6 in. (15 cm) long. 'Sekka' is a male cultivar whose branchlets are sometimes flattened and contorted. It is often used in dried arrangements. Species from Japan and Sakhalin Islands. Blooms in spring. Zone 5.

Sambucus

Honeysuckle family
Caprifoliaceae

Sam-bew'kus. Elder, elderberry. Twenty species of attractive shrubs, grown for their masses of flowers or, in the case of a few species, for their fruit, which is used for making both wine and jelly.

Description
Stems with thick pith and opposite, compound leaves, the leaflets arranged pinnately, all toothed. Flowers small, white, in terminal, much-branched, often flat-topped corymbs or panicles. Corolla small, wheel-shaped, the calyx very small or undeveloped. Fruit berrylike, with 3-5 one-seeded nutlets.

How to Grow
All species are easy to grow in any soil, although most do best in moist sites. Since elders are inclined to be sprawling, they are well suited to informal shrub borders. If they become overgrown, prune them down to the ground and they will renew quickly. Propagate by cuttings or by suckers, which are very common in most of them.

canadensis *pp. 232, 233*
American Elder; American Elderberry. A very common North American shrub, 6–10 ft. (1.8–3.0 m) high, its branches brittle. Leaflets mostly 7, short-stalked, 2–6 in. (5–15 cm) long, tapering at the tip. Flowers small, 1/10 in. (2.5 mm) wide, the cluster slightly convex but essentially flat-topped, nearly 4 in. (10 cm) across. Fruit purple-black, 1/6 in. (4 mm) in diameter. There are golden-leaved varieties, and the cultivar 'Acutiloba' has dissected leaflets. All

forms tolerate city conditions better than most shrubs. E. North America. Blooms in summer. Zone 4.

nigra *p. 232*
European Elder. A shrub, to 30 ft. (9 m) high, sometimes treelike. Leaflets mostly 5, elliptic to ovalish, short-stalked, 2–5 in. (5.0–12.5 cm) long. Flowers yellowish white, heavy-scented, the essentially flat-topped cluster 3 in. (7.5 cm) wide. Fruit black, ¼ in. (6 mm) in diameter. Eurasia and n. Africa. Blooms in spring. Zone 6.

pubens *p. 233*
American Red Elder; Scarlet Elder. A spreading shrub, 8–12 ft. (2.4–3.5 m) high. Leaflets 5-7, generally ovalish or oblongish, 2–4 in. (5–10 cm) long. Flower cluster pyramid-shaped, 1 to 4 in. (10 cm) long. Fruit scarlet, inedible. Common in moist, mountain woods. E. North America, but west to Oreg. Blooms in spring. Zone 4.

Santolina
Daisy family
Compositae

San-to-ly′na. Evergreen, aromatic subshrubs. Most of the 8 species, which are from the Mediterranean region, are useful as ground covers or low hedges.

Description
Leaves alternate, finely divided. Solitary, globe-shaped, yellow flower heads, all without ray flowers.

How to Grow
Santolina is easy to grow in a well-drained, dry soil in full sun. Fertile soil and too much water will cause the plant to become leggy. In any case, some pruning should be done to shape the plant. Do this after flowering if you want flowers; some gardeners prune the flowers off, considering them a distraction from the silver-gray foliage. Propagate by cuttings in spring.

chamaecyparissus *pp. 182, 183*
Lavender Cotton. A silver-gray evergreen woody perennial or subshrub, 1–2 ft. (30–60 cm) high. Leaves cut into very narrow segments. Flowerheads solitary, ¾ in. (19 mm) wide, terminal, the stalk 6 in.

(15 cm) long. S. Europe. Blooms in summer. Zone 6.

Sarcococca
Box family
Buxaceae

Sar-ko-kok′a. Sweet Box. A small group of Asiatic and Malayan evergreen shrubs grown mostly on the Pacific Coast and in the South for their foliage and black or red fruits.

Description
Closely related to *Buxus* but with alternate and longer leaves. Leaves stalked, without marginal teeth, rather leathery. Flowers small, whitish, without petals, the male and female separate on the same plant. Fruit black or dark red, fleshy, berrylike, with 1 or 2 seeds.

How to Grow
Plant sweet box in a well-drained, fertile soil in partial to full shade. Add organic matter for best growth. New stems are produced from the rootstock throughout the life of these plants, so prune out the old stems in early spring to allow vigorous young stems to develop. Propagate by cuttings or seeds.

hookerana *p. 271*
Himalayan Sarcococca. A rhizomatous shrub with erect branches, to 6 ft. (1.8 m) high, twigs hairy when young. Leaves elliptic to lance-shaped, 1–4 in. (2.5–10.0 cm) long. Fruits fleshy, to ⅜ in. (9 mm) long, purple to black. Tibet to the e. Himalayas. Zone 7. Var. *humilis* has stems ½–2 ft. (15–60 cm) high and is considered hardier than the species. China. Zone 6.

Skimmia
Citrus family
Rutaceae

Skim′i-a. Somewhat tender Asiatic evergreen shrubs, several species grown for their showy flowers and attractive foliage and fruit.

Description
Leaves alternate, short-stalked, dotted, without marginal teeth, decidedly aromatic when crushed. Flowers small, white, some of

them unisexual. The male flowers are larger than the others, very fragrant and borne in larger panicles. Female flowers usually have 4-5 sterile stamens. Fruit red, berrylike.

How to Grow
The skimmias are good plants for partially to fully shaded areas. Plant them in moist, acid soil with a liberal dose of organic matter added. Be sure you have both male and female flowers if you expect berries. Propagate by seeds or by fall cuttings over bottom-heat.

japonica *pp. 230, 231*
Japanese Skimmia. A low, densely branching shrub, 3–5 ft. (0.9–1 5 m) high, or often less. Leaves more or less crowded at the ends of the twigs, elliptic or oblongish, 3–5 in. (7.5–12.5 cm) long, yellowish green. Male and female flowers usually on different plants, yellowish white, ⅓ in. (8 mm) wide. Fruit nearly round, ⅓ in. (8 mm) thick, bright red. Japan. Blooms in spring. Zone 8.

Sorbaria
Rose family
Rosaceae

Sor-bair′i-a. False Spirea. Tender or hardy Asiatic deciduous shrubs, similar to *Spiraea,* comprising about 8 species, grown for their columns of flowers that bloom in summer.

Description
Leaves alternate, compound, the leaflets in odd numbers, lance-shaped, with toothed margins. Flowers white, small, numerous, in large branching clusters. Calyx of 5 sepals. Corolla of 5 petals. Stamens many. Pistils 5, joined at the base.

How to Grow
False spireas grow best in full sun or partial shade in moist, rich soil, but they will tolerate poor soil. Give them plenty of room and do not place them near choice low-growing shrubs, since they spread quickly. Prune as necessary, in early spring or after flowering. Propagate by seeds or by hardwood or root cuttings.

sorbifolia *p. 144*
Ural False Spirea. Hardy shrub, to 10 ft. (3 m) high. Leaflets 13–21, lance-shaped,

sometimes hairy on the underside. Flowers white, in dense, erect branching clusters 4–10 in. (10–25 cm) long. N. Asia. Zone 3.

Spartium
Pea family
Leguminosae

Spar′shi-um. A single species of essentially leafless shrubs from s. Europe, related to *Genista* and widely planted in warm climates for its profusion of yellow flowers.

Description
Leaves alternate, with 1 leaflet. Flowers yellow, in terminal racemes. Fruit a flat legume.

How to Grow
Plant Spanish Broom in a well-drained, even dry, soil. It will be an open shrub unless you prune it in spring to make it more dense. Propagate by seeds or softwood cuttings rooted in the greenhouse.

junceum *p. 180*
Spanish Broom; Weaver's Broom. A shrub with grooved, rushlike stems, 6–8 ft. (1.8–2.4 m) high, with alternate, simple leaves (when produced). Flowers fragrant, pealike, 1 in. (2.5 cm) long, mostly in terminal racemes that may be 1½ ft. (45 cm) long, hence very showy. Fruit a flattened pod (legume), 3–4 in. (7.5–10.0 cm) long and hairy. Plant parts are poisonous. S. Europe. Blooms summer to fall, or all year in Calif. Zone 8.

Spiraea
Rose family
Rosaceae

Spy-ree′a. Spirea. An important and valuable genus of handsome, flowering, deciduous shrubs, comprising nearly 100 species, mostly from the north temperate zone, but a few southward to Mexico and the Himalayas.

Description
Leaves alternate, mostly toothed or lobed (rarely altogether without teeth), nearly always stalked. Flower clusters usually showy, mostly of umbel-like racemes, sometimes of

panicles or corymbs. Individual flowers small, prevailingly white or pinkish purple, the sepals and petals 5 each. Stamens 15–60. Fruit a dry pod.

How to Grow
The garden spireas are very easy to grow, since they thrive in a variety of soils and under all sorts of exposures, with less attention than many other flowering shrubs. The best site is a reasonably moist one in open sunshine. Most species require little pruning, unless they happen to winter-kill, in which case they will come back after being pruned close to the ground. They are also easy to transplant. Propagate by seeds, sown when ripe or stratified; or by softwood cuttings in the greenhouse. Many can be easily layered, because they tend to arch over and root at the tips.

× ***bumalda*** *p. 142*
Bumald Spirea. Not over 3 ft. (90 cm) high, the twigs striped. Leaves ovalish or lance-shaped, doubly toothed. Flowers white to dark pink, in clusters 4–6 in. (10–15 cm) wide. Cultivar 'Froebelii', a taller plant with bright crimson flowers, is more often available in the nurseries, as is 'Anthony Waterer', perhaps the most popular of all late-flowering spireas. It is more compact and has narrower leaves and bright crimson flowers. Other varieties are offered, such as 'Gold Flame', with red, copper, and orange new foliage that becomes yellow to yellow green in summer. All bloom in late summer. Zone 4.

japonica *p. 143*
Japanese Spirea. An upright shrub, 4–6 ft. (1.2–1.8 m) high. Leaves ovalish or oblong, wedge-shaped at the base, 1–4 in. (2.5–10.0 cm) long, hairy on the veins beneath. Flowers pink, in much-branched, rather loose corymbs 3 in. (7.5 cm) long. Plants offered as *S. callosa* are *S. japonica.* There are many forms, including var. *alpina,* 1½–2½ ft. (45–75 cm) tall, which is daintier than the species. It is compact and wide spreading, making it useful as a massing or ground cover shrub. Japan. Blooms in spring. Zone 4.

nipponica **'Snowmound'** *p. 150*
Snowmound Spirea. Arching shrub, 4–6 ft. (1.2–1.8 m) high. Leaves elliptic, to 1¼ in. (3 cm) long. Flowers white, in hemispherical

clusters 1½–2 in. (4–5 cm) wide. Japan. Blooms in spring. Zone 4.

× ***vanhouttei*** *p. 151*

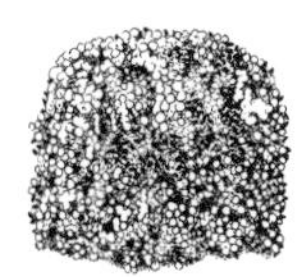

Vanhoutte Spirea. A slender shrub, 6–8 ft. (1.8–2.4 m) high, with beautifully arching branches. Leaves somewhat angularly ovalish, pointed at the tip, to 1½ in. (4 cm) long, pale beneath. Flowers pure white, very numerous, in many-flowered umbels 1–2 in. (2.5–5.0 cm) wide. One of the most commonly cultivated spireas in America, this hybrid tolerates city conditions better than most. Blooms in late spring. Zone 4.

Staphylea

Bladdernut family
Staphyleaceae

Staf-eye-lee′a. Eleven species of shrubs or small trees of the north temperate zone grown for their flowers and fruit.

Description

Leaves opposite, compound, the leaflets arranged pinnately. Flowers white or greenish white, not very showy, arranged in a terminal panicle. Sepals, petals, and stamens, each 5. Fruit an inflated (hence the common name), membranous, usually 3-sided capsule, the seeds bony. The plants are more showy in fruit than in flower.

How to Grow

The species below prefers partial shade and a reasonably moist, rich soil. It is easy to propagate by sowing fresh seeds or by cuttings.

colchica *pp. 100, 101*

Colchis Bladdernut. Usually a shrub, 8–12 ft. (2.4–3.5 m) high. Leaflets 5, or 3 on flowering twigs, oval-oblong, to 3½ in. (9 cm) long, sharply toothed. Flower cluster 2–4 in. (5–10 cm) long, erect or a little pendulous. Flowers ¾ in. (19 mm) wide, greenish white. Fruit much inflated, 2–4 in. (5–10 cm) long. Caucasus. Blooms in late spring. Zone 5.

Stephanandra
Rose family
Rosaceae

Steff-a-nan′dra. Asiatic deciduous shrubs, several species grown for their finely cut foliage and arching habit.

Description
Leaves alternate, more or less lobed and toothed. Flowers small, white, in terminal panicles or corymbs. Calyx cup-shaped, its lobes 5. Petals 5, about the length of the calyx lobes. Stamens 10-20. Fruit a dry pod, with 1-2 shining seeds.

How to Grow
Stephanandras are easy to grow in ordinary garden soil. Consider planting them toward the edges of a shrub border, where their fine foliage can be appreciated. They are easy to propagate by cuttings or by division.

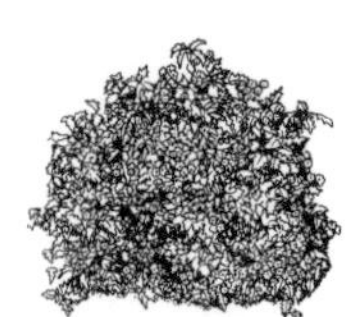

incisa *p. 281*
Cutleaf Stephanandra. An arching shrub, 5–8 ft. (1.5–2.4 m) high, the stems often drooping. Leaves ovalish, long-pointed, 2–2½ in. (5–6 cm) long, lobed almost to the middle, the lobes toothed, reddish purple in the fall. Flowers greenish white, in panicles 1½–2½ in. (4–6 cm) long, the stamens 10. Sometimes offered as *S. flexuosa.* 'Crispa' is a smaller-growing form that is an excellent facer plant, bank cover, or ground cover. Japan and Korea. Blooms in late spring. Zone 4.

Symphoricarpos
Honeysuckle family
Caprifoliaceae

Sim-for-i-kar′pos. Hardy, deciduous, ornamental shrubs, more showy in fruit than in flower. All are American, except for one Chinese species.

Description
Leaves opposite, short-stalked, usually without teeth or lobes. Flowers small, not very showy, mostly in small clusters that are terminal or in the leaf axils. Corolla not over ⅓ in. (8 mm) long, bell-shaped or tubular, the limb 4- to 5-lobed. Stamens 4–5. Fruit a 2-seeded berry, usually borne in pairs or small clusters.

How to Grow
These are excellent shrubs for partly shady or open places and are far more tolerant of city conditions than many other ornamental plants. They will grow in a variety of soils but prefer slightly alkaline ones. Propagate by softwood cuttings.

albus *p. 238*
Snowberry; Waxberry. To 4 ft. (120 cm) high, the branches slender and upright. Leaves ovalish or oblong, 1–2 in. (2.5–5.0 cm) long, blunt. Flowers pinkish. Fruit white. Var. *laevigatus* is nearly twice as tall and has leaves ½–1¼ in. (1.3–3.0 cm) long. Quebec to British Columbia, southward to W.Va., Colo., and Calif. Blooms in spring. Zone 3.

× ***chenaultii*** *p. 239*
Chenault Coralberry. A shrub, 3–6 ft. (0.9–1.8 m) high, the leaves hairy beneath. Flowers pinkish. Fruit white, turning pink on side exposed to the sun. Blooms in spring. Zone 5.

orbiculatus *p. 257*
Indian Currant; Coralberry. A shrub, 3–5 ft. (0.9–1.5 m) high, the branches erect. Leaves elliptic or ovalish, 1½–2½ in. (4–6 cm) long, pale and hairy beneath. Flowers white. Fruit reddish, plentiful. Very attractive in fall with its profusion of fruit and long-persistent crimson foliage. 'Leucocarpus' has greenish-yellow flowers and white fruit. It thrives in poor soil and partial shade. Pa. to Ga. and westward to S. Dak. and Tex. Blooms in summer. Zone 3.

Symplocos
Symplocos family
Symplocaceae

Sim-plo′kos. A large genus of 280 species of trees and shrubs found in most tropical and warm regions, at least one in the se. U.S. The species below is cultivated for its profuse, azure-blue berries in fall.

Description
Leaves alternate, evergreen in some species. Flowers usually small and inconspicuous, but pleasantly fragrant, mostly in stalked or nearly stalkless clusters. Calyx 5-lobed. Corolla 5- to 10-lobed, or with as many

nearly distinct petals. Stamens 15 or more, often in bunches and fastened to the corolla. Fruit orange or blue, berrylike, its stone 1- to 5-seeded.

How to Grow
Plant Sapphire Berry in a well-drained soil that is slightly alkaline in full sun. This plant is difficult to propagate because the seeds germinate erratically even after stratification. Softwood cuttings under glass will grow more easily.

paniculata *pp. 256, 257*
Sapphire Berry. A shrub or small tree, 10–20 ft. (3–6 m) high. Leaves short-stalked, oblongish, 2–3 in. (5.0–7.5 cm) long, the margins finely toothed. Flowers fragrant, white, the clusters 2–3 in. (5.0–7.5 cm) long. Corolla ⅓ in. (8 mm) long. Fruit ½ in. (13 mm) long, bright blue. Japan, China, southward to the Himalayas. Blooms in late spring. Zone 4.

Syringa
Olive family
Oleaceae

Sir-ring′a. Lilac. A large group of decorative, deciduous shrubs and trees from the Old World. Lilacs have long been popular for their fragrant, late-spring blossoms.

Description
Leaves opposite, usually unlobed. Flowers in showy clusters, tubular, with 4 spreading lobes and 2 stamens. They may be white, pink, lavender, or purple and are often fragrant. The fruit is, in most cases, a brown, flattened, oval capsule.

How to Grow
Lilacs will grow in any well-drained soil, but they should be fertilized every 2 years. Old blossoms should be removed as soon as they begin to fade. Pruning can be done any time during the winter by removing all weak wood that does not bear large flower buds or still carries last year's fruit. If you do this every 3 years, a regular sequence of bloom will result. The first year the quantity will be reduced, but each cluster will be very large. The second season there will be more and larger flowers, and the third year still more clusters, but smaller than those produced

the first year. You may prefer to prune more lightly every 2 years, if quality of bloom is more important to you than quantity. Propagate lilacs by softwood cuttings taken in spring.

× ***chinensis*** *pp. 75, 77*
Chinese Lilac. A shrub, usually densely branched, rarely over 10 ft. (3 m) high. Leaves ovalish, 2 in. (5 cm) long, smooth, with a tapering tip. Flowers fragrant, lilac-purple, in clusters 4–6 in. (10–15 cm) long, looser than in the Common Lilac. Zone 4.

meyeri *p. 74*
Meyer Lilac. A handsome lilac with a dense, broad, mounded habit, 4–8 ft. (1.2–2.4 m) high. Flowers are violet-purple, contained in panicles 4 in. (10 cm) long. One of the best lilacs for total flower effect. 'Palibin' is a compact form that is usually offered in the trade as *S. meyeri.* China. Zones 4–8.

microphylla *p. 75*
Littleleaf Lilac. A spreading, slender-branched shrub, growing 7 ft. (2.1 m) high. Leaves ½–3 in. (1.3–7.5 cm) long, roundish-ovate, hairy beneath. Flowers lilac, fragrant, small, in short clusters 1–3 in. (2.5–7.5 cm) long. This species is distinguished by the small size of its leaves and flowers. 'Superba' has profuse, deep pink flowers. China. Zone 5.

***patula* 'Miss Kim'** *p. 73*
Miss Kim Lilac. A small shrub, 4–8 ft. (1.2–2.4 m) high, the leaves elliptic to oblongish, 2–3 in. (5.0–7.5 cm) long, about half as wide, the leafstalk and twigs often glandular, the lower surface of the leaf densely hairy. Flowers in hairy panicles 3 in. (7.5 cm) long, lilac, fading to almost white. Also called *S. palibiniana* and *S. velutina.* Korea and n. China. Zone 4.

× ***persica*** *p. 74*
Persian Lilac. A compact shrub with slender, arching branches, usually 5–6 ft. (1.5–1.8 m) high, though occasionally higher. Leaves lance-shaped, 2½ in. (6 cm) long and sometimes lobed or divided. Flowers pale lilac, fragrant, in short, broad clusters 3 in. (7.5 cm) long. Iran to nw. China. Zone 4.

reticulata *p. 72*
Japanese Tree Lilac. Shrub or tree, to 30 ft. (9 m) high, with smooth, glossy, dark brown

bark. Leaves egg-shaped, to 5 in. (12.5 cm) long, hairy beneath. Flowers white, malodorous, in clusters to 12 in. (30 cm) long, appearing in June. Japan. Zone 4.

villosa *p. 73*
Late Lilac. An upright, strong-growing shrub, to 10 ft. (3 m) high. Leaves 3–6 in. (7.5–15.0 cm) long, more or less oval and pointed at the ends, whitish beneath. The flowers are lilac-pink or paler, borne in terminal clusters 3–7 in. (7.5–17.5 cm) long after most of the other lilacs have passed. China. Zone 3.

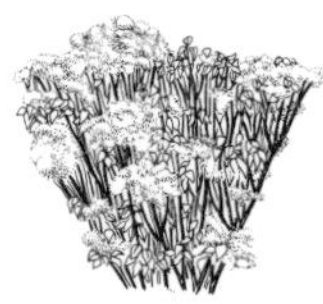

vulgaris *pp. 72, 76*
Common Lilac. A handsome, widely cultivated shrub growing 15 ft. (4.5 m) high, sometimes becoming a small tree. The leaves are heart-shaped to oval, 2–6 in. (5–15 cm) long. The flowers are in clusters 6–8 in. (15–20 cm) long, very fragrant and usually lilac. There are many forms, with white, pink, blue, and purple flowers. Se. Europe. Zone 4.

Syzygium
Myrtle family
Myrtaceae

Sigh-zi′gee-um. A genus of 400-500 species of evergreen trees or shrubs, mostly native to the Old World tropics.

Description
Leaves opposite, simple, and pinnately veined, deep green, often tinged with a coppery color. Flowers with tufts of stamens, giving a brushy look. Fruit a soft and edible berry.

How to Grow
Plant Brush Cherry in well-drained soil in full sun or partial shade. It is useful as a hedge, but requires frequent clipping, and its heavy root system may compete with those of plants nearby. The leaves will be damaged at temperatures below 25° F (−4° C). Propagate by seeds or cuttings.

paniculatum *p. 283*
Brush Cherry. A widely popular ornamental tree, to 40 ft. (12 m) high, but often maintained as a shrub. Leaves oblongish, 2–3 in. (5.0–7.5 cm) long, tapering both

ends, bronzy when young. Flowers ½–1 in. (1.3–2.5 cm) wide, white, the stamens numerous and showy. Fruit edible, purple, ½ in. (13 mm) in diameter. 'Globulus' is a compact form. Often sold as *Eugenia myrtifolia.* Australia. Blooms in spring. Zone 10.

Tamarix

Tamarisk family
Tamaricaceae

Tam'a-ricks. The tamarisks comprise an interesting group of shrubs and trees, all of the about 55 species from Eurasia or Asia Minor. Many of them are salt tolerant, semidesert plants that grow naturally in pure sand.

Description
Very slender branches, the twigs completely covered by the small, scale-like leaves, with which they are shed in fall. Leaves very small, hugging the twigs, scarcely more than 1⁄16 in. (1.6 mm) long, giving a light, feathery effect. Flowers very small, mostly crowded in dense racemes that are grouped in terminal panicles. Fruit a minute capsule.

How to Grow
Tamarisks grow best in full sun and well-drained, acid soil, but they seem to tolerate varied soil conditions. They are particularly suited to seaside plantings because of their salt tolerance. Prune in the early spring, since flowering occurs on branches that develop after the buds break. The root system is especially wide-spreading, so be careful what kind of plants you place near tamarisks. Propagate by cuttings rooted in moist sand.

ramosissima *p. 96*
Five-stamen Tamarisk. A shrub, 10–15 ft. (3.0–4.5 m) high, the foliage purplish. Flowers pink or rose-pink, mostly in dense racemes, which are grouped in a large terminal panicle 1–3 in. (2.5–7.5 cm) long on growth of the current year. Eurasia. Blooms in early summer. Zone 3.

Ternstroemia
Tea family
Theaceae

Tern-stro′mee-a. Tropical evergreen trees and shrubs comprising about 85 species, one of which is grown for its ornamental foliage.

Description
Leaves leathery, simple, spirally arranged. Flowers inconspicuous. Fruit berrylike.

How to Grow
Ternstroemia does best in sun or partial shade but tolerates heavier shade. It requires acid soil. In full sun, provide plenty of moisture. Pinch out the growing tips to produce compact growth. These plants are easy to transplant and to propagate by cuttings.

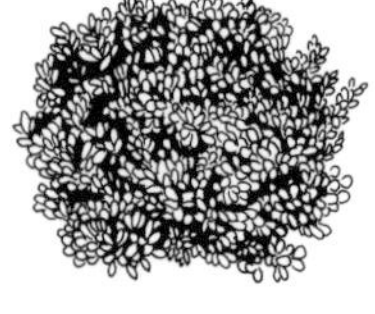

gymnanthera *pp. 236, 237*
Ternstroemia. Usually a low-growing landscape shrub 4–10 ft. (1.2–3.0 m) high. Leaves oval, to 3 in. (7.5 cm) long, glossy, deep green in the shade but almost purple in full sun. Flowers to ½ in. (13 mm) wide, yellowish, borne in leaf axils, fragrant. Fruit ½ in. (13 mm) wide, yellowish or reddish. Also listed as *T. japonica.* India to Japan. Blooms in summer. Zone 7.

Tibouchina
Meadow-beauty family
Melastomataceae

Ti-boo-ky′na. Spiderflower; Glory Bush. Chiefly Brazilian bristly or hairy shrubs, the species here grown in mild climates for its velvety, green leaves and vivid purple flowers.

Description
Leaves simple, flowers large, with 5 petals and 10 stamens. Fruit a capsule.

How to Grow
The Princess Flower will grow best in a well-drained, acid soil. The roots must be kept cool, but the shoots need sun, so place mulch around the plant. Fertilize in spring and after flowering. To reduce legginess, prune after each bloom cycle. Pinch the shoot tips to promote a denser habit. Propagate by cuttings.

urvilleana *p. 128*
Princess Flower; Glory Bush. A handsome, but straggly, hairy shrub, 4–15 ft. (1.2–4.5 m) high, with opposite, densely hairy, ovalish-oblong leaves, 2–4 in. (5–10 cm) long, pale beneath, and with 3-7 main vines. Flowers showy, 3–4 in. (7.5–10.0 cm) wide, solitary or in few terminal clusters, beneath them 2 nearly round bracts. Petals 5, violet or reddish purple. Stamens 10, of unequal length, some of them sticky-hairy. Fruit a 5-valved capsule, surrounded by the calyx tube. Blooms year-round. Zones 9–10.

Vaccinium
Heath family
Ericaceae

Vak-sin′i-um. A very large genus of erect or prostrate shrubs, one grown for ornament, containing both the blueberry and cranberry. Over 150 species range from the Arctic Circle to the summits of tropical mountains.

Description
Leaves alternate, short-stalked, often minutely hairy on the margins. Flowers generally small, not showy, urn-shaped in the blueberries. Stamens 8 or 10. Fruit a many-seeded berry, crowned with the often persistent lobes of the calyx.

How to Grow
Plant Highbush Blueberry in a moist, well-drained, acid soil in sun or partial shade. Mulch around the plants to keep weeds down and to avoid possible damage to the roots, which are close to the surface. Prune plants after fruiting. Propagate by seed or by softwood cuttings in late spring. Transplant as a container or balled-and-burlapped plant.

corymbosum *pp. 258, 259*
Highbush Blueberry. A spreading, bushy shrub, 8–12 ft. (2.4–3.5 m) high, the young twigs yellowish green and warty. Leaves ovalish or elliptic, 2–3 in. (5.0–7.5 cm) long, turning yellow to red in fall. Flowers ⅓ in. (8 mm) long, urn-shaped, white or pinkish. Fruit bluish black, with a powdery bloom. There are a number of cultivars grown for ornament. E. North America, in the swamps or bogs. Blooms in spring. Zone 4.

Viburnum
Honeysuckle family
Caprifoliaceae

Vy-bur′num. A large and valuable genus of shrubs and small trees, many of the 225 known species cultivated for their attractive spring flower clusters and their often showy fruits. They are chiefly deciduous shrubs of the north temperate zone.

Description
Leaves opposite, small, usually with beautiful flowers, generally white, in showy terminal panicles or cymes. Calyx with 5 very small teeth. Corolla bell- or wheel-shaped, or even tubular. Stamens 5. Fruit 1-seeded, fleshy, berrylike, often handsomely colored, persistent, and a favorite food of birds.

How to Grow
The viburnums are generally easy to grow and consequently widely popular. They prefer moist, well-drained, slightly acid soil. Prune after flowering if necessary. Propagate by stratified seeds, cuttings, or by layering.

× ***burkwoodii*** *p. 227*
Burkwood Viburnum. An evergreen (or partly so) shrub, often reaching a height of 6 ft. (1.8 m). Leaves half-evergreen, glossy above but hairy beneath, and with brown veins. Flowers fragrant, white, the cluster nearly 3 in. (7.5 cm) wide. Fruit red, changing to black. Zone 4.

× ***carlcephalum*** *p. 227*
Carlcephalum Viburnum. A deciduous shrub 6–10 ft. (1.8–3.0 m) high, with the rounded habit and the foliage of *V. carlesii.* Flowers very fragrant, white in 5-in. (12.5-cm) clusters. Fruit red, changing to black. One of the latest species to flower. Zone 5.

carlesii *p. 226*
Koreanspice Viburnum. A deciduous shrub, to 5 ft. (1.5 m) high. Leaves ovalish, to 4 in. (10 cm) long, hairy both sides. Flowers fragrant, white or pinkish, the cymes to 3 in. (7.5 cm) wide. Fruit red, changing to bluish black. Korea. Zone 5.

davidii *p. 229*
David Viburnum. An evergreen, compact shrub, to 4 ft. (120 cm) high, the twigs warty. Leaves more or less elliptic, 3–6 in. (7.5–15.0 cm) long, 3-veined, sometimes

faintly toothed on the margin. Flowers dirty white, very small, packed in a flat corymb 2–3 in. (5.0–7.5 cm) wide. Fruit showy, nearly round, ¼ in. (6 mm) long, blue. China. Blooms in late spring. Zone 8.

dentatum *p. 228*
Arrowwood. A shrub, 10–15 ft. (3.0–4.5 m) high. Leaves ovalish or round, 2–3 in. (5.0–7.5 cm) long, coarsely toothed. Flowers in long-stalked cymes that are 3 in. (7.5 cm) wide. Fruit showy, bluish black. This species makes a good, if informal, hedge. E. U. S. Blooms in late spring. Zone 3.

dilatatum *pp. 218, 223*
Linden Viburnum. A shrub, 6–10 ft. (1.8–3.0 m) high. Leaves nearly round, 4–5 in. (10.0–12.5 cm) wide, hairy both sides and coarsely toothed. Flower clusters 5 in. (12.5 cm) wide. Fruit showy, scarlet. An attractive shrub in the fall, for the fruit is long-persistent. Japan. Blooms in late spring. Zones 5–8.

× ***juddii*** *p. 226*
Judd Viburnum. Similar to *V. carlesii,* 6–8 ft. (1.8–2.4 m) high, with a slightly wider flower cluster, pink in the bud but ultimately white and very fragrant. Zone 5.

lantana *p. 219*
Wayfaring-tree Viburnum. A treelike shrub, 10–15 ft. (3.0–4.5 m) high. Leaves ovalish, 3–5 in. (7.5–12.5 cm) long, hairy both sides, coarsely toothed. Flower clusters nearly 4 in. (10 cm) wide. Fruit red, but later turning black. Useful as informal hedge. Eurasia, but naturalized in the e. U.S. Blooms in late spring. Zone 4.

lentago *p. 218*
Nannyberry; Sheepberry. A shrub, but more often treelike, 20–30 ft. (6–9 m) high. Leaves ovalish, 3–4 in. (7.5–10.0 cm) long, finely toothed. Flower clusters nearly 5 in. (12.5 cm) wide, stalkless. Fruit bluish black, with a slight bloom. North America. Blooms in late spring. Zone 3.

opulus *p. 224*
European Cranberrybush Viburnum. A shrub, 7–12 ft. (2.1–3.5 m) high. Leaves maplelike, 3- to 5-lobed, 3½ in. (9 cm) wide, hairy on the underside. Flower clusters nearly 4 in. (10 cm) wide, stalked, the outer flowers nearly ¾ in. (19 mm) wide and sterile. Fruit

red. Eurasia and n. Africa. Blooms in spring. Zone 4. 'Nanum' is a dwarf cultivar, 3 ft. (90 cm) high, that tolerates shade but seldom flowers. It is useful as a low hedge. Cultivar 'Roseum', Common Snowball or Guelder Rose, is 6–10 ft. (1.8–3.0 m) tall and by far the most common in cultivation. Its ball-like flower clusters are 3–4 in. (7.5–10.0 cm) wide and wholly made up of sterile flowers. The plant is sometimes offered as *V. opulus* var. *sterile.* All forms are useful in cities, since they tolerate that atmosphere very well. Zone 4.

plicatum **var.** ***tomentosum*** *pp. 222, 225*
Doublefile Viburnum. A deciduous shrub, 8–10 ft. (2.4–3.0 m) high, with horizontal branches. Leaves to 4 in. (10 cm) long. Flowers creamy white, in flat clusters, to 3 in. (7.5 cm) wide, only those on the edge sterile. Fruit red, changing to black. Very good reddish-purple fall color. More popular than the species, which has round clusters. China and Japan. Zone 5.

× ***pragense*** *p. 216*
Prague Viburnum. Grows 10–12 ft. (3.0–3.5 m) high. Leaves dark green, evergreen in warm climates. Flowers creamy-white, in clusters 2–3 in. (5.0–7.5 cm) wide. Hybrid derived from *V. rhytidophyllum* and *V. utile.* Zone 6.

prunifolium *pp. 216, 217*
Black Haw; Stagbush. A shrub or small tree, 10–15 ft. (3.0–4.5 m) high. Leaves broadly ovalish, 2–3 in. (5.0–7.5 cm) long, finely toothed. Flower clusters nearly 4 in. (10 cm) wide, stalkless. Fruit white at first, turning bluish black, with a slight bloom. Conn. to Fla. and westward. Zone 4.

× ***rhytidophylloides*** *p. 220*
Lantanaphyllum Viburnum. Like *V. rhytidophyllum,* but hardier and with broader and smoother leaves. Flower clusters 3–4 in. (7.5–10.0 cm) wide. Hybrid derived from *V. lantana* × *V. rhytidophyllum.* Zone 5.

rhytidophyllum *p. 219*
Leatherleaf Viburnum. An evergreen shrub, 10–15 ft. (3.0–4.5 m) high. Leaves ovalish or oblong, 5–7 in. (12.5–17.5 cm) long, nearly without marginal teeth, wrinkled above. Flowers yellowish white, the clusters nearly 8 in. (20 cm) wide. Fruit red, later black. China. Blooms in late spring. Zone 5.

sargentii *p. 220*
Sargent Viburnum. 10–15 ft. (3.0–4.5 m) high, resembling *V. opulus,* but with darker bark, thicker and sometimes larger leaves, and 4-in. (10-cm), sterile flowers. Ne. Asia. Zone 4.

setigerum *p. 221*
Tea Viburnum. A deciduous shrub, 7–12 ft. (2.1–3.5 m) high, the twigs smooth. Leaves stalked, ovalish or oblong, 3–5 in. (7.5–12.5 cm) long, faintly toothed or toothless, hairy on the veins beneath. Flowers white, in a cluster about 2 in. (5 cm) wide. Calyx purple. Fruit red. China. Blooms in late spring. Zone 5.

sieboldii *p. 223*
Siebold Viburnum. A deciduous shrub, to 20 ft. (6 m) high. Leaves elliptic, toothed, hairy beneath, to 6 in. (15 cm) long. White flowers in branching clusters to 4 in. (10 cm) long. Fruit rose-red, changing to black. Zone 4.

suspensum *p. 221*
Sandankwa Viburnum. An evergreen shrub, 6–12 ft. (1.8–3.5 m) high. Leaves ovalish, 3–4 in. (7.5–10.0 cm) long, toothed toward the tip. Flower cluster dense, fragrant, pinkish, 1½ in. (4 cm) wide. Fruit red, or black when mature. Tolerates drought. Ryukyu Island. Zone 9.

tinus *p. 229*
Laurustinus. A handsome evergreen shrub, 7–10 ft. (2.1–3.0 m) high. Leaves oblongish or broader, 2–3 in. (5.0–7.5 cm) long, without marginal teeth, dark green. Flower clusters 3 in. (7.5 cm) wide, often faintly pinkish, unpleasantly scented. Fruit metallic blue, turing black. Mediterranean region. Long in cultivation and popular in the South and Calif.; there are several horticultural forms, one with variegated leaves. Useful as a hedge. Blooms winter to spring. Zone 7.

trilobum *p. 222*
American Cranberry Bush. A shrub, 8–12 ft. (2.4–3.5 m) high. Leaves broadly oval, 3-lobed and toothed, 3–5 in. (7.5–12.5 cm) long. Flower cluster short-stalked, nearly 4 in. (10 cm) wide, the marginal flowers sterile and larger than the others. Fruit scarlet. Fruit ripens in midsummer and persists over most of the winter. Closely related to

V. opulus, but the leaves of *V. trilobum* are smooth on the underside and its fruit makes good jellies. N. North America. Blooms in late spring. Zones 3–7.

wrightii *p. 228*
Wright Viburnum. A sturdy, upright shrub, 7–10 ft. (2.1–3.0 m) high, the leaves nearly round, coarsely toothed and generally smooth. Flowers white, in a short-stalked cyme nearly 4 in. (10 cm) wide. Fruit red, showy, especially when the foliage turns red in fall. Japan. Blooms in late spring. Zone 5.

Vitex

Verbena family
Verbenaceae

Vy-tex. Ornamental trees or shrubs comprising about 270 species found chiefly in the tropical and warmer regions of the world.

Description
Leaves opposite, compound, long-stalked, the leaflets 3–7, arranged palmately, sometimes stalked, often grayish green, and slightly hairy. Flowers small, white, blue, yellowish, or red, in dense, showy terminal spikes. Calyx of 5 sepals. Corolla tubular, 4 of its lobes equal, 1 larger, forming a lip. Stamens 4, two long, two short. Fruit plumlike, 4-seeded.

How to Grow
Plant vitexes in any good garden soil. In the North, they may die back, but the roots will send up new shoots that will flower the same year. Propagate by seeds or by cuttings of young shoots inserted in half sand and half soil, shaded from sun and kept in a cool, humid atmosphere until rooted.

agnus-castus *pp. 78, 79*
Lilac Chaste Tree. Deciduous shrub or small tree, 7–20 ft. (2.1–6.0 m) high. Leaves long-stalked, the leaflets 5–7, lance-shaped, the middle leaflets to 4 in. (10 cm) long, covered with short gray hairs on the underside, pleasantly scented when bruised. Flowers fragrant, lilac-blue, in dense, showy terminal spikes 1 ft. (30 cm) long. Cultivar 'Alba', a white form with larger leaves, is one of the best of the cultivated species.

'Latifolia' has shorter, broader leaves. S. Europe. Blooms in summer. Zone 7.

negundo *pp. 78, 79*
Chaste Tree. Deciduous shrub, growing 10–15 ft. (3.0–4.5 m) high, the branches 4-sided. Leaves long-stalked; leaflets 3-5, broadly lance-shaped, covered with small gray hairs on the underside, the margins sometimes toothed. Flowers lilac, ¼ in. (6 mm) long, stalked, in dense, showy terminal spikes 8 in. (20 cm) long. In the variety *heterophylla,* the leaflets are much cut and the flowers less showy. China and India. Blooms in summer. Zone 7.

Weigela

Honeysuckle family
Caprifoliaceae

Wy-gee'la. Very handsome Asiatic shrubs, most flowering in late spring, comprising about 12 species. They are closely related to *Diervilla,* but differ in the larger, much more showy flowers.

Description
Leaves opposite. Flowers more or less funnel-shaped, 1½ in. (4 cm) long, borne very profusely on short shoots, mostly in clusters of 1–3. Corolla slightly irregular. Stamens 5. Fruit a rather woody 2-valved capsule, splitting from the top downward.

How to Grow
These shrubs are easy to grow in any ordinary garden soil, which, along with their attractive bloom, accounts for their wide popularity. Their flowers are borne on shoots of the season, which start from last year's twigs, so prune them only after flowering. Propagate by cuttings taken in summer and put in moist sand in the cold frame or in boxes under trees.

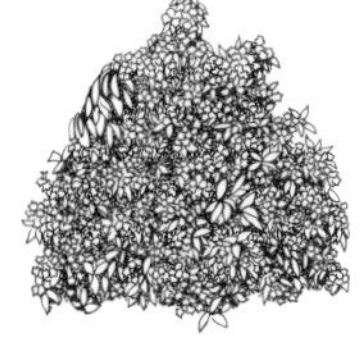

florida *pp. 82, 83*
Old-fashioned Weigela. The most widely planted species, and a shrub 7–10 ft. (2.1–3.0 m) high, the branches spreading. Leaves generally elliptic, tapering at the tip, to 4 in. (10 cm) long, hairy only on the veins beneath. Flowers 1½ in. (4 cm) long, rose-pink in the typical form, but in the many horticultural varieties white, pink, or darker. Korea and n. China. Zone 4.

Xylosma
Indian plum family
Flacourtiaceae

Zy-los′ma. A genus of over 100 species of shrubs and trees, all tropical, some grown for their shiny, yellow-green foliage.

Description
Leaves alternate. Flowers small, unisexual and inconspicuous, without petals. Stamens many, surrounded by a disk. Fruit a 2- to 8-seeded berry.

How to Grow
Easy to grow in most soils in full sun or partial shade. Xylosma is heat and drought tolerant but does best with occasional watering. It responds well to pruning and can be espaliered. It is best to buy small container plants rather than propagate.

congestum *p. 285*
Xylosma. A shrub, to 10 ft. (3 m) high, with the twigs brown-hairy. Spines in the leaf axils slender and sharp. Leaves ovalish, to 3½ in. (9 cm) long, bluntly toothed on the margin. China. Zone 9.

Appendices

Shrub Chart

	Page Numbers	Zone
Abelia 'Edward Goucher'	131	7
Abelia × *grandiflora*	130	5–9
Abeliophyllum distichum	87	5
Acacia longifolia	186, 187	8
Acacia redolens var. *prostrata*	186	9
Acer ginnala	208	2
Acer japonicum	209	6
Acer palmatum 'Dissectum'	208, 209	5
Aesculus parviflora	144	4
Alyogyne huegelii	116	9
Amelanchier stolonifera	86	4
Andromeda polifolia	152	2
Aralia spinosa	230, 231	5
Arctostaphylos uva-ursi	281	2–6
Aronia arbutifolia	196, 197	4
Aronia melanocarpa	196, 197	3
Aucuba japonica	214, 215	7
Baccharis halimifolia	98, 99	6–10
Berberis candidula	266	6–8
Berberis × *chenaultii*	267	6–8
Berberis julianae	266, 267	6–8
Berberis koreana	190, 191	3–7
Berberis × *mentorensis*	192	4–8
Berberis thunbergii	190, 192, 193	4–8
Berberis verruculosa	191	6–8
Brunfelsia pauciflora	128, 129	9
Buddleia alternifolia	150	6–8
Buddleia davidii	148, 149	5–9
Buddleia × *weyeriana* 'Sun Gold'	187	7–10
Buxus microphylla	278, 279	6
Buxus sempervirens	279	5–8
Caesalpinia gilliesii	183	9–10

Under 4 ft.	4–8 ft.	Over 8 ft.	Spring	Summer	Fall	Winter	Dry Soil	Acid Soil	Shade	Evergreen	Fall Color	Showy Fruit	Use for Hedges
	■			■	■			■		■			
	■			■	■			■					
■			■										
		■		■			■						
■			■				■						
		■	■								■		
		■	■								■		
		■			■						■		
		■		■					■				
	■		■	■	■	■	■			■			
	■		■									■	
■			■					■		■			
		■		■								■	
■			■					■		■		■	
	■		■				■				■	■	
■			■				■					■	
		■	■						■	■		■	
		■		■									
■			■							■		■	
■			■							■		■	
	■		■							■		■	■
	■		■				■					■	■
	■		■				■			■		■	■
	■		■							■		■	■
	■		■							■			■
■			■	■				■		■			
		■		■									
		■		■	■								
		■		■									
	■		■							■			■
		■	■							■			■
		■		■						■			

	Page Numbers	Zone
Calliandra haematocephala	94	10
Callicarpa americana	263	7
Callicarpa dichotoma	262	5
Callicarpa japonica	262, 263	6–8
Callistemon citrinus	95	9
Calluna vulgaris	152	5
Calycanthus floridus	92	4
Camellia japonica	120	8
Camellia sasanqua	121	8
Caragana arborescens	178	2
Carissa grandiflora	215	10
Caryopteris × *clandonensis*	154, 155	5
Cassia artemisioides	182	9
Ceanothus cyaneus 'Sierra Blue'	76	8
Ceanothus griseus var. *horizontalis*	77	8
Ceanothus ovatus	137	5
Cephalanthus occidentalis	143	5
Cercis chinensis	82, 83	7
Chaenomeles japonica	110	5
Chaenomeles speciosa	110, 111	5
Chaenomeles × *superba*	111	5
Chimonanthus praecox	165	7
Chionanthus virginicus	88, 89	4
Choisya ternata	136	8
Cistus × *hybridus*	118	8
Cistus ladanifer	117	7
Cistus × *pulverulentus*	119	8
Cistus × *purpureus*	116	8
Clethra alnifolia	145	4
Colutea arborescens	179	6
Comptonia peregrina	184, 185	3
Coprosma repens	280	9

Under 4 ft.	4–8 ft.	Over 8 ft.	Spring	Summer	Fall	Winter	Dry Soil	Acid Soil	Shade	Evergreen	Fall Color	Showy Fruit	Use for Hedges
		■		■	■								
	■		■									■	
■				■								■	
	■			■	■							■	
		■	■	■				■					
■				■	■			■		■			
	■		■						■				
		■	■		■	■		■		■		■	
		■			■	■		■		■		■	
		■	■				■						
		■	■	■	■	■						■	
■				■									
■			■	■			■						
		■	■				■			■			
■			■				■			■			
■			■				■					■	
		■		■									
		■	■										
■			■									■	
		■	■									■	
	■		■									■	
		■				■							
		■	■										
	■		■					■		■			■
■			■	■			■						
■				■			■						
■				■			■						
■				■			■						
	■			■				■					
	■		■	■								■	
■								■					
		■					■						

Shrub Chart

	Page Numbers	Zone
Cornus alba	241	3
Cornus mas	242, 243	5
Cornus racemosa	240, 241	4
Cornus sericea	240	3
Corylopsis glabrescens	167	5
Corylopsis pauciflora	166, 167	6
Corylus avellana	166	4
Corylus maxima	204, 205	5
Cotinus coggygria	96, 97	5
Cotoneaster adpressus	244	5
Cotoneaster apiculatus	244	5
Cotoneaster dammeri 'Skogsholm'	245	6
Cotoneaster divaricatus	246	5
Cotoneaster horizontalis	245	5
Cotoneaster lacteus	246	7
Cotoneaster multiflorus	247	4
Cotoneaster salicifolius	247	6
Cyrilla racemiflora	184, 185	6
Cytisus × praecox	176, 177	7
Cytisus racemosus	176, 177	8
Cytisus scoparius	178, 179	6
Daphne × burkwoodii	135	4
Daphne cneorum	134	5
Daphne mezereum	134	6
Daphne odora	135	7
Deutzia gracilis	103	5
Deutzia × lemoinei	102	4
Deutzia scabra	102, 103	5
Diervilla sessilifolia	174	4
Dirca palustris	164, 165	5
Elaeagnus angustifolia	260, 261	3
Elaeagnus multiflora	261	5

Under 4 ft.	4–8 ft.	Over 8 ft.	Spring	Summer	Fall	Winter	Dry Soil	Acid Soil	Shade	Evergreen	Fall Color	Showy Fruit	Use for Hedges
		■	■									■	
		■	■									■	
		■	■						■			■	
	■		■									■	
		■	■			■		■					
	■		■			■		■					
		■											
		■											
		■		■			■						
■			■				■					■	
■			■				■					■	
■			■				■			■		■	
	■		■				■				■	■	
■			■				■					■	
		■	■				■			■		■	■
		■	■				■					■	
		■	■				■					■	
		■		■				■				■	
		■	■				■						
	■		■				■			■			
	■		■				■						
■			■										
■			■							■			
■			■						■				
■			■						■				
■			■										
	■		■										
	■		■	■									
	■			■									
	■		■						■		■		
		■	■				■						
	■		■				■					■	

	Page Numbers	Zone
Elaeagnus pungens	258, 259	7
Elaeagnus umbellata	260	4
Enkianthus campanulatus	98, 99	5
Erica × darleyensis	153	6
Escallonia rubra	131	8
Euonymus alata	194	4
Euonymus japonica	195	7
Euonymus kiautschovica	194	6
Exochorda × macrantha 'The Bride'	101	5
Exochorda racemosa	100	5
× *Fatshedera × lizei*	136	8
Fatsia japonica	137	8
Feijoa sellowiana	93	8
Forsythia × intermedia	172, 173	5
Forsythia suspensa var. *sieboldii*	173	5
Forsythia viridissima 'Bronxensis'	172	5
Fothergilla gardenii	198, 199	5
Fothergilla major	198, 199	5
Fremontodendron californicum	162	8
Gardenia jasminoides	123	8
Gaylussacia brachycera	153	6
Genista lydia	180	7
Genista tinctoria	181	5
Grevillea 'Canberra'	157	8
Grevillea 'Constance'	156	8
Grevillea rosmarinifolia	156	8
Grewia occidentalis	130	9
Hamamelis × intermedia	170	5
Hamamelis mollis	171	6
Hamamelis vernalis	171	5
Hamamelis virginiana	170	4
Hibiscus rosa-sinensis	121	10

Under 4 ft.	4–8 ft.	Over 8 ft.	Spring	Summer	Fall	Winter	Dry Soil	Acid Soil	Shade	Evergreen	Fall Color	Showy Fruit	Use for Hedges
		■			■		■		■	■			
		■	■				■					■	
		■	■					■			■		
■			■		■	■		■		■			
		■	■	■						■			
		■	■								■	■	■
		■	■						■	■			
		■	■										■
■			■										
		■	■										
	■				■				■	■			
		■			■				■	■			
		■	■				■			■		■	
■			■										
		■	■										
■			■										
■			■					■			■		
	■		■					■			■		
		■	■				■			■			
■			■	■	■			■		■			
■			■					■		■		■	
■				■			■						
■			■				■						
	■		■				■						
	■		■				■						
	■			■			■						
		■	■							■			
		■	■			■					■		
		■				■					■		
		■				■					■		
		■			■				■		■		
		■		■									

	Page Numbers	Zone
Hibiscus syriacus	120	5
Hippophae rhamnoides	256	4
Holodiscus discolor	175	4
Hydrangea arborescens	140	4
Hydrangea macrophylla	141	7
Hydrangea paniculata	140, 141	4
Hydrangea quercifolia	138, 139	5
Hypericum calycinum	159	6
Hypericum frondosum	160	6
Hypericum kalmianum	161	5
Hypericum patulum 'Hidcote'	160	7
Hypericum prolificum	161	4
Ilex × *altaclarensis* 'Wilsonii'	252	8
Ilex aquifolium	248, 249	7
Ilex × *attenuata* 'Fosteri'	250	6
Ilex cornuta	249	7
Ilex cornuta 'Bufordii'	252	7
Ilex cornuta 'Bufordii Compact'	253	7
Ilex cornuta 'Rotunda'	248	7
Ilex crenata	264, 265	6
Ilex decidua	254, 255	5
Ilex glabra	265	5
Ilex × *meserveae*	253	5
Ilex opaca	250, 251	6
Ilex penduncolosa	251	5
Ilex verticillata	254, 255	4
Ilex vomitoria	264	7
Illicium floridanum	92	8
Itea virginica	204, 205	5
Jasminum nudiflorum	163	7
Kalmia angustifolia	114	3
Kalmia latifolia	114, 115	5

Under 4 ft.	4–8 ft.	Over 8 ft.	Spring	Summer	Fall	Winter	Dry Soil	Acid Soil	Shade	Evergreen	Fall Color	Showy Fruit	Use for Hedges
		■		■	■								
		■									■	■	
		■		■			■						
■				■									
	■			■									
		■		■									
	■			■							■		
■				■			■						
■				■			■						
■				■			■			■			
■				■			■			■			
■				■			■			■			
		■										■	
		■								■		■	■
		■	■							■		■	
		■					■			■		■	■
		■					■					■	■
												■	
	■						■						■
		■							■	■			■
		■										■	
	■		■					■		■			■
		■								■		■	■
		■						■		■		■	■
		■								■		■	
		■						■				■	
		■					■			■		■	■
		■	■						■				
	■			■					■		■		
	■		■			■			■				
■			■					■		■			
		■	■					■		■			

	Page Numbers	Zone
Kerria japonica	162, 163	5
Kolkwitzia amabilis	97	5
Lantana camara	158	9
Lavandula dentata	151	9
Leptospermum scoparium	157	9
Leucophyllum frutescens	202	9
Leucothoe axillaris	203	6
Leucothoe fontanesiana	202, 203	5
Ligustrum amurense	276	4
Ligustrum japonicum	124	7
Ligustrum lucidum	277	8
Ligustrum obtusifolium	124, 125	4
Ligustrum × vicaryi	277	5
Ligustrum vulgare	125, 276	4
Lindera benzoin	242, 243	4
Lonicera fragrantissima	282	5
Lonicera maackii	237	3
Lonicera nitida	283	7
Lonicera tatarica	236	4
Lonicera xylosteum	282	5
Loropetalum chinense	174, 175	7
Magnolia × loebneri	90, 91	4
Magnolia quinquepeta	90, 91	5
Magnolia stellata	88, 89	4
Mahonia aquifolium	188	5
Mahonia bealei	189	7
Mahonia lomariifolia	188, 189	9
Michelia figo	164	9
Myrica cerifera	268, 269	7
Myrica pensylvanica	268, 269	3
Myrtus communis	279	9

Under 4 ft.	4–8 ft.	Over 8 ft.	Spring	Summer	Fall	Winter	Dry Soil	Acid Soil	Shade	Evergreen	Fall Color	Showy Fruit	Use for Hedges
	■		■						■				
		■	■										
■			■	■	■	■							
■				■			■						■
		■	■	■			■						
	■			■			■			■			■
■			■					■	■	■			
	■		■					■	■	■			
		■	■				■					■	■
		■	■				■		■	■			■
		■	■				■			■			■
		■	■				■					■	■
		■	■				■						■
		■	■				■						■
		■	■				■					■	
		■	■			■							
		■					■					■	
	■		■										■
		■	■									■	
		■	■				■						■
		■	■					■	■	■			
		■	■										
		■	■										
		■	■										
	■		■						■	■		■	
		■	■						■	■		■	
		■	■			■			■	■		■	
		■	■										
		■					■			■		■	
		■					■					■	
	■			■			■			■		■	■

	Page Numbers	Zone
Nandina domestica	238, 239	7
Nerium oleander	122, 123	8–10
Ochna serrulata	93	9
Osmanthus americanus	270, 273	7
Osmanthus × *fortunei*	272	7
Osmanthus fragrans	273	8
Osmanthus heterophyllus	270, 271, 272	7
Parrotia persica	212, 213	5
Paxistima canbyi	280	4
Philadelphus coronarius	126, 127	5
Philadelphus × *lemoinei*	126	5
Philadelphus × *virginalis*	127	5
Phlomis fruticosa	181	7
Photinia × *fraseri*	206	8
Photinia glabra	207	8
Photinia serrulata	206	8
Photinia villosa	207	5
Physocarpus opulifolius	142	3
Pieris floribunda	200	5
Pieris forrestii	200	7
Pieris japonica	201	5
Pittosporum tobira	275	9
Pittosporum tobira 'Wheeler's Dwarf'	274	9
Podocarpus macrophyllus var. *maki*	286, 287	9
Polygala × *dalmaisiana*	129	9
Poncirus trifoliata	86, 87	6
Potentilla fruticosa	158	3
Prunus besseyi	147	4
Prunus × *cistena*	85	3
Prunus glandulosa	84	5
Prunus 'Hally Jolivette'	84	5
Prunus laurocerasus	145, 146, 147	7

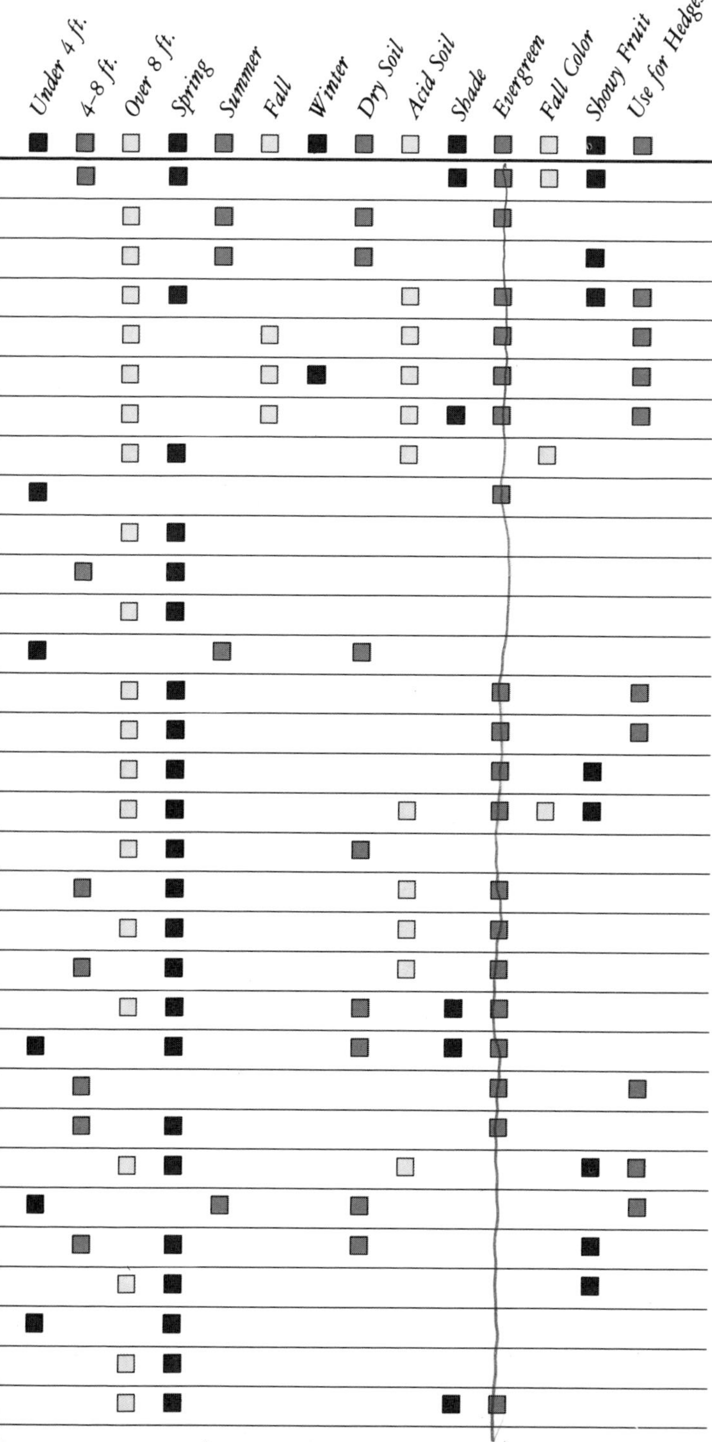
Under 4 ft.
4–8 ft.
Over 8 ft.
Spring
Summer
Fall
Winter
Dry Soil
Acid Soil
Shade
Evergreen
Fall Color
Showy Fruit
Use for Hedges

	Page Numbers	Zone
Prunus tenella 'Fire Hill'	85	3
Punica granatum	94, 95	8
Pyracantha coccinea	234	6
Pyracantha fortuneana 'Graberi'	234	7
Pyracantha 'Navaho'	235	7
Pyracantha 'Teton'	235	7
Raphiolepsis indica	132, 133	8
Raphiolepsis umbellata	132, 133	8
Rhamnus frangula 'Asplenifolia'	286, 287	3
Rhamnus frangula 'Columnaris'	284	3
Rhododendron catawbiense	107	5
Rhododendron Dexter hybrids	cover	5
Rhododendron Exbury hybrids	104, 105	5
Rhododendron Gable hybrids	112	6
Rhododendron kaempferi	109	5
Rhododendron × *kosteranum*	104	6
Rhododendron Kurume hybrids	112, 113	7
Rhododendron mucronulatum	108	5
Rhododendron PJM hybrids	106	4
Rhododendron schlippenbachii	108, 109	5
Rhododendron yakusimanum	106, 107	5
Rhodotypos scandens	122	5
Rhus aromatica	210, 211	3
Rhus integrifolia	285	9
Rhus ovata	284	9
Rhus typhina	210, 211	4
Ribes alpinum	81	3
Ribes odoratum	80	5
Ribes sanguineum	80, 81	6–8
Romneya coulteri	117	7
Rosa hugonis	159	5
Rosa rugosa	119	3

Under 4 ft.	4–8 ft.	Over 8 ft.	Spring	Summer	Fall	Winter	Dry Soil	Acid Soil	Shade	Evergreen	Fall Color	Showy Fruit	Use for Hedges
■	■	□	■	■	□	■	■	□	■	■	□	■	■
■			■										
		□	■									■	
		□	■							■		■	■
		□	■							■		■	
	■		■							■		■	■
		□	■							■		■	■
■			■				■			■			■
	■		■				■			■		■	■
		□											■
		□											■
		□	■					□		■			
	■		■					□		■			
■			■					□					
■			■					□		■			
	■		■					□					
	■		■					□					
	■		■					□		■			
	■		■					□					
	■		■					□		■			
		□	■					□			□		
■			■					□		■			
	■		■						■			■	
	■		■				■				□	■	
		□	■				■			■		■	■
		□	■				■			■		■	
		□		■			■				□	■	
	■		■						■				■
	■		■						■				■
		□	■										
	■			■			■						
	■		■									■	■
	■			■								■	■

	Page Numbers	Zone
Rosa wichuraiana	118	6
Rosmarinus officinalis	154, 155	7
Ruscus aculeatus	214	8
Salix discolor	169	3
Salix gracilistyla	169	6
Salix 'Melanostachys'	168	5
Salix sachalinensis 'Sekka'	168	5
Sambucus canadensis	232, 233	4
Sambucus nigra	232	6
Sambucus pubens	233	4
Santolina chamaecyparissus	182, 183	6
Sarcococca hookerana	271	7
Skimmia japonica	230, 231	8
Sorbaria sorbifolia	144	3
Spartium junceum	180	8
Spiraea × *bumalda*	142	4
Spiraea japonica	143	4
Spiraea nipponica 'Snow Mound'	150	4
Spiraea × *vanhouttei*	151	4
Staphylea colchica	100, 101	5
Stephanandra incisa	281	4
Symphoricarpos albus	238	3
Symphoricarpos × *chenaultii*	239	5
Symphoricarpos orbiculatus	257	3
Symplocos paniculata	256, 257	4
Syringa × *chinensis*	75, 77	4
Syringa meyeri	74	4-8
Syringa microphylla	75	5
Syringa patula 'Miss Kim'	73	4
Syringa × *persica*	74	4
Syringa reticulata	72	4
Syringa villosa	73	3

Under 4 ft.	4–8 ft.	Over 8 ft.	Spring	Summer	Fall	Winter	Dry Soil	Acid Soil	Shade	Evergreen	Fall Color	Showy Fruit	Use for Hedges
■	■	■	■	■	■	■	■	■	■	■	■	■	■
■				■			■					■	
	■				■	■	■			■		■	
■									■			■	
		■	■										
		■	■										
		■	■										
		■	■										
		■		■								■	
		■	■									■	
		■	■									■	
■				■			■			■			
	■								■	■			
■			■						■	■		■	
		■		■									
	■			■	■		■						
■				■									
	■		■										
	■		■										
	■		■										
		■	■									■	
	■		■										
■			■						■			■	
	■		■						■			■	
■			■						■		■	■	
		■	■									■	
		■	■										
	■		■										
	■		■										
	■		■										
	■		■										
		■	■										
		■	■										

	Page Numbers	Zone
Syringa vulgaris	72, 76	4
Syzygium paniculatum	283	10
Tamarix ramosissima	96	3
Ternstroemia gymnanthera	236, 237	7
Tibouchina urvilleana	128	9–10
Vaccinium corymbosum	258, 259	4
Viburnum × *burkwoodii*	227	4
Viburnum × *carlcephalum*	227	5
Viburnum carlesii	226	5
Viburnum davidii	229	8
Viburnum dentatum	228	3
Viburnum dilatatum	218, 223	5–8
Viburnum × *juddii*	226	5
Viburnum lantana	219	4
Viburnum lentago	218	3
Viburnum opulus	224, 225	4
Viburnum plicatum var. *tomentosum*	222	5
Viburnum × *pragense*	216	6
Viburnum prunifolium	216, 217	4
Viburnum × *rhytidophylloides*	220	5
Viburnum rhytidophyllum	219	5
Viburnum sargentii	220	4
Viburnum setigerum	221	5
Viburnum sieboldii	223	4
Viburnum suspensum	221	9
Viburnum tinus	229	7
Viburnum trilobum	222	3–7
Viburnum wrightii	228	5
Vitex agnus-castus	78, 79	7
Vitex negundo	78, 79	7
Weigela florida	82, 83	4
Xylosma congestum	285	9

Under 4 ft.	4–8 ft.	Over 8 ft.	Spring	Summer	Fall	Winter	Dry Soil	Acid Soil	Shade	Evergreen	Fall Color	Showy Fruit	Use for Hedges
		■	■										
		■	■							■		■	■
		■		■									
	■			■				■	■	■			
		■	■	■	■	■		■					
		■	■					■				■	
	■		■							■	■	■	
		■	■									■	
■			■										
■			■							■	■	■	
		■	■								■	■	■
		■	■								■	■	■
		■	■										
		■	■									■	■
		■	■								■	■	
		■	■									■	
		■	■								■	■	
		■	■							■			
		■	■								■	■	
		■	■							■		■	
		■	■							■		■	
		■	■								■	■	
		■	■								■	■	
		■	■									■	
		■	■				■			■		■	■
		■	■			■				■		■	■
		■	■								■	■	
		■	■								■	■	
		■		■									
		■		■									
		■	■										
		■					■						

Pests & Diseases

Because plant pests and diseases are a fact of life for a gardener, it is helpful to become familiar with the common problems in your area and to learn how to control them.

Symptoms of Problems
The same general symptoms are associated with many different diseases and pests, so some experience is needed to determine their causes.

Diseases
Both fungi and bacteria are responsible for a variety of diseases ranging from leafspots and wilts to root rot, but bacterial diseases usually make the affected plant tissues appear wetter than fungi do. Diseases caused by viruses and mycoplasma, often transmitted by aphids and leafhoppers, display such symptoms as mottled yellow or deformed leaves and stunted growth.

Insect Pests
Numerous insects attack plants. Sap-sucking insects—including aphids, leafhoppers, and scale insects—suck plant juices. The affected plant becomes yellow, stunted, and misshapen. Aphids and scale insects produce honeydew, a sticky substance that attracts ants and sooty mold fungus growth. Other pests with rasping-sucking mouthparts, such as thrips and spider mites, scrape plant tissue and then suck the juices that well up in the injured areas.
Leaf-chewers, namely beetles and caterpillars, consume plant leaves, whole or in part. Borers tunnel into shoots and stems, and their young larvae consume plant tissue, weakening the plant. Some insects, such as various grubs and maggots, feed on roots, weakening or killing the plant.

Nematodes
Microscopic roundworms called nematodes are other pests that attack roots and cause stunting and poor plant growth. Some produce galls on roots and others produce them on leaves.

Environmental Stresses
Some types of plant illness result from environment-related stress, such as severe wind, drought, flooding, or extreme cold. Other problems are caused by salt toxicity, rodents, nutritional deficiencies or excesses, pesticides, or damage from lawnmowers. Many of these injuries are avoidable if you take proper precautions.

Controlling Plant Problems
Always buy healthy disease- and insect-free shrubs, and select resistant varieties and those that are hardy in your area. Check leaves and canes for dead areas or off-color and stunted tissue. Give your plants the proper care and you will avoid many problems.

Routine Preventives

By cultivating the soil routinely you will expose insects and disease-causing organisms to the sun and thus lessen their chances of surviving in your garden. Be sure to prune out and destroy infested or diseased stems, remove dead leaves and flowers, and clean up plant debris in the fall. Do not add diseased or infested material to the compost pile. Spray plants with water from time to time to dislodge insect pests and remove suffocating dust. Pick off the larger insects by hand. To discourage fungal leafspots and blights, always water plants in the morning and allow the leaves to dry before nightfall. For the same reason, provide adequate air circulation around leaves and stems by pruning and spacing plants properly.

Weeds provide a home for insects and diseases, so pull them up or use herbicides. But do not apply herbicides, including "weed-and-feed" lawn preparations, too close to landscape plants. Herbicide injury may cause elongated, straplike, or downward-cupping leaves. Spray weed-killers when there is little air movement, but not on a very hot, dry day.

Insecticides and Fungicides

To protect plant tissue from injury due to insects and diseases, a number of insecticides and fungicides are available. However, few products control diseases due to bacteria, viruses, and mycoplasma. Pesticides are usually either "protectant" or "systemic" in nature. Protectants guard uninfected foliage from insects or disease organisms, while systemics move through the plant and provide some therapeutic or eradicant action as well as protection. Botanical insecticides such as pyrethrum and rotenone have a shorter residual effect on pests but are considered less toxic and generally safer for the user and the environment than inorganic chemical insecticides. Biological control through the use of organisms like *Bacillus thuringiensis* (a bacterium toxic to moth and butterfly larvae) is effective and safe.

Recommended pesticides may vary to some extent from region to region. Consult your local Cooperative Extension Service or plant professional regarding the appropriate material to use. Always check the pesticide label to be sure that it is registered for use on the pest and plant with which you are dealing. Follow the label concerning safety precautions, dosage, and frequency of application.

Recognizing Pests and Diseases

Learn to recognize the insects and diseases that plague garden plants. The chart on the following pages describes the most common pests and diseases that attack shrubs, the damage they cause, and the measures to take to control them.

Pest or Disease

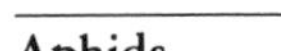

Aphids

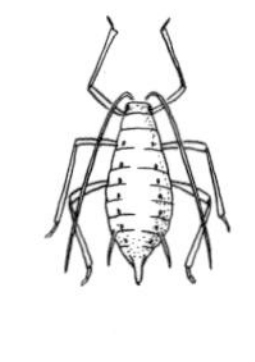

Bagworms

Borers

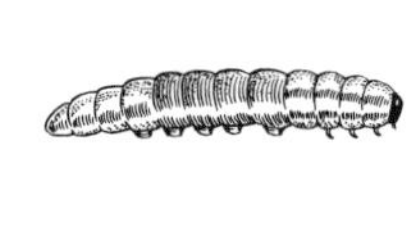

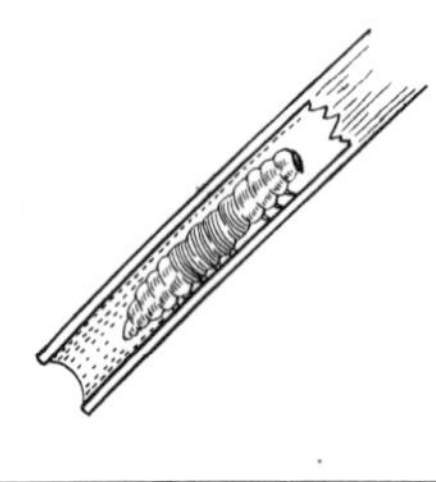

Cankers

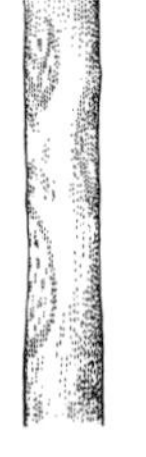

Crown Gall

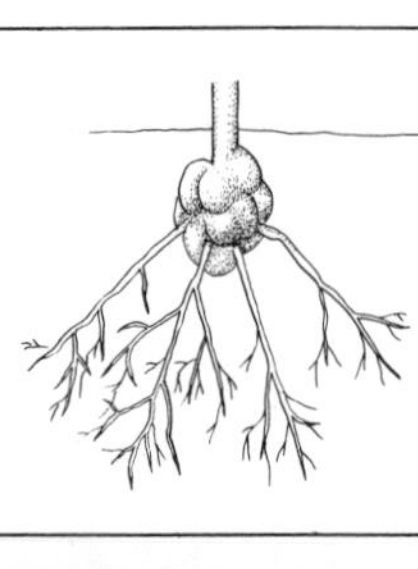

Description	*Damage*	*Controls*
Tiny green, brown, or reddish, pear-shaped, soft-bodied insects in clusters on buds, shoots, and undersides of leaves.	Suck plant juices, causing stunted or deformed blooms and leaves. Some transmit plant viruses. Secretions attract ants.	Spray with strong stream of water, insecticidal soap, sabadilla, neem extract or rotenone/pyrethrin. Encourage beneficial insects, such as lacewings and parasitic wasps.
Larvae of moths that spin a spindle-shaped nest, or "bag," several inches in length.	Larvae feed on shrub foliage and produce unsightly bags on plants.	Prune out and destroy bags. Spray caterpillars with *Bacillus thuringiensis,* neem extract or pyrethrum.
Several kinds of wormlike, legless, cream-colored larvae tunneling in stems.	Swollen bands on stems. Girdling causes dieback of stems and shoots.	Remove and destroy infested branches, pruning several inches below swelling. Fertilize and water deeply to increase vigor. Inject with beneficial nematodes.
Fungal disease causing spots and dead areas on stems. Black dots of fungal spores in dead areas.	Discolored spots on stems. Spots enlarge, becoming light or dark and dry. Shoots wilt and stems die back.	Prune and destroy infected stems. Avoid wounding healthy stems in wet weather. Use proper pruning techniques.
Soil-borne bacterial disease, forming cancerlike growths on plant stems and roots.	Rounded growths on stem near soil line. May also appear on roots and occasionally on branches.	Remove and destroy infected plants. Buy only healthy, certified disease-free plants. Plant in uninfested soil.

Pest or Disease

Fire blight

Fungal Blights

Fungal Leaf Spots

Leaf-feeding Beetles

Leaf-feeding Caterpillars

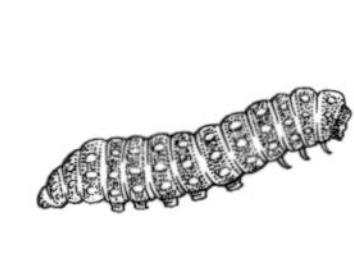

Description	*Damage*	*Controls*
A bacterial disease that causes blackened foliage and oozing stem cankers.	Blackens terminal shoots, causes stem cankers, often kills plants.	Cut out diseased shoots 12 inches below visible infection. Sterilize clippers in bleach solution between cuts. Spray with copper or Bordeaux mixture.
Leaves of deciduous shrubs turn brown and wilt. Branches of evergreen shrubs may be brown or gray.	Affects leaves and shoots of shrubs, killing portions of growth and stunting plant.	Prune badly affected plant parts. Avoid getting foliage wet. Provide adequate air circulation around shrubs.
Spots on leaves caused by fungi and encouraged by humid or wet weather.	Tan, brown, or black spots on leaves. If serious, foliage may drop from plant.	Increase air circulation. Prune off and discard diseased foliage. Avoid wetting the foliage. Spray with sulfur, lime-sulfur, Bordeaux mixture or copper.
Hard-shelled, oval to oblong insects on leaves, stems, and flowers.	Chew plant parts, leaving holes. Larvae of some feed on roots.	Handpick and destroy. Spray with sabadilla, rotenone or rotenone/pyrethrin mix.
Soft-bodied, wormlike crawling insects with several pairs of legs. May be smooth, hairy, or spiny. Adults are moths or butterflies.	Consume part or all of leaves. Flowers and shoots may also be eaten.	Handpick and destroy. Spray with *Bacillus thuringiensis,* neem extract or rotenone/pyrethrin.

Pest or Disease

Leafminers

Nematodes

Powdery Mildew

Root-feeding Larvae

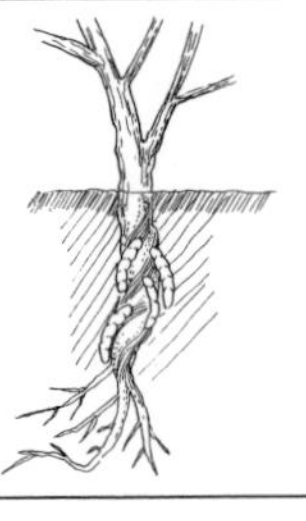

Root Rot

Description	*Damage*	*Controls*
Small larvae of flies or beetles that feed between leaf surfaces.	Leaves show yellow, then brown, oval, or meandering papery blotches. Leaves may drop.	Remove badly infested leaves. Often kept in check by natural enemies. Spray with horticultural oil or neem extract.
Microscopic roundworms, usually associated with roots. They cause various diseases.	Stunted, off-color plants that do not respond to water or fertilizer. Minute galls maybe present on roots.	Remove and destroy badly infested plants. Plant nematode-resistant stock. Treat soil with plenty of organic matter, CLANDOSAN, beneficial nematodes or neem extract.
White, powdery fungal disease on aerial plant parts.	Reddish spots and powdery fungal growth. Leaves may be distorted and drop. Stems, buds, and flowers may also be affected.	Remove and destroy badly infected leaves. Wash weekly with heavy stream of water. Spray with sulfur or Bordeaux mixture.
Small, whitish grubs that feed on plant roots.	Feeding causes root injury and can stunt growth. Plants may be off-color and sickly.	Control adult leaf-feeding beetles. Apply beneficial nematodes.
Fungal or bacterial disease, usually soil-borne, often encouraged by water-logged soil.	Wilting, off-color plants. Roots dark and dry or mushy, rather than firm and white.	Remove and destroy infected plants. Do not plant similar plants in that area. Improve soil drainage.

Pest or Disease

Rust

Scale

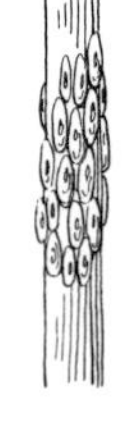

Spider Mites

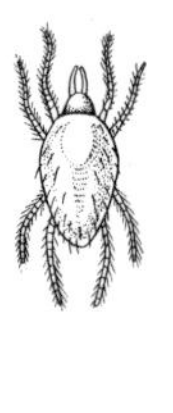

Viruses

Wilts

Description	*Damage*	*Controls*
Fungus causing orange powdery spots on lower sides of leaves.	Leaves and stems may be attacked. Infected leaves may drop.	Increase air circulation. Water at soil-line or early in day. Discard fallen debris. Remove and destroy infected canes and leaves. Spray with sulfur.
Small, waxy, soft- or hard-bodied stationary insects on shoots and leaves. May be red, white, brown, black, or gray.	Suck plant juices, causing stunted, off-color plants. May cover large portion of stem.	Prune off badly infested plant parts. Spray with insecticidal soap, horticultural oil or lime-sulfur. Release lacewings.
Tiny golden, red, or brown arachnids on undersides of leaves. Profuse fine webs seen with heavy infestations.	Scrape leaves and suck plant juices. Leaves become pale and dry. Plant may be stunted.	Spray with strong jet of water, insecticidal soap, horticultural oil or sulfur. Release predatory mites.
Various diseases, including mosaics, that cause off-color, stunted plants. May be transmitted by aphids.	Crinkled, mottled, deformed leaves, stunted plants, and poor growth.	Remove and destroy infected plants. Control the insect vector (usually aphids or leafhoppers), if present. Buy only healthy plants.
Soil-borne fungal or bacterial diseases that cause wilting, stunting, and eventual death of plants.	Leaves turn yellow and entire plant may wilt and die.	Remove and destroy infected plants. Sterilize pruners before reuse. Practice crop rotation. Use resistant varieties.

Nurseries

Camellia Forest Nursery
125 Carolina Forest Road, Chapel Hill, NC 27514
(Rare shrubs; imports from Asia)

Carlson's Gardens
Box 305 GS 586, South Salem, NY 10590
(Mainly rhododendrons and azaleas)

Cedar Lane Farms
3790 Sandy Creek Road, Madison, GA 30650
(Good selection of shrubs)

The Cummins Garden
22 Robertsville Road, Marlboro, NJ 10590
(Specialists in plants of the heath family)

Eastern Plant Specialties
P.O. Box 40, Colonia, NJ 07067
(Many rare and choice items)

Fjellgarden
P.O. Box 1111, Lakeside, AZ 85929
(Alpines and Rocky Mountain natives)

Gosler Farm Nursery
1200 Weaver Road, Springfield, OR 97477
(Magnolia and other rare genera)

Greer Gardens
1280 Goodpasture Road, Eugene, OR 97401
(Huge selection of azaleas, rhododendrons, maples, and choice shrubs)

Heaths and Heathers
Box 850, Elma, WA 98541
(Good selection)

Indian Run Nursery
Allentown Road, Robbinsville, NJ 08691
(Hardy rhododendrons)

Oliver Nurseries, Inc.
1159 Bronson Road, Fairfield, CT 06430
(Rare plants, dwarf shrubs, and evergreens)

Rice Creek Gardens
1315 66th Avenue N.E., Minneapolis, MN 55432
(Alpines and dwarf shrubs)

This list includes some of the best sources of shrubs in the country. Some offer large and varied selections of popular forms, others carry rare variations, and a few specialize in certain groups of plants. Catalogues may be free, or the fee may be refunded with your first order. Try to order shrubs from nurseries in climates similar to your own.

Roses of Yesterday & Today
802 Brown's Valley Road, Watsonville, CA 95076
(Specialists in shrub and species roses)

Roslyn Nursery
211 Burrs Lane, Dix Hills, NY 11746
(Fine selection of very hardy azaleas, rhododendrons, camellias. Also kalmia cultivars, pieris, and other shrubs)

Wayside Gardens
Hodges, SC 29695
(A valuable source and a lovely catalogue)

Weston Nurseries
Hopkinton, MA 01748
(Huge inventory of excellent plants)

White Flower Farm
Litchfield, CT 06759
(Occasional rarity offered)

Winterthur Garden Sampler
Direct Mail Office, Winterthur Museum
Winterthur, DE 19735
(Small but choice selection)

Woodlanders
Dept. RG
1128 Colleton Avenue, Aiken, SC 29801
(Very good source of beautiful and unusual plants)

Glossary

Acid soil
Soil with a pH value of less than 7.

Alkaline soil
Soil with a pH value of more than 7.

Alpine
A plant from mountainous, high altitude regions, often grown in rock gardens.

Alternate
Arranged singly along a twig or shoot, and not in whorls or opposite pairs.

Axil
The angle formed by a leafstalk and the stem from which it grows.

Balled and burlapped
Dug out of the ground with a ball of soil around the roots, which is tied with burlap and string for transport.

Bare-rooted
Dug out of a loose growing medium with no soil around the roots. Some shrubs are sold by nurseries in this condition.

Berry
A fleshy fruit, with one to many seeds, developed from a single ovary.

Bisexual
A flower with functional stamens and pistils.

Bloom
A whitish powdery or waxy covering on some fruits or other plant parts.

Bottom-heat
Heat applied to the bottom of propagating beds or flats to speed or aid the germination of seeds or rooting of cuttings.

Bract
A modified and often scalelike leaf, usually located at the base of a flower, a fruit, or a cluster of flowers or fruits.

Broad-leaved evergreen
An evergreen plant that is not a conifer.

Bud
A young and undeveloped leaf, flower, or shoot, usually covered tightly with scales.

Calyx
Collectively, the sepals of a flower.

Cane
A long, woody, pliable stem.

Capsule
A dry fruit containing more than one cell, splitting along more than one groove.

Catkin
A compact and often drooping cluster of reduced, stalkless, and usually unisexual flowers.

Clone
A group of plants all originating by vegetative propagation from a single plant, and therefore genetically identical to it and to one another.

Compound leaf
A leaf made up of two or more leaflets.

Conifer
A cone-bearing tree or shrub, often evergreen, usually with needle-like leaves.

Container-grown
Raised in a pot that is removed before planting. Many shrubs are sold by nurseries in this form.

Corolla
Collectively, the petals of a flower.

Corymb
A flower cluster with a flat top, in which the individual pedicels emerge from the axis at different points, rather than at the same point as in an umbel, and blooming from the edges toward the center.

Creeping
Prostrate or trailing over the ground or over other plants.

Crown
That part of a plant where the roots and the stem meet.

Cultivar
An unvarying plant variety maintained by vegetative propagation or by inbred seed.

Cutting
A piece of plant without roots; set in a rooting medium, it develops roots, and is then potted as a new plant.

Cyme
A flat or rounded branching flower cluster that blooms from the center toward the edges, and in which the tip of the axis always bears a flower.

Deadheading
Removing old flowers during the growing season to encourage the development of new flowers and prevent seed formation.

Deciduous
Dropping its leaves; not evergreen.

Die-back
The death of tops of plants—naturally, due to climatic conditions, or unnaturally, due to disease.

Dioeceous
Bearing male and female flowers on different plants.

Dissected leaf
A deeply cut leaf, the clefts not reaching the midrib; same as a divided leaf. See also Lobed leaf.

Division
Propagation of a plant by separating it into two or more pieces, each of which has at least one bud and some roots.

Double-flowered
Having more than the usual number of petals, usually arranged in extra rows.

Drupe
A fleshy fruit with a single seed enclosed in a hard covering.

Dwarf
A plant that, due to an inherited characteristic, is shorter and/or slower-growing than normal forms.

Escape
An exotic plant that has spread from cultivation and grows successfully in the wild.

Espalier
A plant that has been trained to grow flat against a wall or framework.

Evergreen
Retaining green leaves for more than one annual growth cycle.

Family
A group of plants in related genera, all of which share characteristics not found in other families.

Fertile
Able to produce seed.

Form
A small but constant variation within a population of plants, such as a white-flowered plant in a normally purple-flowered population.

Fruit
The fully developed ovary of a flower, containing one or more seeds.

Genus
A group of closely related species; plural, genera.

Germinate
To sprout, used to describe the sprouting of seeds.

Habit
The characteristic growth form or general shape of a plant.

Hardwood cutting
A cutting taken from a dormant plant after it has finished its yearly growth.

Herbaceous perennial
A plant with little or no woody tissue that dies to the ground each fall and resprouts each spring.

Horticulture
The cultivation of plants for ornament or food.

Humus
Partly or wholly decomposed vegetable matter, an important constituent of garden soil.

Hybrid
The offspring of two parent plants belonging to different species, subspecies, genera, or clones.

Inflorescence
A flower cluster.

Invasive
Spreading aggressively from the original site of planting.

Keel
A sharp ridge or rib on the underside of a petal, leaf, or other plant part.

Key
A dry, one-seeded fruit with a wing; a samara.

Lanceolate
Shaped like a lance: several times longer than wide, pointed at the tip and broadest near the base.

Layering
A method of propagating plants in which a stem is induced to send out roots by surrounding a section of it with soil.

Leaflet
One of the subdivisions of a compound leaf.

Leaf mold
A type of humus consisting of partially decayed leaves.

Lime
A substance containing calcium added to soil for increased alkalinity and nutrient content.

Loam
A humus-rich soil containing up to 25 percent clay, up to 50 percent silt, and less than 50 percent sand.

Lobe
A segment of a cleft leaf or petal.

Lobed leaf
A leaf whose margin is shallowly divided.

Margin
The edge of a leaf.

Massing
Using large groups of plants to provide mass, visual bulk, or balance to a landscape.

Midrib
The primary rib or mid-vein of a leaf or leaflet.

Mulch
A protective covering spread over the soil around the base of plants to retard evaporation, control temperature, or suppress weeds.

Naturalized
Established as a part of the flora in an area other than the place of origin. Also, of a planting, tended so as to give the appearance of spontaneous or "wild" growth.

Neutral soil
Soil that is neither acid nor alkaline, having a pH value of 7.

Node
The place on a stem where leaves or branches are attached.

Nutlet
One of several small, nutlike parts of a compound fruit; or the hard inner core of some fruits, containing a seed and surrounded by softer flesh.

Offset
A short, lateral shoot arising near the base of a plant, readily producing new roots, and useful in propagation.

Opposite
Arranged along a twig or shoot in pairs, with one on each side.

Ovate
Oval, with the broader end at the base.

Palmately compound
Having veins or leaflets arranged like the fingers on a hand, arising from a single point. See also Pinnately compound.

Panicle
A compound, branching flower cluster, blooming from bottom to top, and never terminating in a flower.

Peat moss
Partly decomposed moss, rich in nutrients and with a high water retention, used as a component of garden soil.

Pedicel
The stalk of an individual flower.

Perennial
A plant whose life spans several growing seasons and that produces seeds in several growing seasons, rather than only one.

Petal
One of a series of flower parts lying within the sepals and outside the stamens and pistils, often large and brightly colored.

Petiole
The stalk of a leaf.

pH
A symbol for the hydrogen ion content of the soil, and thus a means of expressing the acidity or alkalinity of the soil.

Pinna
A primary division or leaflet of a pinnate leaf.

Pinnately compound
With leaflets arranged in two rows along an axis.

Pistil
The female reproductive organ of a flower, consisting of an ovary, style, and stigma.

Pod
A dry, one-celled fruit, with thicker walls than a capsule.

Pollen
Minute grains containing the male germ cells and produced by the stamens.

Polygamous
Bearing male and female flowers on the same plant.

Pome
A fruit with fleshy outer tissue and a papery-walled inner chamber containing the seeds.

Propagate
To produce new plants, either by vegetative means involving the rooting of pieces of a plant, or by sowing seeds.

Prostrate
Lying on the ground; creeping.

Prune
To cut the branches of a woody plant to spur growth, maintain vigor, or shape the plant.

Raceme
A long flower cluster on which individual flowers are borne on small stalks from a common, larger, central stalk.

Rhizome
A horizontal stem at or just below the surface of the ground, distinguished from a root by the presence of nodes.

Rock garden
A landscape created with rocks and plants native to cliffs and mountainous regions.

Root
The underground portion of a plant that serves to anchor it and absorb water and minerals from the soil.

Runner
A prostrate shoot, rooting at its nodes.

Samara
A dry, one-seeded fruit with a wing; a key.

Scarified seeds
Seeds that have been scratched or sanded in order to induce them to absorb water and germinate.

Screen
A single plant or grouping of plants used to bar certain parts of the landscape from view.

Scurfy
Covered with tiny, broad scales.

Seed
A fertilized, ripened ovule, almost always covered with a protective coating and contained in a fruit.

Semi-evergreen
Retaining at least some green foliage well into winter, or shedding leaves only in cold climates.

Sepal
One of the outermost series of flower parts, arranged in a ring outside the petals, and usually green and leaflike.

Shrub
A woody, perennial plant, smaller than a tree, usually with several stems or trunks.

Shrub border
A row of shrubs, usually of mixed species, allowed to grow naturally.

Simple leaf
A leaf with an undivided blade; not compound or composed of leaflets.

Solitary
Borne singly or alone; not in clusters.

Softwood
Immature stems of woody plants.

Species
A population of plants or animals whose members reproduce by breeding with each other, but which is reproductively isolated from other populations.

Specimen
A plant placed conspicuously alone, usually in a prominent place, so as to show off its ornamental qualities.

Spike
An elongated flower cluster, each flower of which is without a stalk.

Spine
A strong, sharp, usually woody projection from the stem or branches of a plant; not usually from a bud.

Spreading plant
A plant whose branches grow in a more or less horizontal direction.

Spur
A tubular elongation of the petals or sepals of certain flowers, usually containing nectar.

Stamen
The male reproductive organ of a flower, consisting of a filament and a pollen-containing anther.

Sterile
Incapable of producing seeds, either because of a lack of stamens and pistils or because of internal genetic incompatibilities.

Stipule
A small, leaflike appendage at the base of some petioles.

Stolon
A horizontal stem growing along or just under the ground from the top of which a new plant arises; a runner or unthickened rhizome.

Stone
A single seed surrounded by a large, hard shell and covered by pulp.

Stratify
To keep seeds under cool, dark, moist conditions in order to encourage them to break dormancy after this treatment.

Style
The elongated part of a pistil between the stigma and the ovary.

Subshrub
A partly woody plant whose stems die back partially in fall.

Succulent
A plant with thick, fleshy leaves or stems that contain abundant water-storage tissue.

Sucker
A secondary shoot arising from underground buds on the roots of a plant.

Suffruticose
Partially woody, with stems that die back partially in fall; see Subshrub.

Terminal
Borne at the tip of a stem or shoot, rather than in the axil.

Thorn
A short, sharp, woody outgrowth of a stem.

Toothed
Having the margin shallowly divided into small, toothlike segments.

Topiary
The art of shearing trees and shrubs into unusual shapes.

Tuber
A swollen, mostly underground stem that bears buds and serves as a storage site for food.

Umbel
A flower cluster in which the individual flower stalks grow from the same point, like the ribs of an umbrella.

Unisexual flower
A flower bearing only stamens or pistils and not both.

Valve
One of the separable parts of the wall of a pod or capsule.

Variegated
Marked, striped, or blotched with some color other than green.

Variety
A population of plants differing slightly but consistently from the typical form of the species, and occurring naturally. More loosely applied to forms produced in cultivation. See also Cultivar.

Weeping
Having drooping branches.

Winter-kill
To be killed by harsh winter weather.

Woody
Producing hard rather than fleshy stems and having buds that survive above ground in winter.

Photo Credits

Ruth Allen
A recent contributor to the Audubon Society Nature Guides.
123A 146B, 193B, 201B, 256B

Gillian Beckett
A well-known English horticultural photographer.
79B, 126B, 128A, 134A, 154A, 156A, 181B, 247A, 261A, 279A

Al Bussewitz, PHOTO/NATS
A photographer for the Arnold Arboretum. Al Bussewitz is former sanctuary director at the Massachusetts Audubon Society.
73A, 73B, 97B, 137A, 142B, 171B, 193A, 204A, 204B, 209A, 243B, 255A, 287B

David Cavagnaro
A freelance nature photographer and author.
249B

Gordon Courtright
A retired nurseryman and landscape architect.
188A, 202A, 280B, 285A, 285B

Jack Dermid
A freelance biological photographer and retired professor.
269B

John Elsley
Assistant Vice-President of Wayside Gardens in South Carolina.
162A

Thomas E. Eltzroth
The co-author of *How to Grow a Thriving Vegetable Garden.* Thomas Eltzroth is a professor of horticulture.
95B, 116B, 130B, 132B, 157A, 182B, 186A, 189A, 215B, 252B, 274A

Derek Fell
A widely published garden writer. Derek Fell's photographs have appeared in numerous articles on gardening.
74B, 76A, 78A, 78B, 82A, 84A, 84B, 87B, 100A, 101A, 102A, 105B, 106B, 107A, 108A, 112A, 112B, 113B, 114A, 117B, 120A, 122A, 140B, 144A, 150A, 154B, 155A, 157B, 163A, 170A, 171A, 175A, 178A, 181A, 182A, 189B, 194A, 200B, 202B, 206A, 210A, 214A, 217A, 219A, 220B, 221B, 222A, 222B, 223A, 224A, 225A, 253B, 254A, 270A, 275A, 278A, 286A

Charles Marden Fitch
A media specialist and horticulturist. Most of Charles Fitch's photographs are taken in his own garden.
93B, 95A, 104A, 105A, 133A, 145A, 151B, 173A, 199A, 213B, 254B, 266B, 267B, 277A, 279B, cover

Judy Glattstein
An instructor at the New York and Brooklyn botanic gardens.
106A, 119B, 152B, 212B, 242A, 269A

Pamela J. Harper
Horticultural writer, photographer, and lecturer. Pamela Harper has an extensive library of plant and garden slides.
72B, 75A, 75B, 77B, 82B, 83A, 85B, 86A, 88B, 94A, 94B, 98B, 99B, 101B, 102B, 103A, 104B, 109A, 111B, 113A, 114B, 115A, 115B, 116A, 117A, 118B, 119A, 120B, 121A, 121B, 122B, 123B, 127A, 127B, 128B, 129B, 131A, 131B, 132A, 134B, 135A, 135B, 136A, 136B, 139A, 139B, 141B, 143A, 143B, 145B, 148A, 149A, 150B, 155B, 156B, 158A, 158B, 159B, 160A, 161B, 164A, 164B, 165A, 166A, 168A, 168B, 169A, 169B, 172A, 176B, 177A, 177B, 179B, 183A, 183B, 184B, 185A, 185B, 187A, 187B, 195B, 197A, 201A, 203A, 205B, 206B, 211B, 215A, 216A, 220A, 221A, 225B, 226B, 227B, 229A, 229B, 230B, 231B, 232B, 234A, 235A, 235B, 236B, 237B, 245A, 246B, 248A, 250A, 252A, 253A, 257A, 257B, 258B, 259B, 263A, 265A, 265B, 268B, 270B, 271A, 271B, 272A, 272B, 273B, 274B, 278B, 280A, 283B, 284A

Walter H. Hodge
Author of *The Audubon Society Book of Wildflowers,* Walter Hodge has photographed plants and animals all over the world.
76B, 79A, 81A, 86B, 92B, 108B, 129A, 133B, 137B, 141A, 147B, 153B, 163B, 174A, 180A, 188B, 192A, 195A, 207A, 231A, 233A, 251B, 258A, 275B, 287A

Philip Keenan
A freelance photographer specializing in horticulture.
223B, 233B, 251A

Helen Kittinger
A nature photographer, conservationist, and lecturer.
174B, 255B, 273A

Ken Lewis, Jr.
A contributor to the Audubon Society Field Guides.
242B, 245B

Dorothy S. Long, PHOTO/NATS
Currently associated with the New England Wildflower Society.
107B

The letter after each page number refers to the position of the color plates. A *represents the picture at the top and* B *the picture at the bottom. Some are also in the Visual Key.*

John A. Lynch
A photographer specializing in gardening and wildflowers.
200A

Robert Lyons, PHOTO/NATS
A professor of horticulture at Virginia Polytechnic Institute.
234B

G. R. Roberts
Author and photographer of books and film strips.
93A

Joy Spurr
Writer, photographer, and owner of a photographic agency.
80A, 87A, 166B, 175B, 179A, 211A, 213A, 238B, 247B, 260B

Alvin E. Staffan
A freelance photographer whose work has appeared in magazines.
210B, 216B, 259A, 261B

Steven M. Still
Contributing editor to this book. Steven Still is a professor and author of articles and books on horticulture.
72A, 74A, 80B, 81B, 83B, 85A, 88A, 90B, 91B, 92A, 96A, 96B, 98A, 100B, 103B, 109B, 110A, 110B, 118A, 124A, 124B, 125B, 126A, 130A, 138A, 138B, 140A, 142A, 144B, 146A, 147A, 148B, 149B, 152A, 153A, 160B, 161A, 167B, 170B, 172B, 178B, 180B, 184A, 190B, 191A, 191B, 192B, 194B, 196B, 197B, 198A, 198B, 199B, 203B, 205A, 207B, 208A, 208B, 209B, 212A, 214B, 217B, 218A, 218B, 219B, 224B, 226A, 227A, 228B, 230A, 232A, 236A, 237A, 238A, 239A, 239B, 240A, 240B, 241A, 241B, 244A, 244B, 246A, 248B, 249A, 250B, 260A, 262A, 262B, 263B, 264A, 264B, 266A, 267A, 268A, 276A, 276B, 277B, 281A, 281B, 282A, 282B, 283A, 284B, 286B

David M. Stone, PHOTO/NATS
A freelance nature and life science photographer.
99A, 111A, 125A, 176A, 186B, 190A, 243A

George Taloumis
Garden columnist for the *Boston Globe* and *Flower and Garden* magazine in Kansas City, Missouri.
77A, 89A, 89B, 90A, 91A, 97A, 151A, 159A, 162B, 165B, 173B, 196A, 228A, 256A

Doug Wechsler
A wildlife biologist and freelance photographer.
167A

Index

Numbers in boldface type refer to pages on which color plates appear.